D1740181

The Future of Capitalism After the Financial Crisis

The Future of Capitalism After the Financial Crisis: The Varieties of Capitalism Debate in the Age of Austerity contains thirteen world leading political economists writing from within eight different countries who critically analyze the current crisis tendencies of capitalism both globally and in particular countries. Given the likelihood of an increasingly crisis prone future for capitalism, it is important not only to rethink capitalism in its current manifestations or varieties, it is also important to rethink research methods and conceptual frameworks in preparation for understanding an increasingly rocky future in which capitalism itself could go the way of the many species that in the past were endangered only to become extinct.

More and more titles of books and articles are suggesting that capitalism or perhaps civilization itself is endangered if we do not make radical changes in the near future. This book breaks with academic path dependency and attempts to open new vistas of political economy and of multidisciplinary analysis that are crucially important if our thought processes are to be effective for a world in jeopardy.

The varieties of capitalism (VoC) debate itself came into being as the Soviet Union unraveled. It drew in scholarship from a cross-section of Marxian and heterodox political economy. The key argument of VoC was that if capitalism was the only global option then those on the Left must get involved in policy discussions on how capitalist economies can be fashioned to become competitive as well as progressive. However, the financial crisis has seen policy across the advanced economies veer toward competitiveness coupled with austerity. The lesson for the Left is that alternatives to capitalism must be sought in the here and now.

Richard Westra is Designated Professor, Graduate School of Law, Nagoya University, Japan.

Dennis Badeen is Instructor, Business Administration, Trent University, Canada.

Robert Albritton is Professor Emeritus, Department of Political Science, York University, Canada.

Routledge Frontiers of Political Economy

The Future of Capitalism After the Financial Crisis

The Varieties of Capitalism debate in the age of austerity

Edited by
Richard Westra, Dennis Badeen,
and Robert Albritton

Routledge
Taylor & Francis Group

LONDON AND NEW YORK

First published 2015
by Routledge
2 Park Square, Milton Park, Abingdon, Oxon OX14 4RN

and by Routledge
711 Third Avenue, New York, NY 10017

Routledge is an imprint of the Taylor & Francis Group, an informa business

© 2015 selection and editorial material, Richard Westra, Dennis Badeen and
Robert Albritton; individual chapters, the contributors

The right of the editors to be identified as the authors of the editorial material, and of
the authors for their individual chapters, has been asserted in accordance with sections
77 and 78 of the Copyright, Designs and Patents Act 1988.

All rights reserved. No part of this book may be reprinted or reproduced or utilized in
any form or by any electronic, mechanical, or other means, now known or hereafter
invented, including photocopying and recording, or in any information storage or
retrieval system, without permission in writing from the publishers.

Trademark notice: Product or corporate names may be trademarks or registered
trademarks, and are used only for identification and explanation without intent to
infringe.

British Library Cataloguing in Publication Data
A catalogue record for this book is available from the British Library

Library of Congress Cataloging in Publication Data
The future of capitalism after the financial crisis : the varieties of capitalism debate in
the age of austerity / edited by Richard Westra, Dennis Badeen, Robert Albritton.
  pages cm. -- (Routledge frontiers of political economy)
Summary: "The Future of Capitalism After the Financial Crisis: The Varieties of
Capitalism Debate in the Age of Austerity contains thirteen world leading political
economists writing from within eight different countries who critically analyze the
current crisis tendencies of capitalism both globally and in particular countries. Given
the likelihood of an increasingly crisis prone future for capitalism, it is important not
only to rethink capitalism in its current manifestations or varieties. It is also important
to rethink research methods and conceptual frameworks in preparation for
understanding an increasingly rocky future in which capitalism itself could go the way
of the many species that in the past were endangered only to become extinct. More
and more titles of books and articles are suggesting that capitalism or perhaps
civilization itself is endangered if we do not make radical changes in the near future.
This book breaks with academic path dependency and attempts to open new vistas of
political economy and of multidisciplinary analysis that are crucially important if our
thought processes are to be effective in a world in jeopardy. The varieties of capitalism
(VoC) debate itself came into being as the Soviet Union unraveled. It drew in
scholarship from a cross-section of Marxian and heterodox political economy. The key
argument of VoC was that if capitalism was the only global option then those on the
Left must get involved in policy discussions on how capitalist economies can be
fashioned to become competitive as well as progressive. However, the financial crisis
has seen policy across the advanced economies veer toward competitiveness coupled
with austerity. The lesson for the Left is that alternatives to capitalism must be sought
in the here and now"-- Provided by publisher.
Includes bibliographical references and index.
  1. Capitalism. 2. Financial crises. 3. Global Financial Crisis, 2008-2009. I. Westra,
Richard, 1954- II. Badeen, Dennis. III. Albritton, Robert, 1941-
  HB501.F79135 2014
  330.12'2--dc23
      2014025933

ISBN: 978-0-415-72284-1 (hbk)
ISBN: 978-1-315-85804-3 (ebk)

Typeset in Times New Roman by Taylor & Francis Books

MIX
Paper from
responsible sources
FSC
www.fsc.org   FSC® C013604

Printed and bound by CPI Group (UK) Ltd, Croydon, CR0 4YY

Contents

List of illustrations

Figures

Tables

List of contributors

Robert Albritton is Professor Emeritus, Department of Political Science, York University, Toronto, Canada. His current interests include Marxian Political Economy in general and in particular, discussions about how best to advance towards socialism. Published books include: *A Japanese Approach to Stages of Capitalist Development* (1991), *Dialectics and Deconstruction in Political Economy* (2001), *Economics Transformed: Discovering the Brilliance of Marx* (2007, translated into Chinese), *Let Them Eat Junk: How Capitalism Creates Hunger and Obesity* (2009). Some recent articles in journals and books include: "Between Obesity and Hunger," in *Socialist Register,* 2010; "Marxist Political Economy and Global Warming," in *International Journal of Pluralism in Economics Education* (2013); "A Practical Utopia for the Twenty-First Century," in Patricia Vieria and Michael Marder eds, *Existential Utopia: New Perspectives on Utopian Though* (2012); and "Two Great Food Revolutions: The Domestication of Nature and the Transgression of Nature's Limits", in Mustafa Koc, Jennifer Sumner and Tony Winson eds, *Critical Perspectives in Food Studies.* He can be reached at ralbritt@yorku.ca.

Grant Amyot is Professor and Head of the Department of Political Studies at Queen's University, Kingston, Canada. He holds degrees from the University of Western Ontario, Oxford University, and the University of Reading. He wrote his doctoral thesis on the Italian Communist Party, for which he undertook research in the field and at the Gramsci Institute in Rome. At Queen's, he teaches primarily on comparative politics, European politics, and the EU. He has also served as co-editor of *Queen's Quarterly* and as a member of the editorial board and executive committee of *Studies in Political Economy.* His recent publications include: *Business, the State and Economic Policy: The Case of Italy* (2004), *Italian Politics: The End of the Berlusconi Era?* vol. 21 of *Italian Politics: A Review,* (ed.) with Luca Verzichelli (2006), and "The Privatization of Alitalia," in G. Baldini and Anna Cento Bull (eds), *Governing Fear,* vol. 24 of *Italian Politics: A Review* (2010).

Dennis Badeen is an instructor at Trent University, Canada. He received his Ph.D. from York University, Canada. His scholarly interests include Marxist philosophy and political economy.

Hans-Jürgen Bieling is Professor of Political Economy at Eberhard Karls University of Tübingen, Germany. He received his Ph.D. and his habilitation from the Philipps University of Marburg. He is board member of the Political Economy section of the German political science association. His main academic interests are in the fields of International Political Economy, European integration and State and Social Theory. He has of recent widely published on the causes and implications of European crisis processes and the struggles over financial market regulation.

Ulrich Brand is Chair of International Politics, Department of Political Science, University of Vienna, Austria. His interests lie in critical state and governance studies, theories of Regulation and hegemony, political ecology, international resource and environmental politics; his regional focus is Latin America. He recently co-edited books on Regulation theory, Political Ecology, and Latin America. He received his Ph.D. at Frankfurt/M. University, Germany, and his habilitation at Kassel University, Germany.

Ian Bruff is Lecturer in European Politics at the University of Manchester, UK. He has published widely on European varieties of capitalism, neoliberalism, and social (especially historical materialist) theory, and is currently researching the political economy of neoliberalism in Europe. He is about to complete a large cross-country project on the diversity of contemporary capitalism(s) with Matthias Ebenau, Christian May, and Andreas Nölke, which produced two German-language collections in 2013 (with Westfälisches Dampfboot and the journal *Peripherie*), an English-language special issue in 2014 (*Capital & Class*), and an English-language volume in early 2015 (Palgrave).

Guglielmo Carchedi is Professor Emeritus, University of Amsterdam. Currently, he is Special Adjunct Professor, York University, Canada. His recent publications include the book, *Behind the Crisis* (2011), along with articles in the journals *International Socialism* and *World Review of Political Economy*.

Makoto Itoh is Professor Emeritus of the University of Tokyo, and a member of the Japan Academy. He has taught at universities around the world, including the New School for Social Research, York University, Canada, and London University. Among his numerous published works are: *The World Economic Crisis and Japanese Capitalism* (1990), *The Japanese Economy Reconsidered* (2000), and "The Historical Significance and the Social Costs of the Subprime Crisis," in Costas Lapavitsas (ed.), *Financialisation in Crisis* (2012).

Maria N. Ivanova is Lecturer in Economics at Goldsmiths, University of London. Her main research interests include political economy of the United States, international political economy, money and finance, and social theory. Her most recent work has appeared in *Review of Radical Political Economics, Science & Society, Critical Sociology*, and *Cambridge Journal of Economics*.

Bob Jessop is Distinguished Professor of Sociology and Co-Director of the Cultural Political Economy Research Centre at Lancaster University, UK. He is best known for his contributions to state theory, critical political economy, the analysis of welfare state restructuring, the political economy of post-war Britain, and, most recently, cultural political economy. His recent books include: *The Future of the Capitalist State* (2002), *Beyond the Regulation Approach* (co-authored with Ngai-Ling Sum, 2006), *State Power* (2007), and *Towards Cultural Political Economy* (co-authored with Ngai-Ling Sum, 2013). His personal website is www.bobjessop.org.

Terrence McDonough is Professor of Economics at the National University of Ireland, Galway. He is author, editor, or co-editor of *Contemporary Capitalism and Its Crises: Social Structure of Accumulation Theory for the 21st Century* (2010), *The HEAP Chart: Hierarchy of Earnings, Attributes and Privilege Analysis* (2009), *Was Ireland A Colony? Economics, Politics, Ideology and Culture in the Irish Nineteenth Century* (2005), and *Social Structures of Accumulation: The Political Economy of Growth and Crisis* (1994). His current interests include globalization, American and Irish economic history, and economics education for labor and community groups. He received his Ph.D. from the University of Massachusetts at Amherst.

Kees van der Pijl is Professor Emeritus in the School of Global Studies and Fellow of the Centre for Global Political Economy, University of Sussex. He studied law and political science in Leiden and taught International Relations at the University of Amsterdam where he also obtained his doctorate in 1983. His latest book, *The Discipline of Western Supremacy*, the third of a prize-winning trilogy on *Modes of Foreign Relations and Political Economy*, was published in 2014.

Tony Smith is Professor of Philosophy at Iowa State University. He received his Ph.D. in Philosophy from the State University of New York at Stony Brook. He is the author of numerous works in Marxism, the philosophy of technology, and social theory, including *The Logic of Marx's Capital: Replies to Hegelian Criticisms* (1990), *Technology and Capital in the Age of Lean Production* (2000), and *Globalisation: A Systematic Marxian Account* (2005). Most recently he co-edited the collection *Marx's Capital and Hegel's Logic* (2014). He is presently working on a book provisionally titled *Beyond Liberal Egalitarianism: Normative Social Theory for the Twenty-First Century*.

Richard Westra is Designated Professor, Graduate School of Law, Nagoya University, Japan. He is author, editor, or coeditor of eleven books. His work has been published in numerous international peer-reviewed academic journals. He is a member of the editorial board for *Journal of Contemporary Asia* and is a manuscript reviewer for major global publishing houses. He received his Ph.D. in the Department of Political Studies at Queen's University, Canada in 2001. He can be reached at westrarj@aim.com.

Preface

This collection follows a tradition commenced by two of the editors over a decade ago in gathering together teams of internationally renowned scholars to deal with the most pressing political economic problems of the day. This volume is the third in that line. The previous volumes were: Robert Albritton, Makoto Itoh, Richard Westra, and Alan Zuege (eds) *Phases of Capitalist Development: Booms, Crises and Globalizations*; and Robert Albritton, Bob Jessop, and Richard Westra (eds) *Political Economy and Global Capitalism: The 21st Century, Present and Future*. What made those books unique within the academic tradition of political economy is that unlike the practices of specialized academic journals or most academic book collections, while the editors selected an important theme which called out for in-depth analysis, contributors had full license to set out the problem as they saw it and apply their own original theoretical approach and empirics.

Following in this tradition, the current book features thirteen world leading political economists writing from within eight different countries. They critically analyze the current crisis tendencies of capitalism both globally and in particular countries either through the analytic frameworks of the Varieties of Capitalism (VoC) literature, or in some cases moving beyond this literature altogether. The VoC school of thought came into being as the Soviet Union unraveled. Its scholarship drew from a cross-section of Marxian economics and a range of Left heterodox economic schools. Its foundational premise was that with capitalism as the only option, the Left had better learn how to live with it and get in on the policy-making action to ensure that while economies were driven to compete, they would nevertheless move in progressive directions, or at least preserve whatever desirable economic arrangements were already in place. The global economic meltdown of 2008–09 and the following half decade of recession has in effect seen much of this Left policy discussion vitiated. For the "progressive" side of the equation has in most cases been replaced by *austerity*, with no end in sight. Much of the Left has responded to this by renewing their calls for radical social change that would ultimately replace capitalism with a gradual unfolding of a democratic, egalitarian, sustainable socialism.

This volume is divided into three parts. In Part 1, Richard Westra, Bob Jessop, Kees van der Pijl, and Terrence McDonough, each operationalize their own cutting edge theoretical framework to contextualize and critically analyze the current political economy of VoC and austerity. In Part 2, Tony Smith, Grant Amyot, Ian Bruff, and Makoto Itoh bring nuanced theoretical approaches to bear upon VoC empirical cases of US, Italy, Germany, and Japan. A basic question here is to what extent are the politics of austerity making capitalism in different countries more similar. In Part 3, Robert Albritton, Maria N. Ivanova, Hans-Jürgen Bieling along with Ulrich Brand, and Guglielmo Carchedi take on questions of the deepening multiple mutually exacerbating crises of capitalism now confronting not only the VoC school of thought, but also placing into doubt the very future of capitalism.

The Editors,
Japan and Canada,
June 2014

Part 1

Varieties of Capitalism from beginning to end?

1 From imperialism to Varieties of Capitalism

Richard Westra

Introduction

The purpose of this chapter is to follow the conceptual trail from the theorizing of imperialism in the field of Marxian political economy to the research agenda of Varieties of Capitalism (VoC).

Marxian political economy is based upon the most significant economic writing of Karl Marx, his monumental three-volume study – *Capital*. Marx, however, passed away before his masterwork was completed. He even bemoaned pressures to publish it before the intricacies of his theories were better worked out. In a letter to Engels, Marx declares (2014c [1865]):

> … I cannot bring myself to send anything off until I have the whole thing in front of me. Whatever shortcomings they may have, the advantage of my writings is that they are an artistic whole, and this can only be achieved through my practice of never having things printed until I have them in front of me *in their entirety*. This is impossible with Jacob Grimm's method which is in general better with writings that have no dialectical structure.

Marx's reference here, as well as in the Afterword to the Second German edition of *Capital* (and elsewhere) to the dialectical epistemology of *Capital* has befuddled both followers and critics alike. Yet it did not entail a self-styled "choice" of where to "start" *Capital* (Marx 2014d [1867]). Rather, as Stefanos Kourkoulakos explains, while formal or axiomatic logic is operable in varied epistemological contexts and may be directed toward explanation of a multiplicity of phenomena across the sciences, the dialectic is a "special purpose" or "content specific" method demanding a theoretical object with unique ontological properties for its operation (Kourkoulakos 2002, pp. 191–94). These properties being, that the object is self-abstracting, self-reifying, and self-revealing (this latter in the sense of the subject matter "telling its own story" from the "inside").

In the *idealist* dialectic of G. W. F. Hegel, the "storyteller" was the Absolute or God revealing piecemeal the truth of the universe across the history of philosophy. For Marx, to deploy the special purpose dialectical epistemology in the *material* world required a theoretical object that is either an Absolute, or evidences "Absolute-like" characteristics. It was Marx's great acumen to discern that *one* such object exists in the material world – capital. As put by Moishe Postone (1996, p. 75):

> Marx ... explicitly characterizes capital as the self-moving substance which is Subject. In doing so, Marx suggests that a ... [materialist] Subject in the Hegelian sense does indeed exist in capitalism ... Marx analyzes it in terms of the structure of social relations ... His analysis suggests that the social relations that characterize capitalism are of a very peculiar sort – they possess attributes that Hegel accorded the *Geist*.

Marx begins *Capital* with the *commodity* because the commodity in the capitalist economy contains the elemental *contradiction* or dialectical opposition of capital – that between *value* and *use-value*. Value is the historically specific, abstract, quantitative principle of capital. Use-value is the transhistorical, concrete, qualitative foundation of all human life. Indeed, it is an ideological ruse of neoclassical economics to study "the economy" (read capitalism) through its yoga of purported "rational" consumer choice, because "consumption" of use-values to materially provision human society is a transhistorical phenomenon. In that fashion, neoclassical economics "naturalizes" its subject matter ("the market," read capitalism). However, to understand *capitalism* requires grasp of its cardinal activity of profit-making. Marx, therefore, rightly theorizes the commodity in the first pages of *Capital* from the perspective of the *seller* as a good becomes a commodity precisely because its owner is *not* interested in its use-value or "consumption," but in its *value*. Value in this sense always manifests an *indifference* to use-value. And it is the contradiction between value and use-value inherent in the commodity that drives the dialectic forward to unfold each and every category of *Capital* so as to expose all the inner secrets of capital as a mode of organizing human economic life. As captured by Robert Albritton (2007, pp. 95–96):

> [A] much misunderstood and sometimes maligned category of dialectics is "contradiction". The use of "contradiction" in dialectical reasoning does not violate the law of non-contradiction in formal logic. To say that within the commodity form there is a contradiction between value and use-value is to say that they are mutually dependent and mutually opposed semi-autonomies. Mutual dependency implies that a value must always be attached to use-value, and mutual opposition implies that as pure quantity, self-expanding value must overcome difficulties posed by incorporating use-value as pure quality. Value must incorporate use-value without compromising its self-expanding quantitativeness, which it does by producing a sequence of categories that overcome and subsume successive use-value obstacles.

Marxian economic theory, in other words, in demonstrating how value surmounts the use-value obstacles confronting it, to reproduce the economic life of a human society as a byproduct of its chrematistic of mercantile wealth augmentation, confirms the historical possibility of capitalism as an "upside-down," "alien" order (as Marx variously refers to it). The dialectical circle closes with capital itself becoming a commodity as represented by the fetishistic concept of *interest*. Where capital appears like the Absolute or *Geist*, divesting itself of all materiality in the labor and production process to become pure, objective quantity bent upon self-expansion. Approached from another angle, dialectical economic theory synthetically *defines* capital in its most fundamental incarnation (Westra 2012/13).

But, while Marx's seeking to operationalize the dialectical epistemology in his three-volume masterpiece, *Capital*, is testament to his interest in capturing the deep causal structure of logical inner relations of capital, Marx's work has been largely apprehended as a theory of history and historical directionality – historical materialism (HM) – with *Capital* pegged as but a subtheory. As argued in greater detail elsewhere (Westra 2009, pp. 46–48), there is no more influential figure in the reconstruction of Marx's work in terms of an overarching theory of historical directionality foretelling a socialist historical outcome than Second International doyen Karl Kautsky. In fact, the very notion of "Marxism" as a field of study predicated upon writings of Marx originates in Kautsky's hands. And it is Kautsky who first codifies Marxism as HM.

Kautsky, it is important to understand, had developed his ideas on Marxism without access to *Capital* as a whole. And, in fact, published a major book, translated into numerous languages with huge influence on a new generation of Marxists, entitled *Economic Doctrines of Karl Marx*, which was based solely on Volume I of *Capital*. Kautsky essentially combined insights from Marx's pithy statement of HM in the Preface to *A Contribution to the Critique of Political Economy* (Marx 2014b [1859]) with Marx's iconic closing words in *Capital* Volume I. Marx proclaimed there: "Centralization of the means of production and socialization of labour at last reach a point where they become incompatible with their capitalist integument. This integument is burst asunder … The expropriators are expropriated" (Marx 2014d [1867]). Mesmerized by the impact of positivism on late nineteenth-century philosophy of science debate, Kautsky argued that *Capital* provides evidence in a given context of the wider teleology of human history as a whole. He unabashedly asserts, "every step in social science has proved it – that, in the last analysis, the history of mankind is determined … by an economic development which progresses irresistibly, obedient to certain underlying laws" (Kautsky 1971, p. 119). According to Kautsky, it is Marx's "law" of accumulation which enforces the historical transition from a so-called "petty commodity society" of independent producers to capitalism. And then it propels capitalism towards its demise by "centralizing" capital in fewer and fewer hands, as the "law" simultaneously enlarges the working class and increases worker impoverishment or "immiseration." In this way it is alleged that capitalism produces its own "gravediggers."

In Volume II and III of *Capital* as left by Marx, however, it is never maintained that the logic of capital or *law of value*, which reproduces economic life in capitalist society as a byproduct of value augmentation, is self-defeating, leading to the demise of capitalism, as Kautsky contends. Even in Marx's own explication in Volume III of the law of the tendency for the rate of profit to fall due to the rising organic composition of capital, Marx never argues that the law *necessarily* spawns combination leading to social class polarization and potential dismounting of capital.

Yet, at the time of his writing, Kautsky's claims were not critiqued on the basis of their logical deficiencies. But from the vantage point of historical transformations they failed to predict. Because the fact was, the extended economic crisis which wracked the European-centered trading world from approximately 1873 into the 1890s, rather than sounding the death knell of capital, and inciting the proletariat to overthrow capitalism, as Kautsky attributed to Marx's analysis, was instead resolved by mid-1890 in a renewed bout of prosperity. This situation became the catalyst for the famous "Revisionist Controversy" within Europe's most formidable socialist party the German SPD (Howard and King 1989, pp. 65–89).

At the center of the "Revisionist Controversy," which essentially pitted Kautsky against his main protagonist Eduard Bernstein, was the question of whether the shifting tide of capital accumulation obliged the socialist movement to revaluate its aims. That is, if historical laws were expanding the working class, instead of devoting energies to fomenting socialist revolutionary overthrow of capitalism, workers and their political party should concentrate their attention on reforming capitalism and "peacefully" transforming it with attainment of political power in electoral victory. While Kautsky emerged victorious in this clash, which was fought not at the level of high theory but over interpretations of empirical trends of capitalism, if one thing did become clear it was the paucity of solid analysis of the changes capitalism was undergoing. It was from within this intellectual vacuum then that the theorizing of *imperialism* exploded.

From *Capital* to imperialism

As the masterful study by Jukka Gronow explains, despite quibbling over the political and strategic implications of imperialism, *all* turn-of-the-century Marxist theoreticians of imperialism accepted the basic assumptions of Kautsky concerning Marx's *Capital* (Gronow, 1986, pp. 57–59, 97–98, 118–19, 161–62). That is, they approached *Capital* as a subtheory of HM, the latter conceived as an overarching theory of historical directionality foretelling a socialist historical outcome. As such, *Capital* is seen as capturing the historical teleology of capitalism beginning with its germination in a supposedly historically existent petty commodity society. From that point of departure capitalism proper is considered by them to be but a short-lived formation wedged between its petty commodity precursor and imperialism. And *Capital*, in this schema, as the theorizing of historical laws applied to the historical period up to the time of Marx's passing, is the theory of that short-lived social formation.

Rudolf Hilferding's book, *Finance Capital* constitutes the opening salvo in the theorizing of imperialism. As recent commentary has it, *Finance Capital* "proved to be the most influential text in the entire history of Marxian political economy, only excepting *Capital* itself" (Howard and King 1989, p. 100). And in fundamental ways, all writers on imperialism follow Hilferding in setting out the unique economic constituents of imperialism (Brewer 1980, pp. 79, 99–100). For Hilferding, what in particular marks imperialism as a new "type" or "period" of capitalism is, first, the morphing of the form of capital from the *industrial capital* treated by Marx in *Capital* to *finance capital* (Hilferding 1981, pp. 223–25). Finance capital, quite simply, involved banks playing an activist role in "socializing" available funds throughout society and deploying the funds to impel the monopolization of commanding heights industries such as steel (over which finance capital exerted control). Second, there is the imperialist state *policy* of acquiring "economic territory" in support of the monopolistic cartels operated by finance capital. To ensure their monopolistic pricing regime in their "national" markets, and forestall competitive devaluations of capital, imperialist policy enabled finance capital to "dump" its excess production in the captive markets, so the argument went (Hilferding 1981, pp. 213, 318–19, 322–23, 328). Nevertheless, Hilferding never wavers on the view that his theorizing of imperialism, as with Marx's *Capital*, is but a subtheory-like intervention or refinement of HM. In the Preface to *Finance Capital* Hilferding states (1981, p. 23):

> Marxism … is only a theory of the laws of motion of society. The Marxist conception of history formulates these laws in general terms, and Marxist economics then applies them to the period of commodity production. The socialist outcome is a result of tendencies which operate in the commodity producing society.

V. I. Lenin is the first Marxist theorist to characterize imperialism as a "stage" of capitalism, though he leaves this conceptualization unrefined (1975, p. 82). As alluded to above, Lenin largely follows Hilferding's analysis of imperialism as a new "type" of capitalism except, on the one hand, Lenin pegs the "monopoly" structure of the firm as the most salient feature of the era. While on the other hand, Lenin emphasizes the geopolitical dimension of imperialism where imperialist powers seek to divide/re-divide the globe into spheres of influence (Lenin 1975, pp. 77–79, 83, 92). Yet, in keeping with our point above on Marxist theoreticians of imperialism, Lenin declares (2014a [1913]):

> [Marx's] historical materialism [HM] was a great achievement in scientific thinking. The chaos and arbitrariness that had previously reigned in

views on history and politics were replaced by a strikingly integral and harmonious scientific theory, which shows how, in consequence of the growth of productive forces, out of one system of social life another and higher system develops ... Marx [then] traced the development of capitalism from embryonic commodity economy, from simple exchange, to its highest forms, to large-scale production.

But, given the understanding of HM as an overarching theory of historical directionality foretelling a socialist historical outcome, and the point that *Capital*, its subtheory of historical directionality, had purportedly been outpaced by historical change with the promise of socialism by its supposed "laws" of accumulation remaining undelivered, the weight of the Marxist qua HM case for socialism fell on the theorizing of imperialism. This transposition has been apprehended in terms of the first "crisis of Marxism" where the theory of imperialism is claimed to "solve" the crisis (McDonough and Drago 1989).

In the explanation given by both Rudolf Hilferding, the formative theorist of imperialism, and V. I. Lenin, who would draw the lessons from theorization of imperialism for socialist practice, the fact that revolution did not follow the first major crisis of capitalism hinged upon the transformed social class conditions of capitalism in its imperialist stage. In his *Finance Capital*, Hilferding pointed to the spawning of salaried "middle classes" that, while constituting a fraction of the working class, increasingly disdained any identification with the proletariat. Instead, they identified with the petit bourgeois middle classes the growth of which was but another class characteristic of the imperialist era (Hilferding 1981, Chapter 23). Lenin, for his part, pointed to the emergence in the stage of imperialism of what he dubbed an "aristocracy of labour," which battened on monopolistic protection in commanding heights imperialist industries (Lenin 2014b [1916]). Like Hilferding's new "middle class," the "aristocracy of labour" felt a vested interest in the fruits of imperialist policies resulting in a bifurcated labor movement with counter-revolutionary inclinations.

It was the above analysis of transmutations in capitalist social class relations that then led Lenin to formulate his theory of a "global imperialist chain." That is, notwithstanding his position on the struggle among rival imperialist states over the division of the globe into economic territories, these territories then slated to become the preserve of "national" imperialist exploitation, the net impact was to create a "chain" of interests among the imperialist bourgeoisie everywhere in the imperialist international capitalist system. The first socialist revolution, according to Lenin, was therefore not going to occur in the most developed "socialized" capitalist state. Instead, Lenin argued, it would occur in that state which constituted the "weakest link" in the imperialist chain. That turned out to be Russia (Milos and Sotiropoulos 2009, pp. 18–20). However, even the Soviet Revolution of 1917 did not solve the credibility problem of Marxism qua HM as an overarching

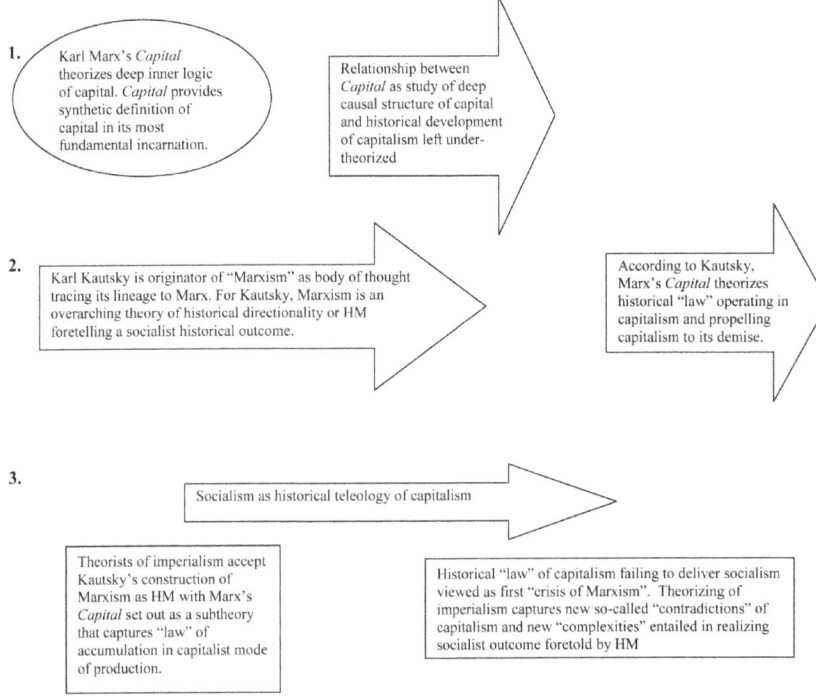

Figure 1.1 From Marx's *Capital* to imperialism

theory of historical directionality foretelling a socialist historical outcome. This is the case because it left the Soviet Union and socialism surrounded by a phalanx of capitalist powers (see Figure 1.1). Even Lenin would lament: "we always said that the victory of the socialist revolution ... can only be regarded as final when it becomes the victory of the proletariat in at least several advanced countries" (Lenin 2014c [1919]).

Imperialism and post-World War II capitalism

The early attempts to theorize transmutations of capitalism as it emerged seemingly once again triumphantly from the ashes of a brutal war, largely blazed the trail taken by theorists of imperialism. Paul Baran and Paul Sweezy, for example, in their major work *Monopoly Capital*, note how Marx's temporal position delimited his focus in *Capital* to "competitive capitalism." Building, then, upon Lenin's formative theorizing of imperialism, that monopoly was the salient feature of capitalism's twentieth-century trajectory (finance capital, according to Baran and Sweezy was but a fleeting symptom of the monopoly tendency), Baran and Sweezy argue that to bring Marxist economic ideas into line with mid-twentieth-century trends, an analysis of the specific modus operandi of monopolization is required. To this effect their work maintains that the "law of falling profits," purportedly identified by Marx as central to competitive capitalism, is supplanted under *monopoly capitalism* by an alleged "law of rising surplus" (Baran and Sweezy 1966, pp. 4, 72). Baran and Sweezy then proceed to extrapolate from their newly identified "law" all the features of monopoly capitalism, such as its hyper-consumerism and proclivity for hypertrophied military investment, which they perceive shape United States (US) accumulation in the post WWII era. In the end, while Baran and Sweezy are not explicit on this, the tenor of their work is that monopoly capitalism, notwithstanding the new purported "law" of capitalism they uncover, entails but further new "complexities" which stand in the way of realizing HM's foretold socialist historical outcome. In the final chapter of *Monopoly Capital* they touch on these in terms of the ideological depoliticizing of society and channeling of human creativity into socially and spiritually destructive activities (Baran and Sweezy 1966, Chapter 11).

Another landmark attempt to deal with transformations of capitalism, while continuing to extrapolate historical outcomes from a purported "law" of capitalism, is the work of Ernest Mandel. Mandel opens his book *Late Capitalism* with this contextualization (Mandel 1978, p. 9):

> The era of late capitalism is not a new epoch of capitalist development. It is merely a further development of the imperialist, monopoly-capitalist epoch. By implication, the characteristics of the imperialist epoch enumerated by Lenin thus remain fully valid for late capitalism.

In his ambitious framework Mandel then proceeds to explain capital accumulation across all historical periods of capitalism by capital's search for "surplus profits" (Mandel 1978, pp. 30, 39, 75). In his own words (Mandel 1978, p. 102):

> The entire capitalist system ... appears as ... the outcome of the uneven development of states, regions, branches of industry and firms, unleashed by the quest for surplus profit ... [However] the main weight of this ramified uneven and combined development takes different forms in different epochs.

These "periods" of capitalism – "freely competitive capitalism," imperialism, and the post-WWII epoch, "late capitalism" – rest, according to Mandel, upon extended economic "cycles" or "long waves" of capitalist development, each incorporating several traditional business cycles, and each predicated upon major "technological revolutions." His elaborations upon these technological revolutions are as follows (Mandel 1978, pp. 120–21): the "machine-made steam engine" (the first technological revolution from 1847 to the 1890s); the "generalized application of electric and combustion engines" (characterizing the period from the 1890s to WWII as the second technological revolution); the "generalized control of machines by electronic apparatuses ... [and] nuclear energy" (being the third technological revolution of the post-WWII period). For Mandel, these long waves are divided into periods of economic upswing and economic stagnation. And, whether capital is able to emerge from a "long wave of depression" to accumulate anew, simply descend into "barbarism," or be superseded by transition to socialism, all depend in Mandel's schema upon the "cycles of class struggle" which interrelate with the economic cycles (Mandel 1995, Chapter Two).

To gather the threads of the discussion thus far, while Marx himself had advanced *Capital* as a dialectical theory exposing the deep structure of inner causal relations of capital, a society that reproduces human economic life as a byproduct of value augmentation, beyond a brief statement of proposed research in the section "The Method of Political Economy" in the post-humously published *Grundrisse* (written prior to *Capital* as its "workbook"), Marx never elaborated upon how his study of the inner logic of capital might be applied to capitalism in all its historical vicissitudes (Marx 2014a [1857]). Following Marx's passing, Second International doyen Karl Kautsky, founder of Marxism as the body of thought tracing its lineage to Marx, fashioned Marx's corpus into an overarching theory of historical directionality or HM, foretelling a socialist historical outcome. In the heady days of the late nineteenth, early twentieth century working class revolutionary aspirations, with the belief widely held that world socialism was nigh, taking a step back to refine Marx's *Capital* as economic theory and potentially develop mediations between the inner logical structure of capital and the hum and buzz of capitalist history was hardly seen as a pressing task. And, when theory did treat the question of historical transmutations of capitalism it did so within a framework that sought to extrapolate from a purported "law" of capitalism an historical outcome a-la-HM. In this sense eliding that which puzzled Marx as a social scientist, which is, how such an "upside down," "alien" society like capitalism could exist and reproduce a human society as a byproduct of value augmentation in the first place.

Stages of capitalism and mid-range theory

In what may be viewed as a seismic shift in Marxian political economic theorizing of capitalism, Michael Aglietta in the founding work of Marxist Regulation Theory sets out his goal of giving "a theoretical foundation to the periodization of capitalism into successive stages of historical evolution" (Aglietta 1987, p. 20). According to Aglietta, capitalism cannot be understood as embodying a solitary trajectory or as being governed by a single inexorable "law." Rather, capitalism develops across its history through a series of discontinuous stages, each stage being marked by a set of socially and historically constituted features or "structural forms." It follows that abstract economic theory alone is insufficient as the sole explanatory locus of capitalist development. It must be supplemented by historical investigation. As Aglietta puts it, "history is no longer an alibi designed to justify certain abstract schemas" (1987, pp. 16–17). To realize its goal, Regulation Theory developed by Aglietta and others approached their study of capitalist stages in terms of "intermediate range" or mid-range concepts which were viewed as analytical devices for mediating the theoretical movement between abstract economic theory and historical studies of capitalism (Boyer 1990, pp. 30–31).

While Regulation Theory treated other stages of capitalism, the operationalizing of its conceptual infrastructure was most exhaustive in analyzing the post-WWII capitalist stage of *Fordism*. In Regulationist terms, Fordism was a "regime of accumulation" or stage of capitalism evidencing a stage-specific "mode of regulation" or ensemble of structural forms ensuring the relatively long-run cohesion of capital accumulation. At the center of the long-run cohesion was the "fix" from crises propensities for capital accumulation provided by the key structural form, the "wage relation" dubbed Fordism. The latter, quite simply, entailed the two-sided coin of semiautomatic electronic mass production and assembly of consumer durables and the "norm" of mass consumption by workers which was integral to accumulation. So much so that the capitalist state enters the picture with herculean supports for accumulation which are accepted by both capital and labor, the latter essentially trading its higher standard of living for political quiescence. The Fordist edifice was then embedded in a wider array of international structural forms such as the Bretton Woods Monetary system and US global hegemony.

Regulation Theory offers an important caution for those like Mandel enamored by so-called long wave theories. The latter arose at the fringes of neoclassical economics (Kondratieff 2010 [1935]). Yet, long wave theories were imbibed by Marxists for their straightforward schema for economic transformation across the capitalist era in terms of long-term profit rate data and technological revolutions. Marx, of course, in his fragmentary elaboration upon business cycle oscillations in Volume III of *Capital*, had shown how rising organic composition of capital accompanied by renewed profitability, particularly surplus profit temporarily garnered by the most innovative firms, marked business cycle upswings (Westra 2012/13). But the economic process treated by Marx in *Capital* entailed incremental changes in technology which were easily absorbed by firms operating competitively in capitalist markets. Technological innovation, however, is endogenous to capitalist market activities. And, the sorts of intervals separating major economic crises of capitalism are punctuated by depression and/or war; thus differ qualitatively from business cycle oscillations dealt with by Marx. Moreover, there is never any guarantee for a renewal of capital accumulation following a major crisis cataclysm such as the concatenating of depression and war from the ashes of which Fordism emerged. Finally, the possibility of a post-WWII stage of capitalism setting in motion the expensive mass production technologies that had in fact become available decades earlier, was predicated upon substantial social, ideological, political, and institutional change without which Fordist accumulation could have never kick-started. In short, the emergence of a new stage of capitalism is never a fait accompli. Nor can it be explained by economic theory alone.

Nevertheless, Regulation Theory, as discussed in my earlier review of the literature, was pounced upon within Marxist theory by currents held in thrall by the Kautskian "orthodox" construction of Marxism that offered a direct and simple explanation of historical change in terms of a "law" of accumulation (Westra 2009, pp. 59–62). Dressed up in philosophical language, the argument was that the "law" of accumulation constitutes the "essence" of capitalism as captured by Marx with history unfolding as the "appearance" of the inner "essence" with its outcomes hence "chain-linked" to the "law." Of course, that makes little more than philosophical nonsense because it convolutes both the meaning of laws in political economy and understandings of history. That is, again, a "law" that is constitutive of capitalism cannot simultaneously be held responsible for the undoing of that which it builds. It would hardly be reasonable to posit resistances to capital whether in terms of working-class organization or climate change as simple "appearances" of an "inner essence" of capital. Further, a multiplicity of social forces operate in modern history alongside capital – race, patriarchy, gender, culture, to name a few – that cannot be grasped in terms of functions or "appearances" of capital's inner logic or "essence."

On the other hand, while Regulation Theory is intuitively correct in its attempt to bridge the gap separating abstract theory (presumably its reference here is to Marx's *Capital* as the "abstract theory" *not* neoclassical economics) from capitalist history in a way that preserves the meaning of law in science (Andrew Collier (1994, p. 43) puts this best: "For a law to be true, it must hold when the mechanism it designates works unimpeded – i.e. in a closed system"), yet does not encumber historical diversity, contingency or agency with crude functionalist constraints, Regulation theory was saddled with a set of fatal elisions.

Regulation Theory never establishes the ontological basis for the analytical separation of base and superstructure or abstract economic theory and its more "concrete" economic along with "political" or "institutional" structural forms in regards to the study of capitalism in the first place. Nor does it answer the question of the epistemological warrant we have for dividing the study of capitalism into "levels" of theory. And as alluded to above, nowhere do Regulationists clearly specify *what* the abstract theory *is* that their mid-range theory supposedly bridges the gap from *to* historical studies. This latter point draws the ire of so-called orthodox Marxists who see the whole mid-range edifice hanging in a kind of abeyance a-la-postmodernism with no "foundation" beyond its own self-styled conceptual scheme. The orthodox proposed resolution a-la-Kautsky to this abiding problem in Marxist theory, however, of "chain-linking" history to a purported inner essence of capital, drags Marxist theory back into the epistemological dark ages. Finally, Regulationists, along with a like theory developed in the US – Social Structures of Accumulation Theory (Gordon *et al.* 1982, pp. 25, 38) – that also sets out to separate analysis of "the capital accumulation process" from that of its "institutional environment" which "conditions" accumulation in "stages of capitalism," are taken to task over their treatment of historical difference and variety in capitalism. Both theories relied heavily upon the US experience to develop concepts about capitalism for which general applicability to broad temporal stages or periods of capitalism is claimed.

Of course, there is nothing necessarily "wrong" with deriving general concepts from a particular empirical case. After all, there was only one "type" of capitalism in Marx's day from which Marx drew his theory of logical inner relations of capital. However Marx was up front with his ontological argument about the peculiar ontological structure of capital which provided the foundation for his "real" abstractions. That is, in maintaining capital converts concrete interpersonal economic relations into abstract "relations among things" as he famously declared, Marx adverts to the ontologically significant fact that as the products of human labor are subsumed by the commodity and money forms, their *qualitative* differences are suppressed as the differentiation of commodities in the capitalist market proceeds in *quantitative* terms. In this way, the resultant abstraction (from the sensuous qualities of things to relate them in quantitative terms) is grounded in action of a particular kind, *not* in thought. It is this *materialist* "force of abstraction" in turn which provides Marx with the epistemological warrant for dialectical economic theorizing of capital. However, not only do Regulation Theory and Social Structures of Accumulation Theory leave the fundamental question of the relation of their mid-range theories to Marx's *Capital* (or any abstract or general theory of capital or "economics" for that matter) unaddressed but, as touched on above, they are not clear on the epistemology of their mid-range theory and how precisely mid-range concepts relate to history. Critics, particularly given the intellectual environment of the late 1980s onward under the spell of postmodernism, attributed that lacuna to Marxism per se which they had always felt was "essentialist" and "totalizing." Put differently, rather than a monotonic "law" of capital from which history was read off a-la-Kautsky, Regulationists and Social Structures of Accumulation theorists were charged with reading history off their mid-range concepts as the new locus of Marxist "essentialism" (Westra 2009, pp. 63–64). Every non-US exemplar of Fordism or structure of accumulation was then claimed to be so divergent with respect to variations on structural forms that one Regulationist and erstwhile Marxist would ultimately proclaim that "there are as many forms of capitalism as there are nation-states" (Boyer 2005, p. 519).

From periodization to Varieties of Capitalism

The unraveling of the Soviet Union in 1989 was a watershed for Left theorizing of capitalism. Not only because of its occurrence as such, but because of its temporal juncture. That is, the global center of socialist revolution in socialism's theretofore most advanced form was scratched out of the picture at the precise time of neoliberal triumphalism and shrill chants among its academic economist proponents that even business cycle oscillations and periodic recessions of capitalism were a thing of the past (Zarnowitz 1999a, 1999b). It thus rocked what had always been a staid conceptualization of Marxist theory since Kautsky, that capitalism was destined to be superseded by socialism and that crises of capitalism were harbingers of that change. Even Aglietta had maintained his study of capitalism in Regulation Theory (1987, p. 16):

> will elucidate the general lesson of historical materialism: the develop-
> ment of the forces of production under the effect of the class struggle, and
> the transformation of the conditions of this struggle and the forms in
> which it is embodied under the effect of that development.

But, in the perfect storm of Soviet disintegration, the seemingly out-of-this-world growth rates posted in the US neoliberal heartland (where analysis had not yet caught on to the house of cards the growth rates were built on), along with the stultifying impact of postmodernism in the academy on "grand theorizing," these kind of deeper, structural concerns over capitalism were largely purged with the birth of VoC. Indeed, many Marxist theorists that transitioned from periodization of capitalism debates to VoC, though, to be sure, certainly not all as the present volume illustrates, left the Marxist fold to engage in the new discourse.

VoC is quite heterogeneous in theoretical and disciplinary orientation. Yet, rather than to Marx, its proponents turned more often than not to disciplinary writings of sociologist Max Weber and economic historian Karl Polanyi. Gone were references to a "level" of abstract economic theory and *in* was the notion of the innate "embedding" of "the market" a-la-neoclassical economics in socially and historically constituted ensembles of institutions. That is, VoC "defines" capitalism in terms where capitalism is a priori understood as an institutionalized order, in which "the market" is simply one institution emplaced in a particular ordering of institutions. This replaces the language of base and superstructure of Marxism. And it largely exorcizes from debate, ironically, questions Marx had posed about the historicity of the *capitalist* market. That is, "markets" of sorts did exist in precapitalist societies in the "interstices" of their worlds, but always as external to the economic principles by which precapitalist societies reproduced their economic life. It is only in capitalist societies that markets assume a dominant role in material reproduction which in turn brings analysis full circle back to attempting to theorize this unique ontological phenomenon as Marx did.

VoC's research agenda essentially avoids the thorny epistemological thicket here and leaps into questions of the ordering of institutions, one among which being "the market," that function to impart a modicum of coherence and direction to an economy as institutional "complementarities." Such complementarities are then purportedly shaped by their emergence in discrete "national" social and historical circumstances and thus embody a so-called "path-dependence." Given these premises VoC considers a wide range of cases and develops a comparative research program from the outset. Further, departing from work by Regulation Theory and Social Structures of Accumulation Theory, VoC debate commenced evincing little interest in institutional complementarities as long-term "fixes" for capitalist crises tendencies. Rather, given the demise of the Soviet Union and increasing belief that capitalism of one kind or another is the only game in town, VoC fixated upon a triage of immediate policy relevant questions: What institutional complementarities optimally promote economic growth and global competitiveness? Is there a particular complementary relationship among institutions which advances competitiveness while yielding a "progressive" variety of capitalism? Given the overall interest in global competitiveness are tendencies afoot toward convergence of economies in a particular variety (see Figure 1.2)?

The production of these "varieties" essentially rested on answers to three basic questions: To what extent is operation of "the market" impacted upon by state intervention? What financing regime characterizes so-called "corporate governance?" And, to what extent and in what fashion is organized labor empowered vis-à-vis business and the state? And the conceptual procedure for arriving at these "varieties" entailed a studied slippage away from notions of mid/intermediate range theory to elaboration in terms of "ideal types" or "stylized facts," tools of analysis the utility of which is essentially the systematizing of empirical/institutional history (Westra 2009, pp. 65–67).

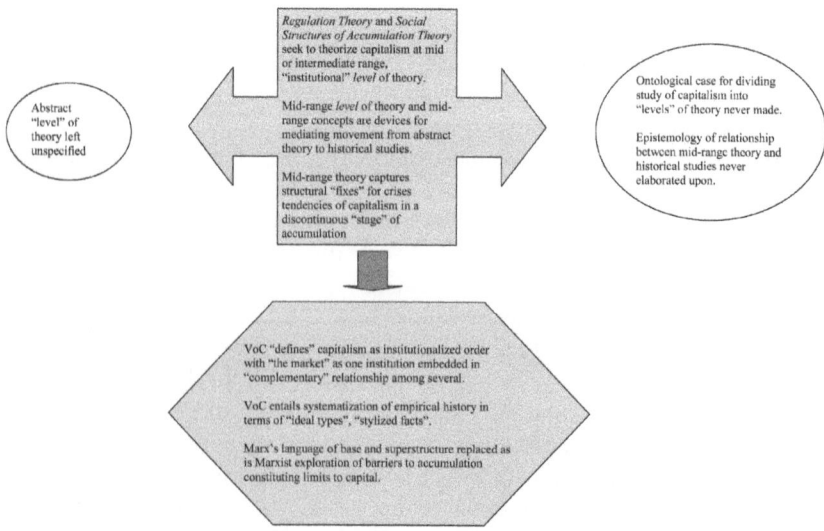

Figure 1.2 From periodizing capitalism to VoC

Conclusion

Following the meltdown of 2008–09 and endless recession, it is not clear where there is to go for the VoC literature which was born at an historical conjuncture of capitalist and neoliberal triumphalism. With all major economies furiously printing money through "quantitative easing" which bolsters financial institution balance sheets but has little impact on the *real* economy; all major economies struggling against the expanding percentage of GDP constituted by government activity which has been necessary to keep them afloat; and all simultaneously calling for policies of austerity which claw back quality of life gains made by average working people across the previous century, it may be time to shift from VoC to discussion of varieties of post-capitalist economies. And we have not even begun to touch in this chapter on questions of biospheric degradation and climate change that not only put capitalism in question, but human existence itself.

Remember, in the *idealist* dialectic of Hegel, "nothing" or *naught* puts up scant resistance to *being* or the Absolute to assure the ultimate triumph of the Absolute in perpetuity (Sekine 2013, pp. 18–19). But in the *materialist* dialectic of capital use-value resists value at every turn. In *Capital*, to "lay bare" the deep causal structure of logical inner relations of capital, Marx assumes a use-value space that value can easily tame with the economic contradictions it poses surmounted. But across the sweep of human history, use-value recalcitrance to value knows no bounds and it may well be that the pathologies of the current era represent death throes of capital finally humbled in its historical march by a conflagration of use-value barriers.

References

Aglietta, M. (1987) *A Theory of Capitalist Regulation* (London: Verso).

Albritton, R. (2007) *Economics Transformed: Discovering the Brilliance of Marx* (London: Pluto).

Baran, P. and P. Sweezy (1966) *Monopoly Capital* (New York: Monthly Review Press).

Boyer, R. (1990) *The Regulation School: A Critical Introduction* (New York: Columbia University Press).

——(2005) "How and Why Capitalisms Differ," *Economy and Society*, 34(4).

Brewer, A. (1980) *Marxist Theories of Imperialism* (London: Routledge and Kegan Paul).

Collier, A. (1994) *Critical Realism* (London: Verso).

Gordon, D., R. Edwards and M. Reich (1982) *Segmented Work, Divided Workers: The Historical Transformation of Labor in the United States* (Cambridge: Cambridge University Press).

Gronow, J. (1986) *On the Formation of Marxism* (Helsinki: The Finnish Society of Sciences and Letters).

Hilferding, R. (1981) *Finance Capital* (London: Routledge & Kegan Paul).

Howard, M. C. and J. E. King (1989) *A History of Marxian Economics: Volume I, 1883–1929* (Princeton, NJ: Princeton University Press).

Kautsky, K. (1971) *The Class Struggle* (New York: W.W. Norton and Company, Inc.).

Kondratieff, N. D. (2010 [1935]) *The Long Waves In Economic Life* (Whitefish, MT: Kessinger Publishing).

Kourkoulakos, S. (2002) "The Specificity of Dialectical Reason (for Hegel)," in R. Albritton and J. Simoulidis (eds) *New Dialectics and Political Economy* (Basingstoke: Palgrave).

Lenin, V.I. (2014a [1913]) *The Three Sources and Three Component Parts of Marxism*, available at: www.marxists.org/archive/lenin/works/1913/mar/x01.htm.

——(2014b [1916]) "Imperialism and the Split in Socialism," available at: www.marxists.org/archive/lenin/works/1916/oct/x01.htm.

——(2014c [1919]) *Seventh All-Russia Congress of Soviets*, December 5–9, available at: www.marxists.org/archive/lenin/works/1919/dec/05.htm.

——(1975) *Imperialism: The Highest Stage of Capitalism* (Moscow: Progress).

Mandel, E. (1978) *Late Capitalism* (London: Verso).

——(1995) *Long Waves of Capitalist Development: A Marxist Interpretation*, Revised Edition (London: Verso).

McDonough, T. and R. Drago (1989) "Crisis of Capitalism and the First Crisis of Marxism: A Theoretical Note on the Bernstein-Kautsky Debate," *Review of Radical Political Economics*, 21(3).

Marx, K. (2014a [1857]) *Grundrisse*, available at: www.marxists.org/archive/marx/works/1857/grundrisse/ch01.htm.

——(2014b [1859]) *A Contribution to the Critique of Political Economy*, available at: www.marxists.org/archive/marx/works/1859/critique-pol-economy/index.htm.

——(2014c [1865]) "Marx to Engels in Manchester," available at: www.marxists.org/archive/marx/works/1865/letters/65_07_31.htm.

——(2014d [1867]) *Capital* Vol. 1, Afterword to the Second German Edition, available at: www.marxists.org/archive/marx/works/1867-c1/p3.htm.

Milos, J. and D. P. Sotiropoulos (2009) *Rethinking Imperialism: A Study of Capitalist Rule* (Basingstoke: Palgrave).

Postone, M. (1996) *Time, Labor and Social Domination* (Cambridge: Cambridge University Press).

Sekine, T. (2013) "Dialectic, Logic, Economics," in J. R. Bell (ed.) *Towards a Critique of Bourgeois Economics: Essays of Thomas T. Sekine* (Berlin: Owl of Minerva Press).

Westra, R. (2009) *Political Economy and Globalization* (London: Routledge).

——(2012/13) "*Capital* as Dialectical Economic Theory," *Journal of Australian Political Economy*, Special Issue on *Capital* against Capitalism: New Research in Marxist Political Economy, 70.

Zarnowitz, V. (1999a) "Theory and History Behind Business Cycles: Are the 1990s the Onset of a Golden Age?" National Bureau of Economic Research (NBER) Working Paper No. 7010 Issued in March, available at: www.nber.org/papers/w7010.

——(1999b) "Has the Business Cycle Been Abolished?" National Bureau of Economic Research (NBER) Working Paper No. 6367, Issued in April, available at: www.nber.org/papers/w6367.

2 Variegated capitalism and the political economy of austerity

Bob Jessop

This chapter develops the notion of "variegated capitalism" and related concepts to analyze differential accumulation on a world scale and, in particular, the dynamics of the "global financial crisis." In this respect it goes beyond varieties of capitalism scholarship to consider how so-called varieties are integrated into the world market and how this shapes crisis-tendencies and efforts at crisis-management. One aspect of this exercise is to take seriously Marx's six-book plan for *Capital*, in which the last three books would address, respectively, the state, foreign trade, and the world market and crises. Extending the analysis systematically through this kind of logical-historical approach brings us closer to a concrete-complex conjuncture than is possible through an exclusive focus on the capital-labor relation or the circuits of capital. It also facilitates the interpretation and explanation of the variegated politics and policies of competitive austerity and their uneven incidence and impact. Variegation both results from and reinforces the multi-scalar interdependence and co-evolution of diverse accumulation regimes, modes of regulation, institutional and spatio-temporal fixes, and societal paradigms in world society. Given the variegated nature of differential accumulation, the political economy of austerity will also be variegated. While austerity policies differ across "varieties of capitalism" (reflecting their specific economic profiles and insertion into the world market), they are also affected by the interdependencies that result from interstate relations (including forms of regional and global governance), foreign trade (and other features of world market integration), the emergent logic of the world market in the current period, and, of course, its inherent crisis-tendencies. The basic argument is illustrated through the cases of the neoliberal US, neo-mercantilist Germany and its influence in the Eurozone, and Greece as a peripheral state. The chapter ends with suggestions for developing the corresponding research agenda.

The diversity and variety of capitalism

Rather than studying discrete varieties of capitalism or comparing capitalisms in a regional or global context (for a survey of such approaches, see Bruff and Ebenau 2014), this chapter explores how the diversity of accumulation regimes is reproduced and transformed in a changing world market. This patterned diversity – or *variegation* – involves a self-organizing ecology of self-organizing economic and political spaces shaped by the interaction of territorialization, place-making, scale, and networks (Jessop *et al.* 2008). It takes the form of a *fractally organized, variegated capitalism*, rather than a disparate set of *national varieties* of capitalism. Variegation is the product of the structural coupling, co-evolution, complementarities, tensions, rivalries, and antagonisms among different types or varieties of capitalism. This sets limits to the varieties that are compossible within a given space–time envelope. While it may be tempting to posit a "flat world" of separate but equal national varieties or, alternatively, a mosaic of rival economies with variable geometry and growth potentials, the world market is marked by many kinds of non-trivial asymmetries with their own forms of structured complexity. For example, some territorial states (e.g., the USA, the People's Republic of China, Germany), some places (e.g., networked global cities), some scales (e.g., the EU), and some spaces of flows (e.g., over the counter trade in interest rate contracts) matter more than others. These different forms of asymmetry may also be combined into relatively distinct bilateral or multilateral economic spaces with their own relatively distinct dynamics. Two cases are the pathological co-dependence of the US and Chinese economies on a global scale and the dysfunctional interaction of a neo-mercantilist German space and the remaining Eurozone, especially Southern Europe.

This "ecological" approach, which differs from an environmental or political ecology approach (but can be linked thereto) posits that current zones of relative stability depend in part on the presence of instability elsewhere, in the past, now, or the future. These are typically related to instabilities that derive from uneven capacities to exploit, displace and/or defer problems, conflicts, and crisis-tendencies. Such differences are related in part to "vertical" relations between core and periphery and other significant asymmetric capacities to shape the world market. This involves more than relative economic efficiency in allocating scarce resources to competing ends. For, alongside the sometimes not so invisible hand of the market, differential accumulation depends on soft power, force, domination, and market rigging to impose specific patterns of valorization, appropriation, and dispossession. In short, world market integration is never just the spontaneous outcome of market forces.

One possible approach to variegated capitalism derives from Marx's "six-book" plan for *Capital*. The planned books were: (1) Capital; (2) Landed Property; (3) Wage-Labor; (4) the State; (5) Foreign Trade; and (6) World Market and Crisis (Marx 1973b, p. 108). The first two books can be reconstructed from Marx's manuscripts but the analysis of capitalist credit money and interest-bearing capital was underdeveloped and also needs updating. Book three would have examined wage-labor considered as an active subject engaged in economic, political, and wider social struggles rather than as a passive object of exploitation in the labor process (Lebowitz 2003). Marx's *oeuvre* also indicates four key issues for inclusion in the state book: capitalist legal and state forms; economic and social policy; fiat money, tax and fiscal crisis; and the relations among great, middle and small powers in the world order (Anderson 2010; Draper 1977; Draper and Haberkern 2005; Krätke 1987; Molnár 1975; van der Pijl 1989). The book on foreign trade might have covered the global division of labor, geo-economics, geo-politics, mercantilism, colonies, and what would later be termed imperialism (Pradella 2013). The absent book on world market and crisis is where "production is posited as a totality together with all its moments, but within which, at the same time, all contradictions come into play" (Marx 1973b, p. 227; see also Smith 2006).

Although never realized (and possibly soon abandoned), the six-book plan implies that a complete analysis of differential accumulation on a world scale must extend beyond the capital–labor relation and the circuits of capitalist production to include the concentration of bourgeois society in the form of the state; the role of taxes (and tax competition); the relation between national monies, international currencies, and an emergent world money; public debt and state credit; colonies; international relations, diplomacy, and war; the international division of labor, foreign trade, and exchange rates; and, of course, the effects of all these factors on the integration and development of the world market and the playing out of capital's contradictions on a world scale. Many of these factors, especially the state, taxes, currency wars, sovereign debt, and international relations bear directly on the interpretation and explanation of progressive competitiveness and its successor, competitive austerity. More generally, growing world market integration makes it ever less appropriate to study "varieties of capitalism" as separate regimes that prove more or less efficient and competitive according to the audit of market forces. For, given that such integration tends to free capital from the frictions of national power containers and national politics and embed it in a space of global flows, the law of value will tend to operate on a global scale by commensurating local conditions and promoting the global search for competitive advantage based on superprofits from one or another kind of innovation.

As indicated above, the dynamics of the world market are related to the dynamics of the world of states. Thus the world market does not constitute a single "world system" with a pregiven logic (as world system theory sometimes presupposes) but actually comprises a tangled, unevenly developing hierarchy of local, regional, national, transnational, and supranational markets corresponding to particular state territories connected through various spaces of flows. While the world market is tendentially unified and integrated through profit-oriented, market-mediated competition based on trade, financial flows, and (capitalist) commodity production, the world political order is still characterized by a "motley diversity" of states that may be "hostile brothers," or deadly enemies, and that vary in size, capacities, and ability to shape the operation of the world market as well as to defend their respective capitals and/or those operating in their economic space. This said, states no more exist in mutual isolation, of course, than do local, regional, or national markets. This is where interdependences and strategic calculation based on geo-economics and geopolitics enter the analysis of the world market and crises.

While the world market is the ultimate horizon of accumulation, it is important to note that variegation, compossibility, and ecological dominance are *fractal*. They emerge and interact in (self-)similar ways at many sites and scales. This requires attention to the changing articulation of territory, place, scale, and flows and to the ways this occurs across time and space in more or less self-similar ways, with similarities attributed to the overall logic of capital and with differences attributed to the particular circumstances in which this logic unfolds. These fractal phenomena are not confined to "national" or, indeed, any single level of territorial organization. And, while there may be one hegemonic or dominant way of organizing economic and political space at a world scale, other patterns may enjoy regional hegemonies and/or dominance within this global framework.

It is in this context that we can explore "ecological dominance." This indicates the relative weight of various economic regimes in the world market and/or the relative impact of different circuits of capital in capital accumulation as a whole. Thus one could investigate the uneven development and structural coupling of capitalist regimes in a regional or global division of labor (e.g., the Rhenish, Nordic, and liberal market models in Europe or the global dominance of the liberal market model); or, again, examine the weight of commercial, industrial, or financial capital in capitalist circuits at different scales. These two kinds of ecological dominance are typically inter-related but vary in their articulation as the world market develops. They are not an automatic, mechanical outcome of market forces but depend on specific economic and political strategies.

For example, the ecological dominance of neoliberal market coordination reflects the politically engineered predominance of finance-dominated accumulation regimes in the world market plus the ecological dominance of financial capital in global capitalist circuits. This is reflected in "accumulation by dispossession" (including the politically licensed plundering of public assets and the intellectual commons), in the history of (varieties of) classical imperialism based on force and domination, and, more recently, in the "special deals with political authority" that facilitated the de-regulation of industrial and financial capital in the neoliberal era. Ecological dominance is especially clear in the positive and negative externalities that each variety generates for the others, in "good" as well as "hard" times. This depends not only on the relative strength of different circuits of capital and their articulation to so-called varieties of capitalism but also on the forms, extent, and intensity of resistance that this generates from the local to the global scale. This calls for more complex spatio-temporal horizons of analysis as well as attention to crisis dynamics.

Indeed, the more extensively and tightly integrated the world economy becomes in real time, the more the contradictions of capital are generalized, become more acute, and the harder it is to displace or defer them (cf. Marx 1973a, p. 227). In short, world market integration is a contradictory process with positive and negative effects.

On the one hand, increasing integration enhances capital's capacity to defer and/or displace the effects of its internal contradictions by the following: extending the scope of its operations; reinforcing its capacities to disembed certain of its operations from local material, social, and spatio-temporal constraints; enabling it to deepen the spatial and scalar divisions of labor; creating more opportunities for moving up, down, and across scales to secure economic and political advantage; re-articulating time horizons; and commodifying and securitizing the future. This helps in turn to emancipate the profit-oriented, market-mediated moment of capital accumulation from extra-economic and spatio-temporal constraints, increases the emphasis on speed, acceleration, and turnover time, and enhances capital's capacity to escape the control of other systems insofar as these are still territorially differentiated and fragmented. Fictitious credit (pseudo-validated loans that are not advanced for productive investment) and fictitious capital (capital as property rather than functioning capital) gain a much larger role compared with Fordism – with the volumes of securitized loans and of credit advanced for financial trading massively boosted by neoliberal banking and financial deregulation (cf. Jessop 2013a). Financial innovation in turn facilitates the increasing acceleration and hyper-mobility of credit money and its escape from regulation. World market integration also weakens the capacity of labor and other subaltern forces to resist exploitation through coordinated action within and across different sites and fields of struggle.

On the other hand, these enhanced capacities reinforce uneven development as the search continues to transcend every barrier to the self-expansion of capital. Capital's efforts to overcome local or national frictions and fetters tend to undermine the power of states to regulate economic activities within their respective territories in the public interest. This tends to weaken local or national competitiveness, especially where it is based on strong competitive advantages (progressive competitiveness); and it also encourages a destructive "race to the bottom" and, as seen in the current crisis, a turn to an equally counter-productive politics and program of competitive austerity. One response to this weakened territorial (and temporal) state sovereignty is to rescale the state but this does not eliminate the pressure to compete for investment or, in conditions of crisis, to impose austerity. Further, insofar as the working class(es) and other subaltern forces are weakened (see above), the potential for overproduction and weak demand tends to rise in line with reductions in the individual and social wage and polarization of wealth and income inequalities in the top decile, percentile, and super-rich (Elsner 2012; Piketty 2014). This reinforces financialization as a driver of world market integration – recreating the immanent barriers to the self-valorization of capital on a larger and more formidable scale.

Finance-dominated accumulation

Money, credit, and debt have existed for three millennia but they acquire new forms and functions with the consolidation of the capitalist mode of production. Indeed, capitalist credit-money is essential to its expanded reproduction. One of its forms is interest-bearing capital (to be distinguished from traditional usury capital) and this, in turn, can generate increasingly fantastic forms of fictitious capital (Marx 1967b; de Madeiros Carneiro *et al.* 2012; Jessop 2013a). The concept of ecological dominance can also be applied to the autonomization of financial capital as the treadmill of global competition has pressured banking capital to turn for profits from the "boring banking" activities of financial intermediation and risk-management to activities concerned with financial speculation and risk-taking (LiPuma and Lee 2004; Haldane 2012; Elsner 2012). However, this did not result solely from spontaneous market forces. It required a series of deliberate economic, political, and social interventions mediated through neoliberalizing states at local, national, regional, continental, and global scales (Duménil and Lévy 2004; Harvey 2003). For financialization was facilitated by successive measures of liberalization and deregulation enacted thanks in part to the role of financial capital in funding political parties and to various "unusual deals with political bodies." This is reinforced through the politically authorized looting of public assets and the sacking of the intellectual commons.

The neoliberal form of world market integration greatly benefits interest-bearing capital because it controls the most liquid, abstract, and generalized resource and has become the most integrated fraction of capital. This points beyond the general significance of capitalist credit-money in the circuits of capital to its specific forms and effects when interest-bearing capital, as opposed, for example, to suppliers of trade or production credit, becomes the dominant force in economic, political, and social life. Where the circuits of interest-bearing capital became increasingly autonomous from those of profit-producing capital (which can only occur in the short- to medium-term before serious crises occur), the impact of fictitious credit, fictitious capital, and fictitious profits has reshaped the wider social formation. They are major vectors of the colonization, commodification, and, eventually, financialization of everyday life. World market integration also reinforces uneven development as financial capital moves on when the disastrous effects of financialization weaken those productive capitals that have to be valorized in particular times and places.

The logic of financialization (wherever it occurs) undermines or restricts the primacy of production in the overall logic of capital accumulation. In contrast with the relative structured coherence of Fordism and the alleged coherence of the once widely heralded post-Fordist "knowledge-based economy," the finance-dominated regime that developed from the 1980s onwards works against the long-term stability of accumulation and its regulation. In particular, it weakens the spatio-temporal fixes through which regimes based on the primacy of productive capital (such as Fordism) produce zones of relative stability. This is evident in the impact of financialization not only in Atlantic Fordism but also in the export-oriented economies of East Asia, the viability of import-substitution industrialization strategies in Latin America and Africa, and the problems in several post-socialist economies in Central and Eastern Europe. This provides one basis for financial crises that develop relatively independently, at least initially, from crisis-tendencies in the circuits of capitalist production. It also promotes rent extraction through excessive leverage, financial arbitrage and innovation, and, as is becoming increasingly evident, various forms of predatory and/or criminal activities (Black 2014; Smith 2010; Will *et al.* 2013). It also expands markets for the "symbionts and parasites" of financial capital in its heartlands, "off-shore," and in the (semi-)periphery (on finance-dominated accumulation, see Jessop 2013b).

In short, as neoliberalism and financialization expand and penetrate deeper into the social and natural world, they transform the micro-, meso- and macro-dynamics of capitalist economies. First, they alter the calculations and behavior of non-financial firms through the rise of shareholder value as a coercive discourse, technology of governance, and vector of competition. One aspect is the growing importance for *non-financial* firms of *financial* activities (e.g., treasury functions, financial intermediation, using retained profits for share buybacks and/or acquisition or expansion of financial subsidiaries) that are not directly tied to their main profit-producing pursuits. Thus financial revenues became more important relative to profits of enterprise for these firms (Krippner 2005; Nölke 2009; Lapavitsas 2013). Second, this process boosts the size and influence of the financial sector. Fee-producing and risk-taking activities increase relative to banking capital's more traditional roles in intermediation and risk management; securitization, leverage and shadow banking with corresponding liquidity risks and weak prudential controls also expand; and so does the significance of new forms of financial capital (e.g., hedge funds, private equity, vulture capital, sovereign wealth funds). Third, everyday life is financialized. The wage is treated primarily as a cost of (global) production rather than as a source of (domestic) demand and this leads to re-commodification of social welfare in housing, pensions, higher education, health insurance, and so on. Growing flexibility of wage labor (especially increasing precarization) and cuts in the residual social wage leads workers to rely on credit (and usury) to maintain their standard of living and provide for daily, life-course, and intergenerational reproduction. Fourth, as successive crises from the mid-1970s show, financialization makes the economy more prone to recession and, in severe cases, more liable to the downward spiral of debt-deflation-default dynamics (Dore 2008; Duménil and Lévy 2004; Fine 2010; Lapavitsas 2013; Rasmus 2010).

But the development of finance-dominated accumulation does not mean that financial capital, let alone capital as property (fictitious capital), can become fully and permanently detached from the need to valorize capital in the "real" economy. On the contrary, because continued expansion depends heavily on the pseudo-validation of highly leveraged speculative and Ponzi debt, this regime contains its own inherent crisis-generating mechanism rooted in the systemic conflict between interest-bearing and profit-producing capital. Elsner (2012) explains this as follows. Financial capital in a finance-dominated accumulation regime has a target rate of return that is several times greater than the historic norm for profit-producing capital and, worse still, in an effort to achieve this target, engages in massive leveraging of ficti-tious credit and capital. In aggregate, the eventual validation of this massively leveraged capital would demand a total volume of surplus-value that far exceeds the productive and exploitative capacity of existing profit-producing capital.

Attempts to square this circle depend on three strategies that are individu-ally and collectively unsustainable. One is to create and manage bubbles, the main redistribution mechanism in finance-dominated accumulation, and then bail out (or get bailed out) at the right moment (Elsner 2012, pp. 146–47; see also Hudson 2012). This requires the complicity of central banks and gov-ernment in the finance-dominated economies. Another is to invoke a system-threatening "financial emergency" that justifies efforts to reduce individual and social wages, impose internal devaluation, and privatize public services and assets to pay off the public debt incurred in massive bailouts (cf. Mirowski 2013). States at different sites and scales have key roles here too and this strategy has reinvigorated neoliberalism and supported the politics of auster-ity. The third approach involves primitive accumulation (e.g., land-grabbing, capitalizing nature and its services enclosing the intellectual commons, priva-tizing accumulated public wealth, colonizing the residual public sector, and so on). This also requires state involvement. In short, the most rarefied and leveraged forms of fictitious credit and capital are now primarily, and sys-temically rather than merely contingently, problem-makers; and the rest of the economy, society, and nature have become problem-takers. It follows, as Marx anticipated, that, the greater and longer the seeming independence of financial capital and the greater the resulting parasitism of finance as prop-erty, the greater and longer the crises created by the forcible re-imposition of the organic unity of different phases of capital's metamorphosis (cf. Marx 1968, p. 509).

The North Atlantic Financial Crisis

I now explore the interaction between a world market organized in the shadow of neoliberal, finance-dominated accumulation and a Eurozone organized in the shadow of neo-mercantilism (on the symbiosis of debt-led and export-led growth, see Stockhammer 2013). Not only does this require attention to the world market, it also requires attention to the role of the state. The global influence of financialization was facilitated by the Washing-ton Consensus, which was heavily promoted by the USA and its allies to roll out liberalization, deregulation, privatization, and market proxies in any residual state services (whether concerned with infrastructure or welfare). This Consensus also promoted cuts in direct taxes (notably for corporations and financial institutions), aided by a fiscal race to the bottom to attract or retain investment (and by greater use of onshore as well as offshore tax havens) and a shift towards indirect taxes. This was supposed to increase the scope for market forces to allocate capital globally but, in conjunction with political capitalism and the logic of shareholder value, it has also re-distributed income and wealth towards the "have-lots" at the expense not only of the "have-nots" but also of the "squeezed middle." This feeds into the politics of austerity.

This can be illustrated by the interaction between the North Atlantic Financial Crisis (NAFC) and the Eurozone crisis. It is not confined to this interaction, however, having many more aspects and far wider ramifications. Although not reducible to the dynamic of financial circuits and more correctly designated as a multi-faceted crisis (*Vielfachkrise*), the NAFC was triggered by accumulating problems generated by a hypertrophied finance-dominated economy in which fictitious money, fictitious credit, fictitious capital (plus fictitious profits derived from control fraud and false accounting) played an increasingly autonomous role outside the circuits of profit-producing capital and the fossil fuel, food, and environmental crises with which the current crisis is associated.

While financialization initially benefitted many economic agents, the collapse of credit bubbles and the implosion of financial speculation have reversed this stimulus effect. As growth in this regime depended on acceleration in fictitious credit, the writing down of bad debt, the repayment of debt, reluctance to contract new debt, and the hoarding of available capital threw the mechanism of pseudo-validated demand into reverse. Thus debt deleveraging, especially when it occurs in both the private and public sectors, creates conditions for a vicious cycle of "debt-default-deflation" dynamics and an eventual epic recession (Rasmus 2010; Keen 2011).

The unwillingness of interest-bearing capital to sacrifice its short-term economic interests to protect its long-term political hegemony or, at least, domination activates the potential antagonism between "Wall Street" and "Main Street" (and their equivalents elsewhere) in three ways. First, too-big-to-fail financial institutions benefit from bailouts and quantitative easing that enables them to rebuild their capital base at low or no cost and to undertake further speculation. Second, small and medium enterprises find it harder to access production and trade credit. And, third, households find it harder to secure personal credit and/or to fund their now privatized health, pension, higher education, and other life-course and intergenerational reproduction needs. Most households also lose from the attack on "entitlements," previously part of the social wage in democratic welfare states, as these are portrayed even more vocally than before as costs that prevent the rundown of public and sovereign debt. This reversal of "private Keynesianism" reinforces the debt-default-deflation dynamics that threaten to shift economies from recession into epic recession or even another depression. Similar results follow in Europe from official attempts to create an "internal devaluation" through cuts in the private and social wage, other production costs, and so on, to compensate for the legal restrictions on devaluation or exit from the Eurozone.

Debt-default-deflation dynamics also strengthen other crisis-tendencies inherent in neoliberalism. The global "reserve army of labor" expands, weakening workers' bargaining power over wages and conditions, and increasing precarious work. Privatization and austerity in areas needed for a productive rather than parasitic economy (e.g., infrastructure provision, education, health, and science) are undermining their capacity to promote growth in the "real economy." A fragile Washington Consensus is challenged by demands for protectionism in crisis-hit metropolitan economies and opposition to free trade in the periphery (sometimes linked to proposals for "post-neoliberalism"). Yet transnational elites continue to present free trade agreements as an essential and purportedly cost-free economic recovery measure and to veil the extent to which such agreements would actually entrench the rights of capital as private property against subaltern groups and less market-friendly states and regimes. The NAFC has also aggravated imbalances in the global economy and shifted its center of gravity to the east and south but even beneficiaries such as the BRICS have suffered contagion from the NAFC in addition to experiencing their own particular, endogenous crisis-tendencies. This can be seen in Brazil and India and the slackening growth and serious hidden debt problems in China as well as the possibly forlorn search for new growth prospects in other large "emerging market" economies, like Mexico, Indonesia, Nigeria, and Turkey (the MINT quartet), which are supposed to escape the worst effects of the global financial crisis.

The political economy of austerity

I now turn to the political economy of austerity. Efforts to impose austerity are an expected and recurrent response to crises in relatively open economies because both the individual wage and social wage are costs of (international) production as well as sources of demand. This can be contrasted with the heyday of Atlantic Fordism, when wage-led growth was feasible within certain limits in relatively closed economies (Jessop 2002; Stockhammer 2013). Austerity may also be pursued, even pro-cyclically and counter-productively, when the economic imaginaries and material interests of interest-bearing capital prevail over those of productive capital (on this distinction, see van der Pijl 1998). What matters below is not austerity in general or general austerity but the specificities of austerity politics and policies and their impact in the NAFC and the Eurozone crisis financial and sovereign debt crisis.

Debt-default-deflation dynamics in the US

The USA and United Kingdom were pioneers in the advanced capitalist states of neoliberal regime shifts (catchwords Reaganism and Thatcherism) and initiated many of the techniques of neoliberal austerity that have since been refined there and elsewhere, including the commitment never to let a good crisis go to waste. They also comprised the economic and political space where conditions favoring a severe financial crisis were strongly nurtured (albeit not with this result in mind) and where it surfaced, initially in the USA and then in the UK (Davies 2014; Jessop 2014; Rasmus 2010, 2012). The features of the crisis in both cases are characteristic of finance-dominated accumulation but the financial sector is less important to the USA than in Britain and it also has the "exorbitant privilege" of the dollar as world money as well as a weakened labor force that had seen no increases in real incomes in over twenty years. In the USA, the crisis passed through several stages: credit crunch, liquidity crisis, financial insolvencies, a generalized financial crisis, a recession that risked becoming an epic recession or great depression, and, most recently, a manufactured "public debt" crisis reflected in a surreal fiscal cliff debate.

The fiscal cliff debate rested on cumulative and wide-ranging efforts over decades to naturalize the need for entitlement reductions to lower public spending and the skilful exploitation of the economic fear and political panic in November 2008 to push this agenda forward in a bicameral, bipartisan manner. Proposals for deficit reduction stoked the fiscal hysteria without seriously examining cuts in defense spending, ending unfunded wars, halting subsidies to a broad spectrum of corporate interests (often with large reserves, often held offshore), or restoring tax rates on the rich to Reagan era levels, despite stagnant wages and increased wealth inequalities to match those of the roaring twenties (Piketty 2014). A key feature of the *public debate* on the front stage of politics was its framing through the "fiscal cliff" metaphor. Back-stage, however, dealings and plotting continued with a view to cutting entitlement programs further and implementing yet more corporate tax breaks. The benefits for the rich of the latter will substantially exceed the "harm" caused by individual tax hikes and this reflects the policy choices favored by interest-bearing capital and transnational profit-producing capital. Little attention was paid to other policy options that might regenerate the economy, enhance competitiveness, improve conditions for the "squeezed middle," and renew the war on poverty.

Even the incoming 2009 Obama Administration, with its strong electoral mandate(s) for change and the potential political resource of public anger, rejected a popular, populist attack on "banksters." Instead it bailed out financial institutions and pursued fiscal austerity to protect corporate tax cuts and defence spending. With many *dramatis personae* recruited from the financial sector (notably from investment banks), the Obama Administration followed the fiscal cliff script, contributing to bipartisan and bicameral immobilism. Yet, despite earlier doom-laden forecasts, the US economy is slowly recovering (although commentators doubt its robustness) and, significantly, the federal budget deficit is falling. This suggests that the deficit hysteria was staged to pressure Congress in an election period to lock in bigger cuts before quantitative easing produced a (weak and still fragile) recovery and that Obama collaborated for his own political ends (and is continuing to do so, despite crowd-pleasing declarations that wealth inequalities are now excessive). In essence, we see the continuation of authoritarian neoliberalism and financialization in the USA that is producing not only rising profits, a weak economy, and welfare cuts in the "exceptional nation" but also causes more economic problems for most other economic spaces in the world market than they can cause for it. This holds both for China, with which it is locked in a relation of pathological co-dependency ("Chimerica," on which see, inter alia, Fabre 2009), and the European Union, its biggest trading and investment partner (Hamilton and Quinlan 2013).

The Eurozone crisis and the fiscal compact

European economic space illustrates well the fractal nature of variegated capitalism. It is organized in the shadow of the German growth regime (*das Modell Deutschland*) as an export-led accumulation regime that, despite significant neoliberal policy adjustments, has remained firmly inside the so-called co-ordinated market economy camp – partly because of the legacies of Ordoliberalism and partly because of the complex material interdependencies in the German space economy, which includes elements of other Rhenish economies in Northern Europe (cf. Bruff, this volume). For example, alongside its own export strengths, the Netherlands provides important commercial and business services that support *Modell Deutschland*; Austria and the new, post-socialist member states in Central Europe also fit into this accumulation regime. European economic space also has important transatlantic links (see above). This provides a basis for strong US interest in the forms and effects of crisis-management in the Eurozone (AmCham EU 2012).

An increasingly heterogeneous EU based on the uneven and combined development of different varieties of capitalism was aggravated by the uneven impact of the crises of Atlantic Fordism and contrasting responses within and across national models from the late 1960s through the 1980s. These were the years of "Eurosclerosis." However, because crisis has proved a crucial driver of European integration, these developments were far from fatal. Indeed, the accession of the Southern European economies (especially Spain) and East and Central European economies enabled the northern member states to moderate their own crises by deepening the regional division of labor within European economic space based on the promotion of peripheral Fordism and the extension of credit. This benefitted the neo-mercantilist German bloc and French industry and also created new investment opportunities for banks and other financial institutions not only from Germany and France but also from Austria, Italy, and Sweden. This strategy was spearheaded politically by the Franco–German axis and the European Commission (Stützle 2013). But the crisis of Fordism also made it harder to re-scale demand management and indicative planning from the national to the European level or to establish a tripartite Euro-corporatism to support a European Keynesian welfare state. This created the space for radical neoliberal regime shifts based on a principled rejection of inherited post-war settlements in some member states and more pragmatic neoliberal policy adjustments in others.

Das Modell Deutschland is distinguished both by the sheer volume and strong share of exports in GDP compared with other trading giants, such as the USA, Japan, and, later, China. Its exports are especially strong in capital goods (notably capital goods for making capital goods) and in diversified, research-intensive, high-quality consumer durables (cf. Porter 1990). Given the limited domestic market in these categories of goods, this export profile has shaped the German state's post-war domestic and foreign economic policy and its general strategy for European integration (Bellofiore *et al.* 2010; Cesaratto and Stirati 2010; Simonis 1998; Streeck 2009). For example, after the initial period of post-war reconstruction, restraining prices and wages was crucial for Germany's capacity to renew its export competitiveness. This has been combined with neo-mercantilist foreign economic policy. In particular, German capital and the German state (initially West Germany, now the re-unified state) have sought to shape the governance of the world market, especially in periods of crisis. This is reflected in the German role in regional and international monetary regimes and the problems of managing the deutsche Mark (and, later, the euro) with a view to maintaining both Germany's export competitiveness and the regional and international stability on which its exports depend. This strategy has been reinvigorated regularly whenever export-led growth has faltered and can be seen most recently in the Hartz labor market reforms introduced in 2002–05 as part of the red-green coalition's Agenda 2010 programme. Real wage suppression made a significant contribution to the increase in German exports to the European Union in the early 2000s, aided by credit-fuelled consumer demand. Greece, Italy, Portugal, and Spain were important sources of demand in this regard (Weeks 2014). It also restrained domestic demand in Germany, contributing to an increasing trade surplus. Paradoxically, then, these and other neoliberal policy adjustments underwrote a neo-mercantilist growth regime.

The development of Economic and Monetary Union (EMU) occurred in the shadow of German neo-mercantilism. Originally agreed for political reasons at the Maastricht Summit and shaped more by political than economic and fiscal principles, EMU was also expected to advance Germany's export-oriented strategy by extending the Deutsche Mark zone across a broader area (Overbeek 2012). The euro would be a weaker currency than the DM on its own and thereby enhance the competitiveness of French and German industrial capital, especially when reinforced by direct wage restraint, a reduced social wage, and lowered domestic consumption. Reflecting the banking tenets of *Modell Deutschland*, EMU operated on two key principles: first, the European Central Bank (ECB) may not act as lender of last resort to insolvent banks or indebted states; and, second, sovereign debts may only be discharged by their respective member states (Varoufakis 2013). In this sense, economic governance of the Eurozone was strongly imprinted by Germanic elements.

Before 2008, the Eurozone appeared to be operating smoothly thanks to global capital and trade flows and the short-term boost to growth produced by EMU. Yet structural incompatibilities and institutional design flaws were already evident before 2009, intensified in 2010–11, and became acute in 2012. Future structural problems were inscribed into the Eurozone at its inception because of tensions among member states that originated in incompatible accumulation regimes, patterns of insertion into European and world markets, modes of regulation, and governance capacities. Several measures taken by member states to produce convergence as a condition of entry into the Eurozone (hidden public debt, cuts in vital infrastructure spending, reduced expenditure on education, health, and welfare to the detriment of long-term competitiveness) reinforced these structural weaknesses. There were other grounds for skepticism too. Monetary union was not accompanied by fiscal union and, additionally, there were no credible institutional arrangements to enforce long-term fiscal discipline, compensate for uneven development and economic performance, or coordinate crisis-management in a situation where conventional national crisis responses such as devaluation were ruled out. In short, the design of EMU "removed internal shock absorbers while … magnifying both the probability and magnitude of a future crisis" (Sotiropoulos 2013).

As Yannis Varoufakis, an astute observer of world market dynamics, notes (Varoufakis 2013, p. 54):

> The combination of accumulating profits in the Eurozone's core (due largely to the repression of Germany's wage share) and abundant toxic, or private, money minted by the financial sector (primarily by the City and Wall Street) ensured that no decent returns could be found in the sluggish Eurozone core itself. So torrents of credit rushed from the surplus to the deficit Eurozone countries in the form of loans and sovereign debt purchases. For 12 years (1997–2008), the capital inflows into the periphery reinforced themselves by strengthening the demand for the core's net exports, part of which was utilised in helping German multinationals globalise beyond the Eurozone (in Eastern Europe, Asia and Latin America)

However, all these tensions were overlooked by the ECB, which placed undue faith in an upward economic convergence induced by monetary integration. Once the NAFC became visible, these factors made the Eurozone especially vulnerable. Thus failure to address the design flaws and the emerging structural problems inherent in a variegated European economic and political space in good times made crisis-management harder with the eruption of the NAFC, the surfacing and intensification of the Eurozone crisis, reinforcing macro-economic imbalances, and provoking the downward spiral of private and sovereign debt-default-deflation dynamics in peripheral economies. Transatlantic contagion effects led to the virtual insolvency of many of Europe's big banks, urgent rescue measures to recapitalize them and nationalize toxic assets, and the threat of sequential bankruptcy of vulnerable member states and their respective banking systems, beginning with Greece and Eire – with the systemically important cases of Spain, Italy, and France looming threats on the near horizon and, without the right to abandon the Euro and regain competitiveness through devaluation (among other measures), the peripheral economies were dangerously exposed to domestic debt-default-deflation dynamics and several pro-cyclical measures taken in other member states and European institutions to address the crisis.

Initial crisis-management responses were pro-cyclical because they made rescue packages contingent on deep cuts in spending and regressive taxation. This reinforced debt-default-deflation dynamics through the feedback between banking and sovereign debt crises. The austerity drive in Southern Europe leads to epic recessions, rising public debt to GDP ratios despite (or, rather, because of) the austerity measures, reduces imports from the core economies, and leads to disinvestment and capital flight so that liquid capital flows from deficit to surplus nations (on the concept of epic recession, see Rasmus 2010). The downward spiral threatened to spread thereby from peripheral member states to the Eurozone's core through the deeply interconnected European credit markets.

This created the space for technocratic governance in southern member states, whether through EU and ECB-inspired *coups d'état* (Greece and Italy) or through *de facto* or formal governments of national unity (Spain, Portugal). These governments are running states of economic emergency that authorize big spending cuts and neoliberal structural reforms. Yet the depth of the crisis and the impact of austerity have prompted growing resistance in the periphery from the unemployed, the poor, the marginalized, savers, etc., with a likely spread northwards. This requires careful modulation of conditionalities to keep the electorates of "donor" states on side and to temper popular unrest that would destabilize the governments of economic emergency in the indebted states. Yet this tends to hide from public view that bailout monies largely return from the PIIGS to financial institutions in Northern Europe.

A series of failed crisis-measures to the Treaty on Stability, Coordination and Governance in the Economic and Monetary Union (or Fiscal Compact) was signed by all but two member states in March 2012. When fully implemented, it will set binding limits (0.5 per cent of GDP) on the structural deficits in the annual budgets of individual member states and thereby constrain national sovereignty in the field of economic policy. The price exacted for the ECB's resort to Long-Term Refinancing Operations (LTRO) and Outright Monetary Transactions (OMT) programs was a Faustian Bargain with the surplus countries. Specifically, to be able to operate as a de facto lender of last resort to banks, central banks, and sovereign states, the ECB had to commit to using its coercive powers in conjunction with the European

Commission and the IMF (operating, then, as the "Troika") to impose the greatest austerity upon the weakest member states (Varoufakis 2013). This will prevent active fiscal policy along Keynesian lines and exacerbate the underlying macroeconomic weaknesses in the Eurozone. The Fiscal Compact removes budgetary policy from national control, establishing technical rules set by experts. By extending disciplinary neoliberalism, it constitutionalizes and entrenches the power of capital, limiting states' political autonomy and transforming budget-making into a more technocratic process subject to legal sanctions as well as market pressures. For the Fiscal Pact's aims to be feasible, however, investment must rise significantly above savings in deficit and surplus countries alike (Varoufakis 2013). There are no prospects of this happening because of the economic and political divisions within the Eurozone.

Greece is a small and peripheral European economy with a weak and clientelist state. It has provided an interesting laboratory for neoliberal austerity policies to see what the political authorities could get away with. The failure of measures imposed on the Greek people to date prompted second thoughts among research staff in the IMF and OECD on the validity and effectiveness of austerity policies. However, despite hopes (and fears) that Greece might exit the Eurozone, permanently or temporarily (to allow for restructuring), the risks and costs of breakup led the German government, European Commission, ECB, and IMF (with US backing) to introduce exceptional measures to preserve this flawed system. Austerity in Greece has been regarded (outside) as a price worth paying to this end, especially as the excluded alternatives (Marshall-plan type capital transfers, a debt moratorium to finance contra-cyclical investment, a state role as employer of last resort, etc.) would have set bad precedents for the larger, more systemically important Southern European economies. In Greece as elsewhere, the "There is No Alternative" mantra restricts the feasible set of economic, political, and social policies. This proved unappealing in Southern Europe (outside the current set of state managers) and is contested by post-Keynesian economists, diverse think tanks, and several major political parties (when in opposition); growing popular unrest, including right-wing populism and xenophobia, and popular reaction against the ECB's attempt to renege on deposit insurance in Cyprus all indicate possible limits of the politics and policies of austerity. But the interpretive authority to translate crisis construals into crisis-management policies remains with the economic and political elites and, as Deutsch (1973, p. 111) once noted, power is the ability not to have to learn from one's mistakes. There is a lot of not learning going on as neoliberal forces emerge stronger strategically from the current crisis – at the expense of storing up bigger problems in the future.

Conclusions

This chapter has offered an alternative to the comparative capitalism and varieties of capitalism literature that affirms the diversity of accumulation regimes and modes of regulation but puts this diversity in its place within the framework of the world market as the presupposition and result of capital accumulation. It further argued that, the greater the integration of the world market (a process promoted by the neoliberal project of market completion), the less plausible it becomes to focus on varieties of capitalism considered in isolation from their structural coupling and co-evolution. Among relevant concepts for analyzing variegated capitalism in the world market are the following: variegation, compossibility, core-periphery relations, the articulation of the space of flows with more territorial or place-based logics, patterns of adhesion and exclusion from the world market, and ecological dominance. This approach promises powerful insights into the alternation between periods of relative stability (at least in some regions and/or some circuits of capital) and periods when contradictions and crisis-tendencies are more visible and into why these dynamics vary over time and space with the ecologically dominant variety of capitalism. It means that varieties of capitalism cannot be accorded equal analytical weight as so many theoretically possible, empirically observable, and more or less internally coherent, harmoniously functioning individual instances of capitalism. Instead they should be studied in terms of their asymmetrical, differential integration into an evolving world market that sets limits to compossible combinations and implies that some "varieties" are more equal than others, that is, cause more problems (or create more "disharmonies") for other varieties than they can cause for it.

Marx's unrealized six-book plan for *Capital* is a useful source of inspiration for developing a "logical-historical" analysis of variegated capitalism. This uses theoretically informed comparison to move stepwise from abstract-simple categories to concrete-complex analyses of historically specific cases. In particular, Marx's plan indicates the importance of exploring, first, how the world market is shaped by the world of states (and hence by foreign trade and other international relations) and, second, how the integration of the world market generalizes the contradictions and crisis-tendencies of capital accumulation and brings closer the time when the ultimate barrier to self-valorization will be the capital relation itself rather than more specific frictions and fetters. This does not amount to a claim about the convergence of capital accumulation around one model but does indicate the scope for crises and contagion effects on a world scale. While this explains the general trend towards austerity in capitalism today, despite its uneven and different development, variegation explains the different forms taken by the pursuit of austerity.

Acknowledgments

Research for this chapter was aided by an Economic and Social Research Council professorial fellowship (RES-051–27-0303).

References

AmCham EU (2012) *Putting Growth Back into Europe. AmCham EU's Strategic Recommendations* (Brussels: American Chamber of Commerce to Europe).

Anderson, K. B. (2010) *Marx at the Margins: on Nationalism, Ethnicity, and non-Western Nations* (Chicago, IL: University of Chicago Press).

Bellofiore, R., F. Garibaldo and J. Halevi (2010) "The Great Recession and the contradictions of European neomercantilism," *Socialist Register 2011*, 120–46.

Black, W. K. (2014) "Madness posing as hyper-rationality: OMB's assault on effective regulation," *New Economic Perspectives*, May 27.

Bruff, I. and M. Ebenau (2014) "Critical political economy and the critique of comparative capitalisms scholarship on capitalist diversity," *Capital & Class*, 38(1): 1–13.

Cesaratto, S. and A. Stirati (2010) "Germany and the European and global crises," *Journal of International Political Economy*, 39(4): 56–86.

Davies, W. (2014) *The Limits of Neoliberalism: Authority, Sovereignty and the Logic of Competition* (London: SAGE).

de Medeiros Carneiro, R., M. Chiliatto-Leite, G. Santos Mello and P. Rossi (2012) "The fourth dimension: derivatives in a capitalism with financial dominance," paper for International Initiative on Political Economy Conference, Paris, July 6.

Deutsch, K. W. (1973) *The Nerves of Government* (New York: Free Press).

Dore, R. (2008) "Financialization of the global economy," *Industrial and Corporate Change*, 17: 1097–1112.

Draper, H. (1977) *Karl Marx's Theory of Revolution: State and Bureaucracy, Part I, in 2 vols* (New York: Monthly Review).

Draper, H. and E. Haberkern (2005) *Karl Marx's Theory of Revolution, vol V: War and Revolution* (New York: Monthly Review).

Duménil, G. and D. Lévy (2004) *Capitalism Resurgent: Roots of the neoliberal revolution* (Cambridge, MA: Harvard University Press).

——(2011) *The Crisis of Neoliberalism* (Cambridge, MA: Harvard University Press).

Elsner, W. (2012) "Financial capitalism – at odds with democracy: the trap of an 'impossible' profit rate," *Real-World Economics Review*, 62: 132–59.

Fabre, G. (2009) "'The twilight of Chimerica'? China and the collapse of the American model," *Economic and Political Weekly*, 44(26–27): 299–307.

Fine, B. (2010) "Locating financialisation," *Historical Materialism*, 18: 97–116.

Haldane, A. (2012) "The doom loop," *London Review of Books* 34(4): 21–22.

Hamilton, D. S. and J. P. Quinlan (2013) *The Transatlantic Economy 2013* (Brussels: American Chamber of Commerce to the European Union).

Harvey, D. (2003) *A Brief History of Neoliberalism* (Oxford: Oxford University Press).

Hudson, M. (2012) *The Bubble and Beyond: Fictitious Capital, Debt Deflation and the Global Crisis* (Dresden: Islet).

Jessop, B. (2002) *The Future of the Capitalist State* (Cambridge: Polity).

——(2013a) "Credit money, fiat money and currency pyramids," in J. Pixley and G. C. Harcourt (eds) *Financial crises and the nature of capitalist money* (Basingstoke: Palgrave Macmillan, pp. 248–72).

——(2013b) "Finance-dominated accumulation and the limits to institutional and spatiotemporal fixes in capitalism," in S. A. Jansen, E. Schröter and N. Stehr (eds) *Fragile Stabilität – stabile Fragilität* (Wiesbaden: Verlag für Sozial-wissenschaften, pp. 301–26).

——(2014) "Margaret Thatcher and Thatcherism: dead but not buried," *British Politics*, 9(4): in press.

Jessop, B., N. Brenner and M.R. Jones (2008) "Theorizing socio-spatial relations," *Society and Space*, 26(3): 389–401.

Keen, S. (2011) "Economic growth, asset markets and the credit accelerator," *Real-World Economics Review*, 57: 25–40.

Krätke, M. (1987) *Kritik der Staatsfinanzen* (Hamburg: VSA).

Krippner, G.R. (2005) "The financialization of the American economy," *Socio-Economic Review*, 3: 173–208.

Lapavitsas, C. (2013) *Profiting without Producing: How Finance Exploits Us All* (London: Verso).

Lebowitz, M. (2003) *Beyond Capital: Marx's Political Economy of the Working Class*, 2nd edn (Basingstoke: Palgrave).

LiPuma, E. and B. Lee (2004) *Financial Derivatives and the Globalization of Risk* (Durham, NC: Duke University Press).

Marx, K. (1967a) *Capital, Vol. 1* (London: Lawrence & Wishart).

——(1967b) *Capital, Vol. 3* (London: Lawrence & Wishart).

——(1968) *Theories of Surplus Value, Vol. 2* (London: Lawrence & Wishart).

——(1973a) *Grundrisse: Foundations of the Critique of Political Economy (Rough Draft)* (Harmondsworth: Penguin).

——(1973b) 'Introduction to the Contribution to the Critique of Political Economy,' in idem, *Grundrisse* (Harmondsworth: Penguin, pp. 88–111).

Mirowski, P. (2013) *Never Let a Serious Crisis Go to Waste* (London: Verso).

Molnár, M. (1975) *Marx, Engels et la politique internationale* (Paris: Gallimard).

Nölke, A. (2009) "Finanzkrise, Finanzialisierung und vergleichende Kapitalismus-forschung," *Zeitschrift für Internationale Beziehungen*, 16: 123–39.

Overbeek, H. (2012). "Sovereign debt crisis in Euroland: root causes and implications for European integration," *International Spectator*, 47(1): 30–48.

Piketty, T. (2014) *Capital in the Twenty-First Century* (Cambridge, MA: Harvard University Press).

Porter, M.E. (1990) *The Competitive Advantage of Nations* (Basingstoke: Macmillan).

Poulantzas, N. (1978) *State, Power, Socialism* (London: Verso).

Pradella, L. (2013) "Imperialism and capitalist development in Marx's *Capital*," *Historical Materialism*, 21(2): 117–47.

Rasmus, J. (2010) *Epic Recession: Prelude to Global Depression* (London: Pluto).

——(2012) *Obama's Economic Recovery: Recovery for the Few* (London: Pluto).

Simonis, G. (1998) "Das Modell Deutschland", in idem (ed.) *Deutschland nach der Wende. Neue Politikstrukturen* (Opladen: Leske, pp. 257–84).

Smith, T. (2006) *Globalisation: A Systematic Marxian Account* (Leiden: Brill).

Smith, Y. (2010) *Econned: How unenlightened self interest undermined democracy and corrupted capitalism* (New York: Palgrave Macmillan).

Sotiropoulos, D. (2013) "Addressing the rationality of 'irrational' European responses to the crisis," paper for the 8th Pan–European Conference on International Relations, Warsaw, September 18–21.

Stockhammer, E. (2013) "Rising inequality as a cause of the present crisis," *Cambridge Journal of Economics*, first published online November 26.

Streeck, W. (2009) *Re-forming Capitalism. Institutional Change in the German Political Economy* (Oxford: Oxford University Press).

Stützle, I. (2013) *Austerität als politisches Projekt. Von der monetären Integration Europas zur Eurokrise* (Münster: Westfälisches Dampfboot).

van der Pijl, K. (1989) *Marx and Engels on International Relations* (Maarssen: Stichting Center for Economic and Political Studies).

——(1998) *Transnational Classes and International Relations* (London: Routledge).

Varoufakis, Y. (2013) "From contagion to incoherence: towards model of the unfolding Eurozone crisis," *Contributions to Political Economy*, 32: 51–71.

Weeks, J. (2014) "Euro crises and Euro scams: trade not debt and deficits tell the tale," *Review of Political Economy*, 26(2): 171–89.

Will, S., D. Brotherton and S. Handelman (eds) (2013) *How They Got Away with it: White Collar Criminals and the Financial Meltdown* (New York: Columbia University Press).

3 Varieties of Capitalism or dominant fractions?

Two forms of money capital in the current crisis

Kees van der Pijl

The current crisis is called "financial" because it originated in the volatile movement of high-risk financial instruments that, since the 1980s, have come to dominate Western economies. Created with ever-more flimsy paper titles, the 2007–08, "financial crisis" saw the house of cards finally collapse. Yet as always, a crisis caused by any particular moment in the cycle of capital accumulation ultimately reveals an underlying limit to accumulation per se, which is the exhaustion of the social and natural base of the capitalist order as such (Funke 1978).

The house of cards is being meticulously rebuilt as I write, and another collapse is imminent. The question in this collection concerns whether we are looking at a world of separate "varieties of capitalism," which would imply that whilst the financial variety is being discredited, another variety, say, one based on production, would be available as an alternative, or whether we are looking at a process in which the market discipline of capital is developing across different societies, and hence unevenly; but that it nevertheless obeys an inner logic that in turn determines a broad historic process. This logic expresses itself through class struggles within and across societies, involving state policy both nationally and internationally. As a result capital in each state operates in a different balance of class forces, through which states also relate to each other. What accounts for these differences, however, is the different degree to which class struggles allow the inherent tendencies of capitalist development to become apparent in various settings – not a mosaic of national/regional capitalisms, each one culturally entrenched within a particular society.

Of course ultimately, we cannot be looking at different realities. So, up to a point, these conflicting approaches can be reconciled at a factual level by translating the different notions used into the other's terminology. For instance, if "culture" denotes habitual patterns of behavior sedimented by cumulative class compromises, the language of institutionalism will merely provide an alternative entry point for the analysis of a concrete instance of capitalist market discipline (in a given society at a given point in time). But if we want to move from case-by-case comparison to comprehensive historical study, the varieties approach suggests possibilities for choice within a capitalist order (say, Sweden reverting to welfare state capitalism), in which the reality suggested by a comprehensive class analysis do not exist.

The institutionalist background of the varieties approach

The Varieties of Capitalism approach belongs to the institutionalist school of political economy. This approach can be traced to the German Historical School that influenced the establishment of institutionalist economics in the United States, associated with Thorstein Veblen and others (I summarize my 2009, Chapter 5, and 2014, pp. 50–52 and 56–58). Its theoretical language was influenced by Pragmatism, which as a quasi-philosophy of trial-and-error built on the anti-metaphysical attitudes of a pioneer society, blended with the evolutionism of Social Darwinism that wafted over from Britain. The functional psychology that US students brought home from their studies in Germany (crucially through G. Stanley Hall's work with the founder of psychology as a separate discipline, Wilhelm Wundt) further shaped the Pragmatist mindset permeating Institutionalism.

The key theoretical sequence at work in this tradition is that people act on account of practical and mental habits – there is no inherent rationality in the human mind, as assumed by Descartes or Immanuel Kant. "Institutions" are habits that have crystallized into more or less permanent fixtures. Hence, a market in the economic sense will not be a matter of straightforward goods-for-money exchange but also involve transaction costs of a non-economic nature that happen to be payable in this or that society. Next, the actions that flow from these habits (and which in turn are dependent on adaptive choices made in specific circumstances) do not obey an objective rationality either, as Spinoza or Hegel would have argued. They are by definition "path-dependent" as they evolve; although Veblen and many contemporaries assumed that an objective principle regulated different lines of action by privileging those adapting best, resulting in the "survival of the fittest" – the Social Darwinist selection criterion actually coined by Herbert Spencer.

The survival of the fittest is a regulative principle "ex post" – in hindsight we can see that it operated. In the same way, the next most important institutionalist thinker after Veblen, Karl Polanyi, assumed an equally hidden principle in the Double Movement. Given that a self-regulating market is not a fact of nature, but must be forcibly instituted, and if applied to the sphere of labor, land or money, actually risks destroying that sphere, it will tend to be accompanied by protective measures sooner or later. These in turn add up to a comprehensive system of social protection through planning. "Laissez-faire was planned, planning was not," was Polanyi's famous aphorism (1957, p. 141).

Social phenomena in the Pragmatist-institutionalist universe are externally related. Finance preys on real production from the outside, the self-regulating market is forcibly "dis-embedded" from society (which Polanyi thought was organically held together by fundamentally different principles than exchange of equivalents – he shared an interest in anthropology with Veblen and many other institutionalists). The Varieties approach can be reconstructed from the variable combination of aspects of capitalist economies in combination with different cultural anthropologies: economies characterized by financial risk-taking or are averse to it, different degrees of social embeddedness of market economies, and so on, all on a path-dependent evolutionary trajectory. Michel Albert's famous comparison between the betting approach to insurance exemplified by those watching ships from the Lloyd's tavern, and the Swiss mountain farmers' habit of chipping in a premium to cover for the occasional lost cow, is the classic example (1991).

A value theory alternative: the cycle of industrial capital

Let me now turn to what I see as the alternative to the Varieties of Capitalism approach. To recap, it agrees with the obvious fact of "variety" but interprets it differently: what we are looking at is not a series of separate capitalisms, but a single market discipline of capital that has unevenly penetrated different societies. Not "culture" but class struggle is the regulator in the process and since the latter is historical, the inherent tendency of capital works its way everywhere. Taking Michel Albert's capitalism versus capitalism thesis again as the reference, "neo-American" capitalism is dominated by finance, risk, individuality, etc., and "Rhineland" capitalism by production, class compromise, and social protection, the question posed in the closing lines of Albert's book, that if only "we" were to form a United States of Europe, we would "have the ability to choose the social-economic model that is best for us all." From this perspective it is an impossibility – unless he means to say that a rise in working class militancy accompanied by a political strategy of the Left, might push back the discipline of capital, say, from the health and education spheres capital has penetrated in the last few decades. But he doesn't, because it follows from an entirely different theoretical discourse, with implications radically different from his own.

The prevalence of finance, risk, individuality, etc. in neo-American capitalism dates from the 1980s, and before with its long prehistory of Lockean liberalism. But then the version of "Rhineland" capitalism that characterized postwar Western Europe, also had its origins in the United States – in Roosevelt's New Deal, the response to the Great Depression of the 1930s, which was exported across the Atlantic in the late 1940s by the Marshall Plan. Of course social protection and the emphasis on production had their own prehistory in Bismarck's Prussia–Germany, but it shared aspects of that history with Disraeli's Britain: what decided the attempt to mitigate the excesses of mass industrialization was not English or continental culture, but fear that the working class might revolt and signs that it was mobilizing to do just that.

The connections between finance and production, then, are imparted by society, and hence are internal, not external. They are necessarily connected. The internal connection between the different forms of capital that we tend to take as markers of a particular "variety" – notably finance and production – occurs through what Marx called the cycle of industrial capital. Industrial capital is centered on the competitive exploitation of living labor power. This, I hardly need to repeat here, is the anchor point of a cycle which otherwise is organized around the exchange of equivalents. These equivalents are measured in labor time, which means that, ultimately, the total output is produced and distributed proportionately to the hours put in (adjusted by a factor accounting for training, machinery and equipment, etc.). Ultimately we are looking at a compound measure beyond practical use except that, in a labor value analysis, the empirical movement of prices takes place against a backdrop of value exchanges. Since labor power is paid what it costs to reproduce it, and not what it produces itself, this type of analysis explains exploitation from the appropriation of surplus value.

Class struggle determines what the reproduction costs of labor are in actuality. In the post-war era, they were relatively high; since the second half of the 1990s the phenomenon of the "working poor" is spreading, wherever the workers have been defeated in wage struggles most thoroughly, irrespective of "culture." Thus according to ILO figures, South Korea has the largest share of working poor (full-time employment paid less than subsistence-level wages), with just above 25 percent of all workers; the United States is second, then Canada, Hungary, Germany, and the UK (with around 20 percent working poor, ILO 2010, p. 34).

Producing new value is the anchor point of capitalist development. Investment for a growing population through capital accumulation is a sign that the economy is working irrespective of whether it is public or private investment. In *Capital* vol. I (*MEW* 23) Marx analyzes the basic process from the angle of capital-in-general appropriating surplus value (the differential between the value of the sold product and the value of labor power). The only limit recognized here is the process of original dispossession of direct producers, so-called original accumulation. Rosa Luxemburg (1966) and more recently, David Harvey (2006) have highlighted this latter aspect as a permanent feature of capitalist expansion.

Next to capital "fixed" in production, there must also be capital in circulation to allow successive rounds of accumulation to take place on an expanded scale (*Capital*, vol. 2, *MEW*, p. 25). So to get at a new productive combination of labor and equipment, supply the process with raw materials and semi-finished inputs, sell the output, etc. we must assume that capital is in constant movement, via a set of circuits in which value circulates in different forms. So behind the physical form of each component mentioned, there is a given amount of value circulating as capital. If we begin with capital in money form (M), via capital in commodity form (C, including labor power), we get to capital engaged in production (P) after which the product enters circulation again as C and then M. These "post-production" values contain the value increment appropriated by capital as surplus value, so C' and M'.

In *Capital*, vol. 3, a further concretization is introduced by identifying money capital as the form of capital-in-general, social capital, in the sense that it operates as "a concentrated, organized mass, which, entirely unlike real production, is subject to the control of bankers representing social capital" (*MEW* 25, p. 382). This may also be called "fictitious capital" because it totalizes the property titles as if they were not tied to actually existing credit relations, commercial activities, or ongoing production (so capital as if abstracted from social relations). Production on the other hand is necessarily embedded in society and nature, through what Harvey (2006, p. 399) calls "human resource complexes ... to which capital must, to some degree, adapt." Once a particular capital has been attached to a human resource complex, its managers will tend to be concerned with productivity, the availability of inputs, and, via commercial capital or directly, sales. Profitability from real value production (in contrast to merely commercial profit) thus depends on the spatio-temporally specific availability of a human and natural resource complex.

In Figure 3.1, the different "moments" of the cycle are depicted. Note that capital in money form has a dual quality: it represents social capital, the (fictitious) totality of all value distributed over different branches of activity; and it is, as bank/insurance, etc. capital, a particular "fraction" of capital with an interest of its own – to get its capital into those activities that yield the highest profit. It thus also constitutes its own "circuit," from one productive (or transport) investment cycle to the next, although per se it does not add value. Capital in commodity form on the other hand is not strictly speaking a "circuit"; it does not direct the process of production, as money capital will, but only operates as a (necessary) medium through which value-creating capital passes without creating value itself (it partakes in profit distribution through the price system).

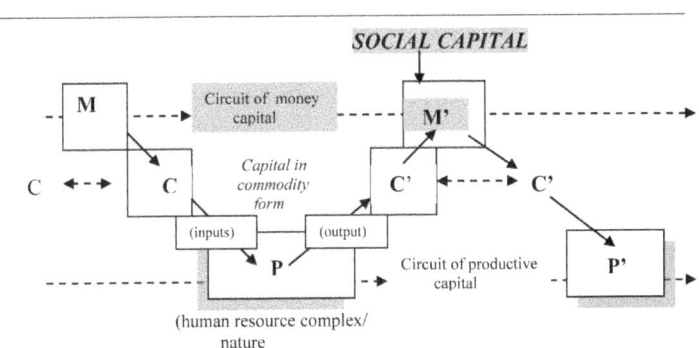

Key: M: capital in money form; C: capital in commodity form; P: capital arranged for production (or transport). Dual role of money capital highlighted; anchorage of productive capital in human resource complexes and nature indicated by shading.

Figure 3.1 Fractional "moments" in the cycle of industrial capital

The above implies that money capital in the sense of "bankers representing social capital" constitutes the wellspring of capitalist market discipline, imposed on individual "particular capitals" via competition. Particular capitals (like corporations) then pass market discipline onto the workers through the labor market and work discipline (Milios and Sotiropoulos 2009, pp. 82–83 & passim). Yet it will be clear that "the" capitalist interest is not easy to pin down: it is in continuous movement, assuming different forms (money, goods and services, actual production and transport); each activity is pursued under conditions of competition; new sources of wage labor have to be created by expropriation ("original accumulation"); and established groups of workers have to be "expropriated" again through deskilling, job reorganization, and the like, in order to maintain a rising rate of exploitation. So not only is the capitalist class interest dynamic owing to the constant movement and re-composition, but it is also "fractious," composed of tenuously combined competitive capitalists whose common interests are tentative at best.

Historic hegemonies and concepts of control

Over time, different fractions of capital have succeeded in making their particular interests appear as the general interest, not just of the capitalist class, but also of society as a whole (Hickel 1975). Their ability to do so has necessarily been the result of class struggle and class compromise, and can be reconstructed from the different moments of the cycle as depicted in Figure 3.1. The key regulator is the strength of the industrial working class. So far, it has enjoyed *one period in which it was able to force a class compromise on capital* – the period following World War I, the Russian Revolution, and the Great Depression, and comprising World War II and its immediate aftermath. Never had disasters of such magnitude struck Western society, and the weakening of the stature of the capitalist ruling class and its ability to direct society was likewise unprecedented. Organized labor in these circumstances was able to limit capitalist discipline, and via its presence in the state machinery, create conditions such as collective bargaining, trade and job market protection, and capital controls, by which the conditions centrally underpinning the class compromise, that is, in production (and transport), were also imposed on other forms of capital, notably speculative money capital, or "money-dealing capital."

After World War I had demonstrated the viability of an economy entirely organized around production in all belligerent countries, and in Russia led to the collapse of an autocracy structurally unrelated to (domestic) capitalism altogether, the 1929 stock market crisis and the Depression demonstrated that any attempt to resurrect nineteenth-century-style liberal internationalism was doomed. The reorganization of the cycle of industrial capital around the needs of production, forced by the strength of working class power, among other things, entailed the separation of speculative, money-dealing capital from money capital for productive investment. The stock market crisis had been caused by the excesses of the international circuit of money-dealing capital, which in terms of our circuits, must be understood as part of capital in commodity form, trade; indeed in contemporary terms, trade in services and more particularly, *trade in financial services*. Money-dealing capital thus belongs to the movement of capital in commodity form, C. ... C, which as we saw, does not add value but only chases the rewards from price differentials. I denote it as C^M ... C^M. So it looks like money, it functions like money in the hands of banks, but it is trade.

In 1933 this form of capital and the class fraction it catered to (the "rentiers"), were subjected to repression under the Glass-Steagall Act, a centerpiece of Roosevelt's New Deal in the United States. The act separated investment banking (money and precious metals trade, stock and bond brokerage, and syndicated loan provision) from commercial banking, taking deposits and lending for investment. Thus money capital in the proper sense, as a moment in the accumulation cycle (M. ... M'), became protected from the vacillations of speculative movement of funds in order to serve the investment and operational needs of large-scale production.

Its role as social capital, the fictitious level at which all capital merges into a single structure in which investment decisions are made, moreover passed under state auspices – a state in which organized labor also had a voice. The state also had the ability to conduct a countercyclical economic policy through monetary and tax policies, although from 1938, it was obvious that the US administration again prioritized class interests by slamming the brakes on a productive economy that was "overheating" from the perspective of the balance between profit and the labor market position of organized workers (Boddy and Crotty 1974; cf. Kalecki 1943). Yet the financial repression, separating money-dealing capital from investment credit, was not therefore less important. Keynes famously called it a "euthanasia of the rentier," the "functionless investor" (Keynes 1970, p. 376) which he claimed would stabilize the capitalist order.

This crucial adjustment was dictated by the vantage point of production as a moment in the cycle. It obtained its salience by the ability of the industrial working class to force a class compromise on capital; all other forms of capital were therefore compelled, formally or informally, to adjust their role to the needs of production. Thus the concept of control of *corporate liberalism*, that is, a liberalism of large "bodies" (organized interests, states, blocs) that are internally organized bureaucratically, "corporeally" replaced nineteenth-century liberal internationalism. Certainly it took the defeat of the Axis powers before a too radical state monopoly tendency, in which liberalism is suspended altogether (still for the same reasons as those argued by Keynes in the *General Theory*), was crowded out and corporate liberalism became truly comprehensive, covering all aspects of class relations including the transnational and international ones of the non-communist industrial world.

A concept of control thus articulates an underlying balance of class forces that is translated into a particular balance of fractions, involving the state(s), and projecting the needs of the sphere in which the class compromise is achieved, in this case that of production, on all others. The propagation of the principles which guide this set of linkages – in corporate liberalism, Keynesianism, and internationally, integration of the West, containment of the Soviet bloc, and disciplinary wars and interventions in the Third World – allows the reconstruction of the concept of control as ideology too. These policies, however incomplete and contradictory in their actual execution, force all classes and states to define their interests and objectives in terms of the hegemonic concept of control even if this does not by itself square with their purely individual-functional interests; thus an individual company may find itself constrained by the generalization of the industrial interest it is part of (Bode 1979).

The point is that all these connections are not a matter of externally applied "power" between different social forces in given cultural contexts, as "Varieties" institutionalism assumes. They are internally linked by necessity rather than choice. From the "initial" balance of class force (between quotation marks because it is not necessarily chronologically first), mutations are passed on through the network of interconnections. This will become clear once we turn to the advent of *neoliberalism* and the role of the two forms of money capital in it.

Restructuring class compromise and the freeing of money capital

One aspect of the Keynesianism of the 1930s and 1940s would have been an international central bank that would compel national economies with a structural trade surplus to adjust for the benefit of overall international stability and perform a countercyclical policy on the scale of the industrialized West as a whole. However Keynes, representing a Britain effectively bankrupted by World War II, was not able to prevail over the US position which in the end even fell short of the proposals of his interlocutor at Bretton Woods, Harry Dexter White. The outcome of an IMF placing the burden of adjustment in the case of trade imbalances on a country with a structural trade deficit rather obeyed the interests of US bank capital and large corporations. However in one respect, even US banks could not alter the balance of forces tilting towards production and class compromise with organized labor – the imposition of exchange controls by states. "They were unable to alter the fact that Bretton Woods did *permit* states to control capital movements across their borders if they so wished" (Burn 2006, p. 4, emphasis in the original).

However, as Gary Burn shows in his study, merchant bankers in the City of London from the late 1950s began accepting dollar deposits circulating outside the jurisdiction of the US monetary authorities (and other foreign currencies) and began using them to get money-dealing capital flows going again. In the early 1960s, in addition to short-term money flows (the Eurodollar market, i.e., $C^M \ldots C^{M)}$, a capital market (the Eurobond market, $M \ldots M'$) also began to operate with offshore dollars, albeit this market was around one-tenth in size of the Eurodollar one. Of course "Euro" is confusing today because of the currency of that name, but at the time it merely referred to all foreign currencies, mainly the US dollar, deposited in the City of London.

After the oil price hike, petrodollars began to be recycled through these City markets and greatly expanded their size. The OPEC price rise was a response to the uncoupling of the US dollar from its gold cover and the resulting inflation (the growth of the mass of dollars in circulation ran at a rate of more than 10 percent a year, Parboni 1981, pp. 38 and 81, Table 8), but the beneficiaries of oil income had only limited use for it at home, as crash industrialization projects such as Iran's demonstrated the risks of precipitate social change (Amineh 1999). Between 1960 and 1983, total net Euro-deposits in the City grew 1,000 fold to $1 trillion (Burn 2006, p. 17). However, like all inflationary episodes in history, this vast mass of unregulated finance also worked as a powerful mechanism of redistribution. In the 1970s it worked to prejudice the political primacy of the West, already battered by the US defeat in Vietnam, revolutions in Portugal and in Africa against Portuguese colonialism, and revolts in Central America. Simultaneously the easy credit available in the Euromarkets served, internationally, to finance catch-up modernization and/or industrialization of the Soviet bloc and the Third World members of the Non-Aligned Movement. Domestically, corporate liberalism rested centrally on a dynamic, productivity-pegged class compromise in Fordist mass production (Duménil and Lévy 2004, pp. 30–31; Rupert 1995). In the 1970s, this compromise was no longer supported by productivity hikes or investment but increasingly prolonged by inflation.

The uncontrolled expansion of dollars in the course of the decade therefore bolstered the class forces, domestically and internationally, that resisted capitalist-imperialist discipline. Importantly, the flows of money circulating through London were also not primarily operating as financial investments, in other words, as money capital proper, seeking value-adding investment but rather as "fundamentally commercial" activity in which bank houses are after profits made through short-term money movements, without exercising actual discipline on borrowers (Burn 2006, p. 100, citing G. Ingham). Therefore this discipline had to be imposed politically because, as social capital, money must function to distribute investment funds over profitable activities bolstering the capitalist order through real accumulation.

This then was the meaning of Paul Volcker's August 1979 intervention as chairman of the Federal Reserve Board. By slamming the brakes on the expansion of money that fuelled the expansion of the international circuit, he sought to bring the interests of internationally operating bank capital again under the discipline of money capital as social capital, amidst protests of the big US banks which had lent to states now faced with debt service at sharply risen real interest rates (van der Pijl 2006, p. 188–91). This historic intervention, rightly assigned the status of a change towards a new concept of control (neoliberalism in combination with other measures such as the NATO missile decision, the election of Margaret Thatcher, and others instances all part of

the same groundswell of a capitalist class offensive), did not however consolidate the repression of speculative finance. Quite the contrary. As we saw,
that measure (through Glass-Steagall in the US and related interventions
elsewhere in the same period) ultimately translated a changing balance of
forces in production into a shift in relations among capital fractions.

The Volcker Shock, on the other hand, was part of an assault on the
working classes in the developed world, on state socialism, and so on, so with
the abrogation of the class compromise with organized labor in production,
the balance among fractions also shifted to money capital qua money, and
without the restrictions of domestically anchored class compromise. As
R. T. Naylor writes, "Tight credit encouraged, even forced, legitimate money
into patterns of behaviour historically associated with the cash hoards of drug
peddlers, tax evaders, contraband traders, and others who have something to
hide – namely, the search for short-term havens in highly liquid assets, instead
of seeking opportunities for long-term productive investment" (Naylor 1987,
p. 13). So whatever Volcker's intentions may have been (and I would argue on
account of his frequent explanations, that they centered on restoring the discipline of social capital globally, cf. Greider 1989, pp. 75, 101 and passim),
the actual outcome also included the growth of money flows, stealthily at
first, that must be categorized as money-dealing capital.

Yet initially, the priority awarded to restoring global class discipline lent
Volcker-style neoliberalism a *systemic* quality. The abrogation of the class
compromise with organized labor in production also gave way to a new core
class compromise, of which Duménil and Lévy mention the two key aspects.
"First, ... a strict alliance with top management ... achieved by paying out
astounding remunerations, as "wages" and stock options." Second, by giving
the asset-owning upper middle classes a chance to profit from capital incomes
and asset price rises, "either directly or through investment funds" (Duménil
and Lévy 2004, p. 30). Here house prices and mutual funds all enter into the
picture; obviously, through them the new class compromise reaches into the
upper layers of the working class as well, including, through pension funds,
even less favored segments of labor in selective cases.

Still this is no longer a matter of a class compromise anchored in production, but plays out in the sphere of money. And even if initially the main
thrust was systemic, anchored in the role of money capital as social capital
(and the circuit of money capital as investment in value-adding activities), I
would argue that in the absence of a social discipline emanating from production, the different forms of money slowly blended into each other again,
not least because the two functions (of money capital and of money-dealing
capital, "trade in financial services") merge in the practical day-to-day activities
of banks. In the course of the 1990s, when the defeats of the working classes
and the dissolution of the Soviet bloc and the Third World coalition fatally
weakened the forces resisting capitalist imperialism, neoliberalism entered a
new stage centrally anchored in speculative, money-dealing capital. This we
may call, for want of a better term, *predatory neoliberalism*.

As the compromises of corporate liberalism (centred on production) continue to be abrogated, the defining nodes in the circuit shift to money and on to money-dealing capital. In Figure 3.2, the interconnections are identified and the shift visualised.

Since productive labor now could be found anywhere in great quantity and with decreasing social protection (or none at all), the interest in securing real value-added production and protection of its human resource base gives way to short-term profit interests. Again as before, the links in the cycle are connected by necessity. The defeat of the Left moves the epicenter from which class interests are generalized further and further away from production, transforming the states in the process, and producing new, highly destabilizing international policies compared to which even the New Cold War under Reagan and Thatcher was still a concerted, consistent policy.

Under the rule of hot money

What happened in 1979, then, was the emancipation of money capital from the repression imposed on it in the 1930s. In the intervening years, capitalism with a human face (at least in the developed West) worked its wonders competing against Soviet-style state socialism. As we saw, releasing money capital from the Keynesian constraints also entailed the emancipation of money-dealing capital, "trade in financial services," which does not add value but obtains its profit share from price movements. Yet as long as the USSR and its bloc remained on their feet, and the non-aligned South had not yet been fatally weakened by the debt crisis (or in the case of the cash-rich oil-producing countries, by devastating wars such as Iraq–Iran and the First Gulf War following Iraq's attempted annexation of Kuwait), the systemic neoliberalism

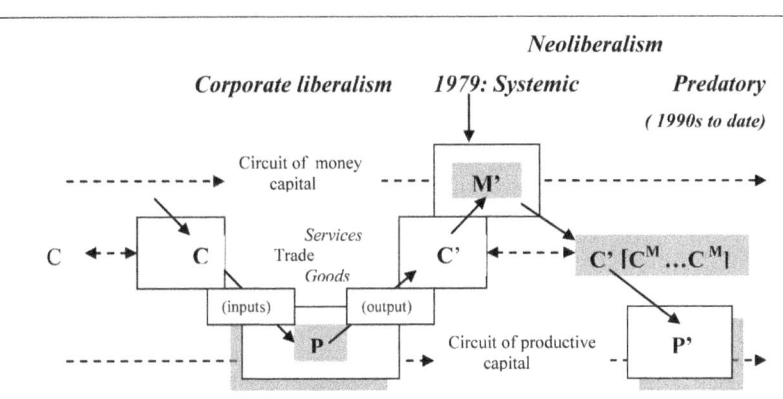

Key: as Fig 3.1. Leading fraction highlighted.

Figure 3.2 A periodization of postwar capitalism by reference to directive nodes in the cycle of industrial capital

obeying the comprehensive class perspective of social capital prevailed. Also in the 1980s, organized labor in the West had not yet lost its ability to resist the neoliberal offensive entirely.

However, with the collapse of the Soviet bloc and the implosion of the USSR, a critical brake was removed. Not just in terms of NATO aggression in Yugoslavia, or the expansion of the alliance (retooled as an "out-of-area" intervention bloc) into the former Soviet sphere – a reckless advance that only today is being checked by a new Russian assertiveness. Also the concern with real accumulation was further eclipsed and predatory money flows came to prevail. The "logic" of such a trend, from production to money capital concerned with production, to money-dealing capital, is suggested by the interconnections illustrated in Figure 3.2. They point to an inner "necessity" that is not a matter of competing Varieties anchored in cultural complexes, but of a logic of exploitation inherent in the capitalist mode of production and Western imperialism; a logic that was uniquely constrained in the period from the 1940s to the 1980s.

The development of a full-blown comprehensive concept of control this time too obtained a scholarly–literary dimension. Whilst Keynes was brutally removed from his pedestal (not unlike the Lenin statues in Europe's east), the thinking of Friedrich Hayek, which had survived the corporate liberal era as a chapter in the academic micro-economics curriculum, now rose to prominence. In 1947, at the first of a series of Mont Pèlerin conferences in which Hayek's neoliberals hibernated, the "power of the trade unions" had been the main item on the agenda (Cockett 1995, pp. 113–14; cf. Walpen 2004). Only in the struggles elicited in the inflationary 1970s did the capitalist class seize the initiative again and attack the working classes while freeing up money capital, in addition to the bloody Pinochet coup in Chile, then Argentina, and then, via elections, Thatcher and Reagan. If the ensuing assaults on capital-labor compromise were still contested, the collapse of the Soviet bloc and the Non-Aligned coalition, and of course the turn to capitalism in Mainland China, pulled out the rug from under working-class resistance. Compared to 1980, the reservoir of globally available labor would eventually triple to 3 billion plus.

With the class compromise with organized labor out of the way, a new compromise with asset-owning middle classes slowly took its place to provide compensating political stability. The privatization policies of neoliberal governments bolstered stock markets and fuelled a process of neoliberal class formation of middle-class households, complementing the restoration of the discipline of capital and the profit rate. The "rentiers," recipients of rent, interest, dividends, and beneficiaries of capital gains on assets, destined for euthanasia in Keynes' heyday, now regained strength as wages declined. Rentier income had never actually been absent, write Epstein and Power, but "the big acceleration in its rise began around 1979 or 1980."

During the period of the Volcker monetary policy of high real interest rates and the Reagan policy of large budget deficits, the rentier share leaped. It declined during the early 1990s but then started to increase again, driven mostly by an increase in the share of entrepreneurial income (Epstein and Power 2002).

On the basis of their calculations (2002, Table 3.1), we can see an across the board increase of rentier income shares, led by the United States in absolute terms (38.3 percent of GDP in the 1980s, 33.5 percent in the 1990s). The only significant exception in the Atlantic economy was Germany, which still in the 1990s, when its eastern half was being re-incorporated, stuck to a 7.4 percent rentier income share compared to percentages of around 20 percent for the other five founding members of the EEC. For those leaping to this fact as an example of the commitment of German society to real production and a cultural resistance to unearned income, the sequel after the creation of the Eurozone should dispel any such thoughts. For by then Germany's abrogation of the compromise with organized labor had allowed it to emerge as the European bulwark of neoliberalism (Bruff 2010). The beggar-thy-neighbor policies towards its partners then slowly undermined the trade and payments balances of the South European Eurozone member states, refinancing them through short-term capital movements until the 2007–08 crisis struck (Lapavitsas *et al.* 2012).

So across the board, but with delays due to unique events like German reunification, neoliberalism replaced post-war corporate liberalism at first as a systemic correction to restore capitalist–imperialist interests but, in the 1990s, giving way to the unrestrained, predatory rule of hot money. In 1987 Volcker was succeeded as Chairman of the Federal Reserve by Alan Greenspan of JP Morgan, whose primary concern was to accommodate "the irrational exuberance of markets," as he saw it (cited in Gamble 2009, p. 1). On his watch, the growth of the financial sphere relative to actual production in the United States transpires in the rise in the value of stock market assets relative to GDP from \$3.1 trillion in 1990 (just under half of GDP) to \$16.6 trillion in 1999, almost twice GDP (Houben 2004, p. 48). Derivatives (such as futures and options on interest rates, currency and stock market indexes) tripled from 1992 to \$12.2 trillion outstanding in 1997. Interest rate swaps and options and currency swaps in combination grew from \$5.3 to 28.7 trillion in the same period (Duménil and Lévy 2001, p. 143; Wildenberg 1990, p. 44, Fig. 3).

Within the banking sector, expanded by allowing various exceptions to Glass-Steagall (it would eventually be abolished by the Clinton administration in 1999), the different types of money flows, regulated bank credit and offshore money-dealing capital movements as pioneered by the Eurodollar market, were often indistinguishable. The actual subordination of regular bank capital to "trading" was highlighted when John Meriwether took his experience in "proprietary trading" (speculating with the bank's own money, also through leveraged operations) developed at Salomon Brothers, to his own hedge fund, Long Term Capital Management (LTCM) with two "Nobel" (Swedish central bank) laureates in economics. Peter Gowan captures the shift when he writes that "trading activity here does not mean long-term investment ... in this or that security, but buying and selling financial and real assets *to exploit – not least by generating – price differences and price shifts*" ("speculative arbitrage," Gowan 2009, p. 9, emphasis added; cf. 8 and 8n). Or as one broker comments, "a large part of the financial sector's growth in the last three decades has been mere rent-seeking, figuring out ways to charge much larger fees and returns for performing a service with only modest economic value added" (Hutchinson 2013).

On the eve of the financial crisis the parallel universe of off-balance-sheet, shadow banking entities like hedge funds (often located in offshore jurisdictions and operating beyond regulatory oversight) had grown to a trading volume twice the size of transactions in the regulated banking system (Chesnais 2011, pp. 71–72; Palan *et al.* 2010). The crisis of 2007–08 interrupted but ultimately did not stem the ascent of speculative money-dealing capital, although it clearly had been at the origin of the debacle. Already in 1998 it had become clear that hot money now had a firm grip on state regulatory policy in the financial sphere. When the aforementioned hedge fund, LTCM, crashed in 1998, it was saved by Greenspan's Fed with $3.6 billion of public money. In combination with the handling of the Asian Crisis (a predatory raid on economies that had not yet joined the neoliberal move away from production) this "allowed the financial turmoil to transmute into yet another stock market/housing bubble" (Rude 2008, p. 211).

This sequence, then, prefigured the solution to the 2007–08 financial crisis. Indeed whatever adventures money-dealers might undertake in terms of predatory asset inflation and deflation, they would be covered by the state and Central Bank authorities. These "rescues" served to refuel the speculative cycle, suggesting a fundamental alignment of state economic policy with the interests of money-dealing capital. The socialization of bank losses from the 2007–08 credit crash fits into the pattern. Encouraged by a license to lower their debt-to-equity ratios in the decade preceding the crash (Panitch and Gindin 2012, p. 306), financial institutions were restocked with public money when the crisis struck. Thus saving the insurance company, AIG, in September 2008 by a $85bn rescue package in exchange for a 80 percent Federal share, included paying out outstanding credit default swaps at face value, with Goldman Sachs receiving between $12.9bn and $20bn according to different sources; Merrill Lynch and its new owner, Bank of America together $12bn, Société Générale (France) and Deutsche Bank $12bn each, Barclays $8.5bn, to name only the largest beneficiaries (Nesvetailova 2010, p. 35; Panitch and Gindin 2012, p. 315 give higher figures).

The bill was presented to society, with austerity policies blocking a return to social protection for the foreseeable future. Certainly, by shrinking the economy, austerity policies only make de-leveraging more difficult (Mirowski 2013, p. 350). But then, economic rationality in a class society is never a matter of taking the objective situation as the basis for action. For lest anyone think that the predatory neoliberalism of the money-dealers would no longer be a form of class rule, it may be worthwhile to recall that already in 1960 the Bank of England "viewed "hot money" flows as almost a mechanism by which the financial markets discipline profligate government" (Burn 2006, p. 89).

Yet the limits of indebtedness, whether public or private, are clearly being reached by the post-crisis resurgence of money-dealing capital. In 2010 the total amount of outstanding over-the-counter derivatives already surpassed the pre-crisis level, reaching $700 trillion (Mirowski 2013, p. 351, Fig. 6.4). As Hutchinson writes (2013):

> the leverage bubble has gone about as far as it can. Leverage rates in the US and worldwide are at record levels, "stimulated" by all the cheap credit. Once interest rates start to return toward more normal levels so that it is no longer profitable to borrow money, the world will be forced into another painful round of de-leveraging, with government budgets forced towards balance, consumers pulling in their horns and overleveraged businesses going bankrupt.

In September 2013 a Dutch website interviewed journalist Joris Luyendijk, who had completed a two-year anthropological study of the City of London for the Guardian newspaper. Reflecting on the resurrection of crisis-ridden speculative finance after the explosion of the sub-prime bubble and its trail of bank collapses, Luyendijk explains that the danger of another, potentially terminal crisis is as big as ever. But the ability to see it coming has been neutralized by a public discourse tailored to serve the crisis' needs. "Neutrality works beautifully in a neutral or equal world. But neutrality in an unequal world makes you the mouthpiece of the status quo … A systemic crisis must be dealt with systematically" (Luyendijk 2013). Or in the terms used here, the exhaustion of a concept of control built around the interests of money-dealing capital requires that its narrative outer shell too must be replaced to make way for a new one.

It is my argument that within the limits of capitalist class society, there is no new configuration of forces waiting in the wings to take over once the great deflation sets in. That is why we must move from an analysis of varieties of capitalism to one of varieties of alternative economic orders, and begin to think of how to move beyond capitalism by rolling back its discipline on society and nature.

References

Albert, M. (1991) *Capitalisme contre capitalisme* (Paris: Ed. du Seuil).

Amineh, M. P. (1999) *Die globale kapitalistische Expansion und Iran. Eine Studie der iranischen politischen Ökonomie 1500–1980* [trans. E. Rakel] (Hamburg: Lit Verlag).

Boddy, R. and J. Crotty (1974) "Class Conflict, Keynesian Policies, and the Business Cycle," *Monthly Review*, 26(5): 1–17.

Bode, R. (1979) "De Nederlandse bourgeoisie tussen de twee wereldoorlogen," *Cahiers voor de Politieke en Sociale Wetenschappen*, 2(4): 9–50.

Bruff, I. (2010) "Germany's Agenda 2010 reforms: Passive revolution at the crossroads," *Capital & Class*, 34(3): 409–28.

Burn, G. (2006) *The Re-emergence of Global Finance* (Basingstoke: Palgrave Macmillan).

Chesnais, F. (2011) *Les dettes illégitimes. Quand les banques font main basse sur les politiques publiques* (Paris: Raisons d'agir).

Cockett, R. (1995) *Thinking the Unthinkable. Think-Tanks and the Economic Counter-Revolution, 1931–1983* (London: Fontana).

Duménil, G. and D. Lévy (2001) "Costs and benefits of neoliberalism. A class analysis," *Review of International Political Economy*, 8(4): 578–607.

——(2004) "Neo-Liberal Dynamics–Towards a New Phase?" in K. van der Pijl, L. Assassi, and D. Wigan (eds) *Global Regulation. Managing Crises After the Imperial Turn* (Basingstoke: Palgrave Macmillan).

Epstein, G. and D. Power (2002) "The Return of Finance and Finance's Returns: Recent Trends in Rentier Incomes in OECD Countries, 1960–2000," *Research Brief, Political Economy Research Institute*, University of Massachusetts Amherst no. 2, November.

Funke, R. (1978) "Sich durchsetzender Kapitalismus. Eine Alternative zum spätkapitalistischen Paradigma," in T. Guldiman, M. Rodenstein, U. Rödel and F. Stille (eds) *Sozialpolitik als soziale Kontrolle* [Starnberger Studien, vol. 2] (Frankfurt: Suhrkamp).

Gamble, A. (2009) *The Spectre at the Feast. Capitalist Crisis and the Politics of Recession* (Basingstoke: Palgrave Macmillan).

Gowan, P. (2009) "Crisis in the Heartland. Consequences of the New Wall Street System," *New Left Review*, 2nd series (55): 5–29.

Greider, W. (1989 [1987]) *Secrets of the Temple. How the Federal Reserve Runs the Country* (New York: Simon and Schuster Touchstone).

Harvey, D. (2006 [1982]) *The Limits to Capital*, rev. edn (London: Verso).

Hickel, R. (1975) "Kapitalfraktionen. Thesen zur Analyse der herrschenden Klasse," *Kursbuch*, 42: 141–54.

Houben, H. (2004) "Het nieuwe hoofddoel van de Europese Unie: de Lissabon-strategie," *Marxistische Studies*, 65: 11–72.

Hutchinson, M. (2013) "Finance sector fading," *AsiaTimes Online*, December 10. Available at: www.atimes.com/atimes/Global_Economy/GECON-01–101213.html [accessed December 11, 2013].

ILO (2010) *Global Wage Report 2010/11. Wage policies in times of crisis* (Geneva: International Labor Office).

Kalecki, M. (1943) "Political Aspects of Full Employment," *Political Quarterly*, 14 (4): 322–31.

Keynes, J. M. (1970 [1936]) *The General Theory of Employment, Interest and Money* (Basingstoke: Macmillan).

Lapavitsas, C., A. Kaltenbrunner, G. Labrinidis, D. Lindo, J. Meadway, J. Mitchell, J.P. Panceira, E. Pires, J. Powell, A. Stenfors, N. Teles and L. Vatikiotis (2012) *Crisis in the Eurozone* [intro. S. Kouvelakis] (London: Verso).

Luxemburg, R. (1966 [1913]) *Die Akkumulation des Kapitals. Ein Beitrag zur Ökonomischen Erklärung des Imperialismus* (Frankfurt: Neue Kritik).

Luyendijk, J. (2013) "Dit gaat helemaal fout," *Volzin* 44. Available at: http://volzin.nu/index.php/redactie/44-redactie/387-dit-gaat-helemaal-fout [accessed September 18, 2013].

MEW: *Marx-Engels Werke*, 45 vols (Berlin: Dietz).

Milios, J. and D. P. Sotiropoulos (2009) *Rethinking Imperialism. A Study of Capitalist Rule* (Basingstoke: Palgrave Macmillan).

Mirowski, P. (2013) *Never Let A Serious Crisis Go to Waste. How Neoliberalism Survived the Financial Meltdown* (London: Verso).

Naylor, R.T. (1987) *Hot Money and the Politics of Debt* (London: Unwin Hyman).

Nesvetailova, A. (2010) *Financial Alchemy in Crisis. The Great Liquidity Illusion* (London: Pluto Press).

Palan, R., R. Murphy and C. Chavagneux (2010) *Tax Havens. How Globalization Really Works* (Ithaca, NY: Cornell University Press).

Panitch, L. and S. Gindin (2012) *The Making of Global Capitalism. The Political Economy of American Empire* (London: Verso).

Parboni, R. (1981) *The Dollar and Its Rivals. Recession, Inflation and International Finance* [trans. J. Rotschild] (London: Verso).

Polanyi, K. (1957 [1944]) *The Great Transformation. The Political and Economic Origins of Our Time* (Boston, MA: Beacon).

Rude, C. (2008) "The Role of Financial Discipline in Imperial Strategy," in L. Panitch and M. Konings (eds) *American Empire and the Political Economy of Global Finance.* (Basingstoke: Palgrave Macmillan).

Rupert, M. (1995) *Producing Hegemony: The Politics of Mass Production and American Global Power* (Cambridge: Cambridge University Press).

Van der Pijl, K. (2006) *Global Rivalries from the Cold War to Iraq* (London: Pluto and New Delhi: Sage Vistaar).

——(2009) *A Survey of Global Political Economy.* Pdf web-text, Version 2.1. Available at: www.sussex.ac.uk/ir/gpe/gpesurvey [accessed September 10, 2014].

——(2014) *The Discipline of Western Supremacy.* Vol. III of *Modes of Foreign Relations and Political Economy* (London: Pluto).

Walpen, B. (2004) *Die offenen Feinde und ihre Gesellschaft. Eine hegemonietheoretische Studie zur Mont Pèlerin Society* (Hamburg: VSA).

Wildenberg, I. W. (1990) *De revolte van de kapitaalmarkt. Over fusies, overnames en de terugkeer van de eigenaar-ondernemer* (Schoonhoven: Academic Service).

4 Comparative capitalisms and the theory of capitalist stages

Terrence McDonough

The reinvigoration over the last three decades of institutional economics has its roots in the question of capitalism's survival. Institutionalists' essential argument has been that capitalism survives through its variation. This variation can take place across time and was in a sense the original concern of the literature. This original literature concerned none other than the French Regulation school's distinction between Fordism and post-Fordism. This school concerned itself with the possibility of capitalist recovery from crisis. Historically this was accomplished through innovations in the institutional regimes that provided "regulation" to the capital accumulation process. The crisis of Fordism could be overcome through the transition to post-Fordism.

As it became clear that post-Fordism was being organized around an aggressive neoliberal project carried out in the context of increasing globalization, the concern with capitalism's survival became more specific. The question shifted from the survival of capitalism to the question of the survival of an alternative to neoliberalism in a globalized world. This question was posed starkly in the United States with the momentum of the Reaganite dismantling of the postwar New Deal order. Parallel developments were taking place in an even more disruptive fashion in Thatcher's Britain. At the same time, globalization seemed to set different national economies in direct competition with one another in world markets. Analysts began to wonder whether this global competition would force a convergence to a neoliberal model of capitalism on a world-wide basis. After all, the earlier postwar Keynesian settlement had found expression, to one degree or another, throughout the developed world and through import-substituting industrialization in much of the developing world. In North America, the question revolved around creating a counter-argument and an alternative set of policies as comprehensive as the neoliberal programme. The question in Europe concerned the survival of the European social model's transition to post-Fordism.

The issue moved from whether there was a capitalist alternative to a Fordism that was now in crisis to whether there was a viable alternative to neoliberalism. A discussion arose as to whether there was a variety of capitalism which could compete globally alongside the developing neoliberal order in the Anglo-Saxon countries. This reposing of the question of capitalism's survival shifted the emphasis of capitalism's ability to vary across periods of time to whether capitalism could vary across space, or more particularly across national boundaries. Did national varieties of capitalism exist which could persist as alternatives to neoliberalism? Could an economy be globalized but not in essence neoliberal? Could the unpalatable social transformations wrought by global neoliberalism be avoided?

Building on a discussion of corporatist labor relations in Germany and similar economies in mainland Europe, the Varieties of Capitalism (VoC) school argued that an alternative variety of capitalism existed to the Liberal Market Economies (LMEs) which dominate the Anglo-Saxon economies like Britain and the United States. This variety takes the form of a Coordinated Market Economy (CME) as exemplified by Germany. CMEs consist of a constellation of institutions both consistent and synergistic with a corporatist approach to labor relations. These economies are characterized by non-market, negotiated forms of coordination, corporatist labor relations, an emphasis on skill formation, inter-firm networks, long-term finance and "patient" capital (Hall and Soskice 2001).

The questions of capitalism's survival across time and the potential for persistent capitalist variation across space both arose in the wake of the stagflationary crisis of the 1970s. Today's crisis, increasingly characterized as the persistence of the Great Recession, raises both questions again. At the time of writing we are six years into the crisis and there are few signs of any permanent recovery. At the same time, the forces of neoliberalism have used the crisis as a platform to attack and erode the remaining vestiges of any social alternative to neoliberalism. These political forces are seemingly oblivious to the fact that austerity policies have only deepened the crisis. The question of whether a non-neoliberal social model can survive the crisis is particularly acute in Europe. If capitalism can survive but the European social model can't, is capitalism finally transitioning toward a unitary market led model even if that model is characterized by continuing stagnation?

This chapter argues that the VoC school and its somewhat broader comparative capitalisms' manifestation arose to address a narrower question than the historical survival of capitalism beyond periods of structural crisis. Its chief concern was the possibility of the survival of alternatives to a neoliberal model in the face of globalization. In the process of addressing this difficult question, the comparative capitalism school has developed a number of problematic theoretical positions and omissions which serve to hobble it as a vehicle for the discussion of the future of capitalism beyond the current crisis. Instead, an analysis of the current crisis is better served by an application of the original vision of the variation of capitalism across time as well as across space. This vision was originally found in the French Regulation school discussion of Fordism and post-Fordism. This article will contend that a contemporary variation of this stages of capitalism perspective, the Social Structures of Accumulation (SSA) framework holds more promise in anticipating the future outcomes of the crisis.

This chapter will first discuss the comparative capitalisms perspective focusing on the VoC school by identifying problems which challenge the VoC school's ability to analyze the current crisis. It will then develop the stages of capitalism alternative concentrating on its Social Structure of Accumulation (SSA) variant. It will also consider the relationship of this approach to the French Regulation school. An argument will be made that the stages of capitalism approach to capitalist variation does not suffer from the same problems as the VoC school. The chapter will conclude by drawing insights from the stages of capitalism approach about the future prospects of the current crisis.

Comparative capitalisms

Bruff (2011) defines the comparative capitalisms literature as "a body of knowledge comprised of contributions which take institutions as their starting point when considering the evolution of national political economies" (p. 482). Three analytical assumptions are identified by Deeg and Jackson (2007, pp. 152–53). The first is that economic action is necessarily embedded in social institutions. The second is an examination of the relationship between different institutional structures and differential economic outcomes resulting in theories of comparative institutional advantage. The third is that the institutions are non-random, interdependent sets which create a particular logic of economic actions. These non-random sets resolve into a number of typologies.

Three broad brush critiques have emerged of this literature that bear on the question of its suitability to address issues raised by the current crisis. The first is that the framework is biased towards an assumption of stability rather than change (Deeg and Jackson 2006, p. 150; Bohle and Greskovits 2009, p. 368). This is, to a certain extent, inherent in institutional approaches generally. Institutional theorizing starts by postulating that human behavior is determined by institutional constraints or is perhaps more loosely directed down certain paths by the availability of institutional resources. In addition to being economic institutions, these institutions usually include political structures and, often, ideological orientations. Thus the constraining institutions make up the whole of society. It is hard to see where there is traction here for institutional transformation.

In the case of Hall and Soskice's (2001) varieties of capitalism approach, this is exacerbated by the inclusion of a theory of economic microfoundations. Action is by and large limited to firms. Firms act as the rational utility maximizers of neoclassical microeconomic theory. If firms confront a Liberal Market Economy (LME) institutional structure which encourages and rewards arms-length market transactions and strategies; it will only be rational to invest in developing the skills and capacities which lead to success in such an environment. Having invested in such capacities, firms will oppose changes to a new institutional environment and only support change within an overall liberal framework. Even when a national LME faces a crisis, resolutions will be sought through deepening the existing institutional orientation. A similar logic applies in the case of firms which confront a Coordinated Market Economy (CME). Firms will develop capacities for coordinated behavior and a path dependence will be established where future choices are constrained by past choices.

Further, the complementary character of the institutions within an LME or CME can be understood to mean that intermediate institutional frameworks which combine institutions from the two types of political economy lose the advantages of complementarity. Thus any transitional state between the two types of economy will perform less well than the pure types. It is hard to envision a successful transition path from one to the other in the absence of a complete institutional breakdown. Bohle and Greskovits sum up this impasse in the following way (2009, p. 370):

> From the very moment that factor-based and specific asset-based models are imputed into history, they set in motion a "perpetuum mobile" of systemic logics, which then allow LMEs and CMEs to survive as clear alternatives world wars, global economic crises and political cataclysms.

A second broad critique is that in its concern to establish the viability of different national models of capitalism, the comparative capitalisms literature has not sufficiently taken on board the changes associated with globalization. This is not an assertion that globalization dictates convergence to a single, most likely Anglo-Saxon, model. The critics generally accept the comparative literature's observation of continued variation in the face of globalizing pressures to be one of its major contributions. The critics do, however, point to several developments which create problems for the varieties of capitalism literature. The first is the emergence of multi-level governance. Governance is no longer confined to the national or sub-national level. Regional organizations like the European Union or the North American Free Trade Agreement (NAFTA) are increasingly influential. Above these supra-national regional organizations global institutions like the World Trade Organization (WTO) have taken on greater weight.

While it was possible and appropriate in the postwar era to view the interaction of states as taking place in a separate and subordinate *inter*national arena, in the current era *trans*national institutions are increasingly dominant. This does not eliminate the space for national institutional variation. Indeed to a certain extent it demands national variation, as there would be little motivation for transnationalization of investment if the world was actually homogenous from place to place. Nevertheless, this transnational environment should have a significant impact on the dynamics of national institutional configurations.

In addition to these critiques, a more foundational criticism has been advanced. This is that the comparative capitalisms literature has become so enamored with its discovery of the trees that it has started to ignore the forest to its cost. Bohle and Greskovits conclude their consideration with the following (2009, p. 382):

> More fundamentally, the instability of contemporary capitalism in all its variants suggests the need for a return to very old literatures and debates, which had had crucial insights into the system's expansionary nature, specific vulnerabilities, destructive and irrational tendencies, and recurrent crises: that is, features of capitalism *tout court* that got lost in the course of the extensive study of its varieties.

Those writing more explicitly within a Marxian tradition can more directly bring this concern to the surface. Bruff (2011) argues that it is important to see the institutional varieties of capitalism as varieties *in* capitalism, that is, institutions are clearly grounded in capitalist conditions of existence. The need is to recognize the importance of institutions but to search for a convincing account "regarding the place of institutions *within*, not external to or separate from, capitalism" (p. 486, emphasis in original). Radice underlines that "capitalism is historically founded on a separation of workers from ownership and possession of the means of production" and that this means that "economic and political institutions and practices centre on the core dynamics of competition, accumulation and reproduction, which characterize historical capitalism" (p. 736). It is precisely within the theorizing of stages within capitalist history that this work has been most explicitly done within the Marxian tradition.

Marxian stage theory

There is a fundamentally continuous tradition of Marxian stage theory from the beginning of the twentieth century until the present day. This tradition begins with the pioneering work of Rudolf Hilferding (1910) on finance capital, Nicolai Bukharin (1915) on the world economy and V.I. Lenin (1917) on imperialism. All three argued that the capitalist economy had, with the advent of monopoly capitalism, entered into a new and higher stage of capitalism. The second wave of Marxian stage theorizing emerged with the end of the post-World War II expansion. Ernest Mandel's Long Wave Theory (LWT), the Social Structure of Accumulation Framework (SSAF), and the Regulation Approach (RA) analyzed the stagflationary crises of most of the advanced capitalist countries as the end of a long wave of growth following the end of the war. This long wave of accumulation[1] was underpinned by the emergence of a new stage of capitalism after World War II which was analogous to the reorganization brought about by monopoly capital at the turn of the century. Since this new stage was the resolution of the crisis of the monopoly stage, these new schools were reluctant to predict the non-resolution of the then current crisis, thus opening up the possibility of further stages of capitalism in the future.

At the end of the 1970s, David Gordon (1978, 1980) published two articles linking long cycle theory with the concept of stages of capitalism. In this context, the advent of monopoly capital at the turn of the century coincides with the completion of the long wave trough at the end of the nineteenth century and the inauguration of the long wave expansion which ended with the Great Depression of the 1930s. The new question which the adoption of a long wave perspective posed to the monopoly stage of capitalism tradition was whether the postwar expansion was associated with a similar set of multidimensional institutional changes. Gordon (1978) answers this question by proposing a set of postwar institutions whose establishment accounted for the long period of postwar prosperity. These institutions included, among others multinational corporate structures, dual labor markets associated with a bread-and-butter industrial unionism, American international economic and military hegemony, easy credit, conservative Keynesian state policy, and bureaucratic control of workers.

In this way, Gordon established the possibility of articulating a postwar set of institutions which conditioned the subsequent expansion of the economy in a way similar to the manner in which the set of institutions analyzed by Hilferding, Bukharin, and Lenin accounted for the turn of the century expansion. Thus the multi-institutional analysis of monopoly capital is implicitly used by Gordon as a model for explaining the postwar expansion.

The repetitive use of this kind of explanation raised the question of whether the assembling of such sets of institutions could be generalized as the basis of a comprehensive theory of stages of capitalism. Gordon (1978, 1980) answers this question by proposing that both the institutions comprising monopoly capital and those making up the postwar social order constituted examples of Social Structures of Accumulation (SSAs). The construction of a new SSA provided the basis for a new stage of capitalism. The disintegration of this set of institutions marks the end of each stage. The SSA approach achieved its definitive form shortly thereafter with the publication of Gordon, Edwards, and Reich's *Segmented Work, Divided Workers* (1982). This volume used Gordon's SSA approach to capitalist stages to reformulate these authors' earlier analysis of the history of capital-labor relations in the US.

In this version, stage theory undertakes an intermediate level of analysis in the sense that it identifies periods intermediate in length between the conjuncture and overall capitalist history. This intermediate period of analysis is founded on the observation that while all economies are embedded in the broader array of social institutions, this is especially important in the capitalist era because of the conflictual foundations of capitalism in class division and capitalist competition. For accumulation to proceed relatively smoothly these sources of instability must be countered through the construction of a set of stable institutions at not only the economic but also the political and ideological levels.

The construction of such a social structure underpins the profit rate and creates the secure expectations that make long-term investment possible. Nevertheless as accumulation proceeds the institutions are undermined by class conflict, capitalist competition, and accumulation itself. These forces and the interdependence of the institutions lead to a breakdown of the set of institutions, a fall in the profit rate, and the collapse of accumulation, initiating a period of crisis and stagnation which is only overcome with the construction of a new set of institutions. Thus capitalist stages are constituted by the sets of interdependent economic, political, and ideological institutions which underpin relatively successful accumulation separated by intervening periods of crisis.[2]

The SSA Framework and the Regulation Approach

The relationship between the Regulation Approach and the Social Structure of Accumulation Framework (SSAF) was recognized early. Bob Jessop lists the SSAF as one of his seven schools of the RA (Jessop 1990). Still the most widely cited source for SSA theory, the 1994 *Social Structures of Accumulation: the Political Economy of Growth and Crisis* (Kotz et al. 1994), prominently featured a comparison between the SSA approach and regulation theory authored by one of the editors (Kotz 1994).

Kotz identifies the similarities between the two approaches. Both theories set out to explain long-run patterns of capital accumulation by analyzing the relationship between that process and sets of social institutions which condition or "regulate" it. The dynamic of the accumulation process over relatively long periods of time depends on the success or failure of these institutions in creating the conditions for profitability, reinvestment, and growth. Kotz observes that the SSA is roughly analogous to some combination of the regulation theory terms "regime of accumulation" and "mode of regulation." Both schools view capitalism "as moving through a series of stages, each characterized by a specific form of the accumulation process embedded in a particular set of institutions" (p. 86). Stages end in a long-term structural crisis which involves a significant reduction in the rate of accumulation over a prolonged period of time. These structural crises result from a failure of the institutions to continue to successfully secure the conditions of accumulation. The crisis ends when a new more successful set of institutions is put in place. Finally according to Kotz, both theories "offer an intermediate level of analysis, more general and abstract than a detailed historical account of capitalist development would be, but more specific and concrete than the usual abstract theory of capitalism-in-general" (p. 87).

Among the major differences, Kotz identifies the following contrasts. The RA had maintained a closer fidelity to the Marxian approach through an emphasis on production relations and the class distribution of income within "the regime of accumulation" while the SSAF had emphasized a more Keynesian concern with the determinants of the capitalist investment decision.

The RA located the origin of long-term crises within the regime of accumulation whereas the SSAF located the origin of the crisis in the breakdown of the institutions of the SSA (closer to "the mode of regulation" in the RA). Consistent with its Althusserian roots, the RA emphasized structure while the SSAF placed more emphasis on agency and class struggle. We will consider the fate of these differences in light of developments within both schools.

A concern with class relations rooted in the production process has never been alien to the SSAF. *Segmented Work, Divided Workers* (Gordon *et al.* 1982) concerned itself primarily with the historical development of capitalist strategies of controlling workers within the labor process. This emphasis has been carried forward in more recent work on the emergence of "spatialization" as a new form of labor control which it is argued is one of the important underlying institutional factors conditioning the construction of a new SSA in the United States (Grant and Wallace 1994; Brady and Wallace 2000; Wallace and Brady 2010). In his 1997 retrospective and prospective on the SSAF, Michael Reich (1997, p. 4) identifies the early theoretical perspective as rooted in "Marxian insights concerning class conflict over production and distribution at the workplace and in the political arena, and by Marxian and Keynesian macroeconomic analyses" and advocates a fidelity to this heritage. Inquiries into the historical background to the SSA approach have given it a much more specific and explicit Marxian pedigree (McDonough 1995, 1999).

While the SSAF has been re-emphasizing its roots within Marxism, something of the opposite movement has taken place in some wings of the RA. This is most pronounced in the founding Parisian school. The publication of *Regulation Theory: The State of the Art* edited by Boyer and Saillard (2000 [1995]) demonstrated the emergence of two quite distinct theoretical strands within the RA. One of the introductory articles by Henri Nadel (2002) contends strongly that the Regulation research program is "clearly linked with the Marxian project" (p. 28). Many of the other contributors are less convinced. In discussing the wage-labor nexus, Boyer and Saillard (2002, p. 46) let the cat out of the bag:

> … its initial basis was none other than the Marxist theory of exploitation which in the 1990's is no longer a major reference point. Today the theory centres on relations between power, wage compromise and the institutional determinants of the wage-profit division.

Several other chapters discuss the RA as a variety of institutionalism. This trend was perhaps most dramatically confirmed when in an afterword to the re-publication of *A Theory of Capitalist Regulation*, Aglietta (1998) discussed the issues involved in a distinctly un-Marxian manner. In the Boyer and Saillard volume, Olivier Favereau (2002, p. 315) draws a straightforward and helpful distinction between Regulation Theory 1 (RT1) as "similar to the Marxist analysis of the capitalist mode of production" and RT2 as "separate from this analysis and based on dynamic aspects of institutional forms." The Marxian strand still dominates with Anglophone adherents working within radical sociology and geography.

Interestingly, the movement by the RA towards institutionalism has, at the same time, lessened some of the other differences identified by Kotz. A greater emphasis has been placed on the role of institutions (found predominantly within the mode of regulation) both in constituting the period of successful regulation and in the emergence of crisis (Aglietta 1998, p. 56) The RA has become much more concerned with the question of the relationship of agency to structure. In the Anglophone RA tradition, this trend is represented by Jessop's (2002, pp. 34–36) advocacy of a "strategic-relational approach" which includes the capacity of actors to engage in struggles which "overflow" structural forms. Dialogue between the two traditions continues (Boyer 2010).

Marxian stage theory and the Varieties of Capitalism literature

In addition to providing a Marxian tradition of the integration of institutions into the creation of a dynamic capitalist variety, the Marxian stage theoretic tradition, and the SSA framework more specifically, have the potential to resolve many of the problems identified earlier in the varieties of capitalism literature. The most fundamental critique is that institutional analysis needs to be rooted in a conception of the basic underlying nature and dynamics of capitalism. This is indeed the starting point of the stage theoretic tradition and the SSA framework. Gordon et al. define capitalism "as a wage-labor system of commodity production for profit" (Gordon *et al.* 1982, p. 18). As such capitalism has five principle tendencies (pp. 19–20, emphasis in original):

1. Capitalist accumulation continually attempts to *expand* the boundaries of the capitalist system ...
2. Capitalist accumulation persistently increases the size of large corporations and *concentrates* the control and ownership of capital in proportionately fewer hands ...
3. The accumulation of capital *spreads wage labor* as the prevalent system of production, draws a larger proportion of the population into wage-labor status, and *replenishes the reserve pool of labor* ...
4. Capitalist accumulation continually *changes the labor process* ...
5. In order to defend themselves against the effects of capitalist accumulation, workers have responded with their own activities and struggles ...

In addition, the realization of these tendencies has institutional preconditions and capitalism contains multiple conflicts, instabilities, and crisis tendencies which need to be moderated and channeled through institutional means. At the same time, capital accumulation tends to erode its own institutional preconditions. This creates an historical dynamic of both the success and failure of capital accumulation, alternating periods of growth and crisis.

It is the onset of capitalist crisis tendencies that allows the stage theoretic tradition to escape the first critique of the comparative capitalisms literature, that the interrelated character and complementarity of the institutions predicts a stasis and inability to transit from one institutional regime to another. The SSA framework in a sense predicts precisely the opposite dynamic. Capitalist contradictions eventually come to the fore, eroding the institutional conditions of capitalist accumulation and precipitating crisis. The failure of institutional resources as well as conflict in the context of the developing crisis further erodes the institutions. The stagnation will only be overcome eventually through the construction of a new SSA. Contrary to any stability thesis, the new SSA differs fundamentally from the previous SSA.

Wolfson and Kotz (2010, pp. 81–89) draw a striking contrast with the Hall and Soskice (2001) conceptualization of Liberal Market Economies (LMEs) and Coordinated Market Economies (CMEs) and their relationship over historical time. Wolfson and Kotz elaborate a conception of Liberal SSAs and Regulated SSAs. These Liberal SSAs and Regulated SSAs roughly parallel Hall and Soskice's LMEs and CMEs.

Liberal SSAs tend to enter into crisis because capital's ability to dominate labor leads to stagnant wages, inadequate demand, and overcapacity. Unregulated economies often fall prey to financial crises. These Liberal crises are most easily resolved through an increase in the strength of labor, a limited redistribution of income, and the regulation of demand and finance; that is, the establishment of a Regulated SSA. Regulated SSAs by contrast are prone to "profit-squeeze" crises, due to rising wages and popular demands for intervention by government in the markets. These crises are most often resolved through the reassertion of capital's dominance over labor and the promotion of deregulation through the creation of a Liberal SSA. Thus the dynamic is directly the opposite of that hypothesized in the VoC argument. Types of capitalism are not internally reproduced over the medium term. Rather they enter into crisis and succeed one another, sometimes in a repeated leap-frog fashion.

The second broad critique is that the national focus of the comparative capitalisms literature makes it difficult to account for the advent of transnational modes of regulation in the recent era of globalization. The SSA framework has shared the focus on the national level. Treating the boundaries of the SSA as contiguous with those of the nation-state was justified through an appeal to the basic structure of the theory. McDonough (1994, p. 79) argued this initial preference for a nation-centric analysis as follows:

Since political and ideological institutions are an important part of any SSA, and politics and ideology are often specific to particular regions or even nations, it seems appropriate to consider SSAs as national or regional phenomena rather than as ones encompassing the whole of the capitalist world.

International institutions and arrangements existed but they were considered as shared aspects of the different national SSAs. However, this type of analysis may be in need of revision in order to better conceptualize the emergence of global and transnational (as opposed to national and international) patterns of production and consumption. This reconsideration would argue that SSA theory originally, and justifiably, articulated country-specific cases. Contemporary developments, however, place new emphasis on those elements of capitalism that have a tendency to transcend national boundaries.

The fundamental elements of national capitalisms (class relations, production, commerce, finance) have *over-spilled* national institutional confines. Following from this, the "inter" national economy framework that governed economic and political activity among nation-states has also evolved beyond previous institutional constraints. An emerging global SSA can no longer be appropriately theorized as the culmination of nationally sited SSAs, with their individual logics of accumulation driving the world's economy. These global developments coupled with the spread of neoliberalism have constituted the core of the SSA which, since the early 1980s, succeeded the Fordist postwar stage of capitalism.

This new SSA is based in the transnationalization of class relations. A globalized capitalist class has emerged from the interpenetration of previously national bourgeoisies. The common confrontation with this transnational capitalist class has brought a truly transnational working class into being. The internationalization of various configurations of class relations involves the internationalization of the state. As national classes increasingly interpenetrate one another, the need for state structures that address this activity becomes prominent. A transnational state apparatus has emerged with institutions like the European Union, the World Trade Organization, and the international financial institutions (Robinson 2001; Nardone and McDonough 2010).

This transnational SSA is not, however, homogenous across national boundaries. In addition, this transnational framework is limited in scope. It has been primarily concerned with the liberalization of the movement of goods and capital across national boundaries. The so far limited remit of transnational governance allows the creation of national differences, which paves the way for capital to site various parts of the accumulation process in the most profitable locations. In the current period, when state action is examined at the national level, differences in form, policies, and operation may be still very apparent. However, the significance of these differences has been transformed. These sets of policies and bodies may be viewed as drawn from a more or less extensive menu of instruments, which is itself part of the global SSA and effectively determines production, competition, regulation, and consumption within both domestic and global spaces.

Other major features of this global neoliberal SSA include the declining economic and political strength of labor as well as the intensification of financialization. Globalization and neoliberalism were central to the emergence of these other core features of the transnational SSA. As mentioned earlier, "spatialization" has emerged as a major strategy in the disciplining of labor. In the era of globalization, capital has substantially increased its mobility relative to labor. Movement, or the credible threat of movement, has become the central strategy for rolling back the achievements of the labor movement. The deregulation and increasing mobility of financial capital specifically has also played a role in the rising importance of finance and the increasing proportion of total profitability flowing through the financial system.

The prospects for the current crisis

The problems we have discussed within the Varieties of Capitalism approach, whatever their effect on the analysis of capitalist diversity across space in the era of neoliberal globalization, have blocked effective approaches to anticipating the outcomes of the current capitalist crisis. These blockages stem from the reluctance to recognize the potential for – further the necessity of – substantial institutional change across time which goes beyond incremental adjustment. In addition, any resolution of the current crisis, whether within capitalism or beyond it, must take account of the current global context of economic activity.

In dealing with post-crisis developments, an account must be made of both what has happened to this moment and what is expected to occur in the longer term. There is insufficient space here to consider in any detail the multiple national and regional responses to the crisis both in its immediate aftermath and subsequently. It is, nevertheless, fair to characterize the broad response as one designed to further consolidate the neoliberal order. This is despite the fact that the initial response could be and has been characterized as Keynesian in nature.[3] Governments intervened aggressively to bail out failing financial institutions, taking many at least temporarily into state ownership. Large amounts of liquidity were pumped into national economies despite the warnings of inflation hawks. Demand management was implemented through public investment programs, though Keynesian analysts regarded these efforts as far from adequate.

These actions have at least temporarily stabilized financial markets. Once this was accomplished, much of the momentum for policy change was rapidly lost. Financial markets were subjected to much opprobrium but limited additional regulation. Financial institutions were returned to private control and stimulus programs cut back.

Most consequentially, the increases in government debt and deficits, essential to arresting the downward spiral of the economy, were quickly regarded as unacceptable both ideologically and practically. Large deficits and debts were regarded as portending a failure of governments to successfully borrow in international financial markets, threatening national bankruptcy.[4] The failure of economies to recover was ascribed to a lack of confidence by business and other investors in the probity of government decision making. A radical retrenchment was undertaken which has come to be known as the implementation of "austerity." Austerity programs sought to reduce current deficits and to ultimately generate surpluses to pay down debt. This effort has generally been concentrated on cutting expenditure rather than raising taxes. Social spending has been targeted and welfare recipients demonized. Money has been raised through the sale of remaining state assets. Public employment has been reduced and state employees' income slashed. This has in turn weakened labor in the private sector. Competitiveness as a goal has been used to justify further reductions in pay across the economy. In the Eurozone this has been characterized as a necessary "internal devaluation" in the absence of flexible exchange rates.

This intensification of neoliberalism, even in the strongholds of the Coordinated Market Economies on continental Europe, poses a problem for the Varieties of Capitalism literature. The current crisis would seem to have rapidly undermined the integrity of the CMEs. For this result to be consistent with the VoC approach, the past five or six years must be one of those rare periods in which varieties of capitalism can be seriously de-stabilized. Alternatively, a transition to a type of Liberal Market Economy must have taken place earlier on the European mainland.[5] But this possibility undermines the *raison d'etre* of the VoC analysis. The impulse behind the theory was to establish the possibility of the survival of non-neoliberal economies in the context of global competition. It may be that the distinction between the Anglo-Saxon economies and the continental economies after the 1980s was one of varieties *within* neoliberal capitalism rather than more qualitative differences between capitalisms. Perhaps the rhetoric of the "social market economies" more accurately depicted a variety of social neoliberalism. Within a social neoliberal economy, governments recognize the need for intervention by the state in society, but restrict their actions to those which can be pursued within the parameters of a low taxation regime and a basic market orientation. Much is made of the "efficiency" of the private provision of government functions, changes in public management structures to improve "customer service," and the hypothetical possibility of clever policy interventions which aim to achieve goals without expending additional resources. New Labour in Britain can be seen as one paradigm of this approach to implementing neoliberalism.

The crisis-driven intensification of neoliberalism also poses a challenge to the SSA framework. Crises are precipitated by contradictions which develop in the institutional configuration of the SSA which conditioned the previous period of relatively unproblematic capitalist expansion. Crises are then potentially resolved by the partial replacement and the *reorganization* of the institutional conditions of accumulation resulting in the inauguration of a *new* SSA. An intensification of the institutions whose eventual malfunction led to the crisis is highly unlikely to play a successful role in resolving the crisis.

If the intensification of neoliberalism were to lead to a sustained capitalist recovery from the current crisis, the SSA framework would certainly have some explaining to do. However, the theory does not predict immediate effective institutional innovation consequent on the emergence of crisis. The crisis period is merely predicted to mark a boundary between stages of capitalism. The theory in fact predicts that the resolution of the crisis period should *not* take place over a relatively short period of time. There is a built-in inertia in institutions even if they are not as inflexible as some versions of the VoC school contend. The creation of new institutions takes time. The demand that institutions be consistent with one another and jointly effective in recreating the conditions for capitalist expansion also generally adds to the time it would take to structurally resolve a capitalist crisis (Lippit 2005). These factors tend to extend the crisis period and are the reason that capitalist history is characterized by alternate periods of growth and stagnation. In addition, following Kotz and Wolfson, crises of liberal social structures are more often resolved with the creation of regulated social structures. These are more difficult to put in place than liberal structures which concentrate on the less complicated task of dismantling previous regulatory structures. Thus the crisis of the Great Depression was not resolved until the years following World War II, while global neoliberalism was well established in about a decade after the beginning of the stagflationary crisis (Kotz and McDonough 2010, p. 97)

Thus a period of floundering or misdirected change in the immediate aftermath of the crisis is not surprising in an SSA theoretical framework. The stages of capitalism approach would predict a longer crisis than the VoC school. The resolution of the crisis from the VoC perspective would involve the restoration of the previously effective complementarities of the ultimately continuing pre-crisis varieties of capitalism thus preserving capitalist variation across space. The stages of capitalism approach predicts the construction of a new stage thus creating capitalist variation over time. The failure of global neoliberalism so far to begin to resolve the crisis on its own terms lends credence to the SSA theory's prediction of an extended crisis.

A case can be made that advocacy of a basically liberal economic framework is the default political position of the capitalist class. Other more regulatory frameworks tend to demand state action which, even when wholly oriented to capital's interest, raise the possibility of working class capture of the direction of government policy. In addition, these more regulated frameworks need to be based on an ideology of collective action even if this is motivated by more reactionary forms of collectivity like aggressive nationalism or fundamentalist religion. Support for unalloyed possessive individualism can potentially be undermined.

It is questionable whether the current drive to austerity is linked by its advocates to any attempt to meaningfully address the crisis. Arguments for "expansionary fiscal contraction" (Giavazzi and Pagano 1990) have not stood up to closer scrutiny and academic apologists for austerity have had to resort to the assertion that these policies will create "confidence." These arguments present no reason why investors should be so naïve as to think that cutting spending and raising taxes in an economy deficient in domestic demand should promote recovery and favorable business conditions. Consequently, it is hard to believe they are a prime motivating factor in the formulation of policy. It is much more likely that the crisis is being treated as a global opportunity for "disaster capitalism" (Klein 2006). Catastrophes can create an opportunity to implement conservative policy using the unfavorable situation as a cover and a rationale.

Wolfson and Kotz (2010) argue that the effective resolution of a crisis of liberal capitalism is likely to be a variety of regulated capitalism. There are two serious obstacles to the achievement of this type of outcome. The first, ironically, is the general absence of a serious social threat to capitalist domination of the economic and political spheres. The second consists of problems created by the global nature of the SSA now in crisis.

To the extent that strategies alternative to liberalism have been pursued by capitalist elites, these have most often been motivated by a sense of threats to capitalism itself. The malfunctioning of capitalism itself is usually not a sufficient motivation to prompt the search by elites for an alternative strategy if a basically liberal institutional structure is already in place.[6] Non-capitalist forces have to be sufficiently mobilized and active so as to present at least a strong potential threat. This creates a certain historical irony. On their own, capitalist elites will not depart from the pursuit of a neoliberal solution to the current crisis. A neoliberal solution to a neoliberal crisis is almost certain to fail. Therefore an effective response to this crisis of capitalism is only likely to arise in response to a potentially revolutionary threat from working and popular forces. The longer it takes to create such a movement, the longer the crisis is likely to last. Despite significant stirrings in Greece, Spain, and Latin America, a sufficiently threatening movement is not yet in evidence.

A regulatory regime must have an agency which is sufficiently united and powerful so as to be able to exercise the regulatory function. In the age of globalization, it is not clear that such an agency exists. The disintegration of production across national borders and its reintegration through trade has created a global capitalist class and transnational state-like institutions through which its hegemony has begun to be exercised.[7] This does not mean that states have completely lost power or influence. It means that that power is exercised within the constraints of a globalized economy and, to the extent that the state is representing capitalist class interests, that class is the global capitalist class rather than remnants of the previously national bourgeoisies. The transnational institutions of the global economy have been oriented specifically to the *de*-regulation of the international economy, promoting the unfettered movement of goods and capital, if not of labor. It is unclear to what extent these institutions could be deployed to collectively set limits to the actions of transnational capital. Meanwhile, the policies of nation-states have been built around attempts to competitively attract inward investment. This tends to create a race to the bottom. Reversing this momentum creates a collective action problem. Nations will be reluctant to be the first to act to restrain the freedom of international capital for fear of discouraging investment.[8]

These blockages create barriers to the construction of a new and successful SSA. If these barriers were overcome what would a future more regulated SSA look like? Kotz (forthcoming) argues that regulated SSAs can potentially take two forms. One is a capitalist-dominated regulated institutional structure and the other is one which eventuates when working and popular classes are able to negotiate a kind of class compromise. An example of the first kind of regulated institutional structure was the monopoly capitalist SSA in the US following the turn of the twentieth century. A sharp break with a competitive market structure was organized by bringing industry under the hegemony of finance capital. Unrestrained competition was eliminated by the creation through merger of giant market-dominating corporations. This was accomplished under the leadership of banking capital which led the merger movement and benefited materially from its creation. The new monopoly corporations were able to mobilize against the working class, secure favorable regulation from the state and secure a successful policy of imperial domination of foreign territories and markets. A militant labor movement was repressed rather than partially incorporated in these new structures. The New Deal Order which was the foundation of the postwar SSA along with American international dominance was, by contrast, created partially through the integration of organized labor into the emergent structures. Labor traded shop floor control for union recognition and productivity linked wage increases. Labor provided one of the electoral bases of a Keynesian policy which balanced employment and price stability. Cold War ideology replaced more radical alternatives and justified the aggressive assertion of American control over the international economy.

One possibility for the future is continued crisis and stagnation under the hegemony of global neoliberalism. A further capitalist-dominated alternative is a capitalist-dominated regulated SSA which may emerge in the face of a challenge to capitalist dominance which is successfully repressed. Such an alternative holds few attractions for popular forces. It would likely continue the repression of working class living standards and be accompanied by an authoritarian state hostile to independent working class political influence. This repressive apparatus could supplement private demand but some form of national infrastructure investment would also have to be organized. Chinese capitalism currently resembles this kind of formation but relies for its stability on the proceeds of large export surpluses. It is clearly impossible to replicate such a strategy across the capitalist world. As observed earlier, the global character of the economy today stands as an obstacle to any regulated solution to the current crisis.

A renewed New Deal or "green" New Deal is supported by certain social democratic forces.[9] Such an alternative is possible but will not be based on persuading elites of the abstract superiority of this kind of economy for creating growth, "social cohesion," and stability. It will be minimally based on a reversal of the current trend of increasing income inequality. A movement to this end would have to overcome the ideological dominance of neoliberalism, the increasingly hollowed-out character of the domestic state, and the competitive pressures induced by globalization. It is hard to see this happening in the absence of widespread revolt by working class and other popular forces. If such an uprising comes to pass, it would behoove radical participants to advocate pushing forward to the replacement of capitalism itself rather than to speculate on how such a revolt could contribute to creating a restored capitalist SSA.

Conclusion

A by now wide body of academic literature on the importance of institutions in capitalist economies has suffered from traditional divisions of labor within the social sciences. Economics has by and large seen capitalism as a system directed by market interactions which both are and ought to be disembedded from influences emanating from the rest of society. More sociological traditions do not suffer from an inability to perceive the importance of institutional determination in relation to the economy, but have had a tendency to ignore work on the fundamental nature and dynamics of capitalism as a system and a mode of production. As a way of overcoming this dichotomy, Bruff and Horn (2012, p. 163) call for a move away from "institutionalist theories of capitalism" towards "capitalist theories of institutions" in treatments of capitalist variation. The Marxian tradition as a whole has developed as a comprehensive theory of capitalist history, thus integrating political, ideological, and cultural concerns and consequently holds considerable promise in this regard. Nevertheless even here academic divisions of labor have discouraged the full integration of political and ideological institutions into the basic theory of capital accumulation.

The Marxian theory of stages of capitalism, while less prominent in the literature than the Marxian theory (or theories) of capitalism, holds one important key to overcoming this weakness. The modern form of Marxian stage theory finds expression in continuations of the early Marxian version of Regulation Theory and the Social Structure of Accumulation (SSA) framework. The SSA framework develops an historically intermediate analysis of capitalist stages which are particular to specific periods in capitalist history and differ from one another in the character of the institutions which condition the reproduction of capitalism and the capitalist accumulation process. The framework thus crosses paths with institutional theories of capitalist variation.

Importantly, however, the SSA framework does not lose sight of the basic dynamics of capitalism in general. In addition to periods of relatively healthy capital accumulation, capitalist social formations also undergo periods of extensive crisis due to multiple crisis tendencies inherent in capitalism in general as well as some peculiar to the particular SSA. Indeed, it is these crisis periods which separate SSAs or stages from one another. Variation is thus theorized over time as well as geographical space. The tendency of some of the literature to see capitalist varieties as static and unchanging is thus absent from the SSA framework. The overcoming of the crisis tendencies of the previous stage demands that a resolution of the crisis and a new period of growth is premised precisely on a new and different institutional basis. The discovery of this basis is the result of class conflict over the crisis period and no limit is placed on the variety of institutional complementarities that might be created. The emergence of global neoliberalism as the resolution of the stagflationary crisis of the 1970s was a contingent outcome of struggles during this period. This particular outcome has demanded that the theory consider the possibility of the emergence of an SSA founded on transnational class relations and the inauguration of transnational institutions which both transcend and include the traditional nation-state. For these reasons, the SSA theory of capitalist stages is better positioned to analyze the potential outcomes of the current capitalist crisis than other institutional approaches to capitalist variation.

Notes

1 Within a Marxian framework accumulation is not simply the accumulation of physical capital but the extension of capitalist social relations. Nevertheless the term is often used synonymously with reinvestment and growth.
2 For a useful collection of articles explaining, reviewing, and applying the SSA approach see Kotz *et al.* (1994). See also McDonough *et al.* (2010).
3 Robert Skidelsky entitled his 2009 book, *Keynes: Return of the Master.*
4 Several members of the Eurozone did indeed face bankruptcy, but this stemmed a lack of control over a national currency and the refusal of the Eurozone authorities to back these countries during the crisis.
5 While a full discussion of these institutional changes would not be appropriate here, many of them, such as an independent central bank with no remit for growth or employment and "debt breaks" on public expenditure, have been implemented at the European Union or Eurozone levels. These basically neoliberal institutions have been established, however, without opposition from authorities from the CMEs in Europe and have in fact been modelled on institutions drawn from Germany, the pre-eminent CME example.
6 This may also be the case if a capitalist dominated regulatory structure is in place as in the case of the Monopoly SSA which preceded the Great Depression.
7 For instance the World Trade Organization (WTO), the International Financial Institutions (IFIs), the European Union (EU), the North Atlantic Free Trade Association (NAFTA), etc.
8 The failure to so far implement a Tobin tax on financial transactions in the developed world is a case in point despite widespread if not unanimous agreement as to its desirability.
9 As distinct from "social market" supporters, who often share (or dominate) (former) social democratic political parties.

References

Aglietta, M. (1998) "Capitalism at the Turn of the Century: Regulation Theory and the Challenge of Social Change," *New Left Review*, 232: 41–90.

Bohle, D. and D. Greskovits (2009) "Varieties of Capitalism and Capitalism Tout Court," *European Journal of Sociology*, 50: 355–86.

Boyer, R. (2002) "Is regulation theory an original theory of economic institutions?" in R. Boyer and Y. Saillard (eds) *Regulation Theory: The State of the Art* (London: Routledge).

——(2010) "The Rise of CEO Pay and the Contemporary Social Structure of Accumulation in the United States," in T. McDonough, M. Reich and D. M. Kotz (eds), *Contemporary Capitalism and Its Crises: Social Structure of Accumulation Theory for the 21st Century* (Cambridge: Cambridge University Press).

——(2002) "Regulation theory: stasis or confirmation of a research programme?" in R. Boyer and Y. Saillard (eds) *Regulation Theory: The State of the Art* (London: Routledge).

——and Y. Saillard (2002) *Regulation Theory: The State of the Art* (London: Routledge).

Brady, D. and M. Wallace (2000) "Spatialization, Foreign Direct Investment and Labor Outcomes in the American States, 1976–1996," *Special Forces*, 79: 67–100.

Bruff, I. (2011) "What about the Elephant in the Room? Varieties of Capitalism, Varieties in Capitalism," *New Political Economy*, 16(4): 481–500.

Bruff, I. and L. Horn (2012) "Varieties of capitalism in crisis?" *Competition and Change*, 16(3) July: 161–68.

Bukharin, N. (1973 [1915]) *Imperialism and World Economy* (New York: Monthly Review Press).

Deeg, R. and G. Jackson (2007) "The State of the Art: Towards a more dynamic theory of capitalist variety," *Socio-Economic Review*, 5: 149–79.

Favereau, O. (2002) "Conventions and regulation," in R. Boyer and Y. Saillard (eds) *Regulation Theory: The State of the Art* (London: Routledge).

Giavazzi, F. and M. Pagano (1990) "Can Severe Fiscal Contractions Be Expansionary? Tales of Two Small European Countries," *NBER Macroeconomics Annual* 5: 75–111.

Gordon, D. M. (1978) "Up and Down the Long Roller Coaster," in Union for Radical Political Economics (ed.) *Capitalism in Crisis* (New York: Union for Radical Political Economics).

——(1980) "Stages of Accumulation and Long Economic Cycles," in T. Hopkins and I. Wallerstein (eds) *Processes of the World System* (Beverly Hills, CA: Sage Publications).

Gordon, D. M., R. C. Edwards and M. Reich (1982) *Segmented Work, Divided Workers* (Cambridge: Cambridge University Press).

Grant, D. S. and M. Wallace (eds) (1994) "The Political-Economy of Manufacturing Growth and Decline across the American States, 1970–85," *Social Forces*, 73(1): 33–63.

Hall, P. A. and D. Soskice (2001) *Varieties of Capitalism: The Institutional Foundations of Comparative Advantage* (New York: Oxford University Press).

Hilferding, R. (1980 [1910]) *Finance Capital* (London: Routledge and Kegan Paul).

Jessop, B. (1990) "Regulation Theories in Retrospect and Prospect," *Economy and Society*, 19(2) May: 153–216.

——(2002) *The Future of the Capitalist State* (Cambridge: Polity).

Klein, N. (2006) *The Shock Doctrine: The Rise of Disaster Capitalism* (New York: Picador).

Kotz, D. M. (1994) "The Regulation Theory and the Social Structure of Accumulation Approach," in D. M. Kotz, T. McDonough, and M. Reich (eds) *Social Structures of*

Accumulation: The Political Economy of Growth and Crisis (Cambridge: Cambridge University Press).

—— and T. McDonough (2010) "Global Neoliberalism and the Contemporary Social Structure of Accumulation," in T. McDonough, M. Reich and D. M. Kotz (eds) *Contemporary Capitalism and Its Crises: Social Structure of Accumulation Theory for the 21st Century* (Cambridge: Cambridge University Press).

——, T. McDonough and M. Reich (eds) (1994) *Social Structures of Accumulation: The Political Economy of Growth and Crisis* (Cambridge: Cambridge University Press).

Lenin, V. I. (1968 [1917]) "Imperialism, The Highest Stage of Capitalism," in *Selected Works* (Moscow: Progress Publishers, pp. 169–262).

Lippit, V. D. (2005) *Capitalism* (Abingdon: Routledge).

McDonough, T. (1994) "Social Structures of Accumulation, Contingent History, and Stages of Capitalism," in D. M. Kotz, T. McDonough and M. Reich (eds) *Social Structures of Accumulation: The Political Economy of Growth and Crisis* (Cambridge: Cambridge University Press).

——(1995) "Lenin, Imperialism, and Stages of Capitalist Development," *Science and Society*, 59(3).

——(1999) "Gordon's Accumulation Theory: the Highest Stage of Stadial Theory," *Review of Radical Political Economics*, 31(4): 6–31.

——, M. Reich and D. M. Kotz (2010) *Contemporary Capitalism and Its Crises: Social Structure of Accumulation Theory for the 21st Century* (Cambridge: Cambridge University Press).

Nadel, H. (2002) "Regulation and Marx," in R. Boyer and Y. Saillard (eds) *Regulation Theory: The State of the Art* (London: Routledge).

Nardone, E. and T. McDonough (2010) "Global Neoliberalism and the Possibility of Transnational State Structures," in T. McDonough, M. Reich and D. M. Kotz (eds) *Contemporary Capitalism and Its Crises: Social Structure of Accumulation Theory for the 21st Century* (Cambridge: Cambridge University Press).

Radice, H. (2000) "Globalization and national capitalisms: theorizing convergence and differentiation," *Review of International Political Economy*, 7(4): 719–42.

Reich, M. (1997) "Social Structure of Accumulation Theory: Retrospect and Prospect," *The Review of Radical Political Economics*, 29(3): 1–10.

Robinson, W. I. (2001) "Social Theory and Globalization: The rise of a transnational state," *Theory and Society*, 30(2): 157–200.

——(2004) *A Theory of Global Capitalism, Production, Class, and State in a Transnational World* (London: University of Baltimore Press).

Skidelsky, R. (2009) *Keynes: Return of the Master* (New York: Public Affairs).

Wallace, M. and D. Brady (2010) "Globalization or Spatialization? The Worldwide Spatial Restructuring of the Labor Process," in T. McDonough, M. Reich and D. M. Kotz (eds) *Contemporary Capitalism and Its Crises: Social Structure of Accumulation Theory for the 21st Century* (Cambridge: Cambridge University Press).

Wolfson, M. H. and D. M. Kotz (2010) "A Reconceptualization of Social Structure of Accumulation Theory," in T. McDonough, M. Reich and D. M. Kotz (eds) *Contemporary Capitalism and Its Crises: Social Structure of Accumulation Theory for the 21st Century* (Cambridge: Cambridge University Press).

Part 2

Varieties of cases, convergence of outcomes?

5 The end of one American century ... and the beginning of another?

Tony Smith

In *Capital* Marx sketched a trajectory followed by a succession of leading regions of the world market since the sixteenth century (Marx 1976, p. 920):

> [T]he villainies of the Venetian system of robbery formed one of the secret foundations of Holland's wealth in capital, for Venice in her years of decadence lent large sums of money to Holland. There is a similar relationship between Holland and England. By the beginning of the eighteenth century, Holland's manufacturers had been far outstripped. It ceased to be a nation preponderant in commerce and industry. One of its main lines of business, therefore, from 1701 to 1776, was the lending out of enormous amounts of capital, especially to its great rival England. The same thing is going on today between England and the United States. A great deal of capital, which appears today in the United States without any birth-certificate, was yesterday, in England, the capitalized blood of children.

In the century after these lines were written the United States (US) came to be "preponderant in commerce and industry," culminating in the so-called golden age after World War II. According to many observers it then entered the next stage in the sequence, "years of decadence" dominated by a financial sector overseeing cross-border flows of "enormous amounts of capital." From this perspective it would appear that future US decline is more or less inevitable, as Venice, Holland, and England declined before it.

The first part of this paper discusses developments in US capitalism that fit this narrative. There are, however, good reasons to expect US capitals to retain significant relative advantages in the coming period, as Part 2 will argue. In the third and final part I suggest that the future of US capitalism may be determined less by these relative advantages than by the limits of the world market in the coming period, reflecting the historical limits of capitalism itself.

Part 1

The post WWII "golden age" of capitalist development, characterized by high levels of profit, investment, and real wages (for some, at least), came to an end in the 1970s. By then Japanese and European capitals were more efficient producers of higher-quality products than established US firms in many sectors. The latter, however, did not cease production.[1] The result was an *overaccumulation crisis*, manifested in excess productive capacity and a decline in rates of profits, investment, and growth.

Ordinarily we would expect an overaccumulation crisis to set off a severe recession or depression, destroying excess productive capacity and devaluing previous capital investment. Ruling circles in the US had powerful incentives to avoid this path. Given the relatively weak position of US capitals, devaluing capital on the scale required would have inflicted very serious harm on the US economy, calling into question both the dollar's privileged position as world money and the US's geopolitical primacy.[2] After a period of trial and error an alternative path was found, *neoliberalism.*[3] An absolutely central component of neoliberalism was an attack on labor that significantly increased the rate of exploitation.[4] Commentators, however, have especially stressed neoliberal *financialization*, echoing Marx's description of the "degenerate" phase of previously hegemonic powers.

Nixon's 1971 break from the gold standard began an astounding and unprecedented explosion of debt in the US, reaching $50 trillion in 2007 (Duncan 2012, p. 34). Deficit state spending created demand for productive capacity that would otherwise be unused ("military Keynesianism"). Greater household debt stimulated a paroxysm of hyper-consumerism by wealthy households, while helping working families maintain living standards. Credit money allocated to non-financial corporations funded stock buy-backs and highly leveraged mergers and acquisitions, lifting stock prices to the great joy of investors (and executives with stock options). The primary beneficiary of the credit money created within the financial sector, however, was the financial sector itself.[5] Increased liquidity directly led to an inexorable inflation of the prices of financial assets (Toporowski 2000). The high fees appropriated from the construction and sale of these assets provided the motivation to construct ever-more exotic synthetic financial instruments, all promising high returns at relatively low risk ("collateralized debt obligations cubed," anyone?). In these circumstances frequent self-sustaining financial bubbles were as assured as their subsequent bursting. The Federal Reserve quickly discovered that if it pumped massive amounts of liquidity into financial markets after these bubbles burst, the damage to the financial sector would be minimized and a new round of financial asset inflation could soon commence. By 2005 financial firms accounted for more than 40 percent of the earnings of companies listed in the Standard and Poor 500. The combined income of *all* 500 CEOs of those leading non-financial companies totaled less than that of just the top twenty-five hedge fund managers. In 2008 one in every thirteen dollars in compensation in the US went to people in finance, as opposed to one in forty in the "golden age" after WWII (Roubini and Mihm 2010, p. 190).

Fueled by the income gains of the wealthy and the increased debt of all households, the US consumer market became the primary "engine" of global growth. US trade deficits and the surpluses of exporting nations expanded in sync.[6] Mainstream economics predicted that there would eventually be a steep appreciation in the currencies of surplus countries relative to the dollar, raising the prices of their exports in dollar terms and thereby hurting exports to the US. Japan, and China. Other surplus nations avoided this result by investing their reserves in US Treasury Bills, with the increasing demand for dollars preventing a decline in its relative value.[7] These and other capital inflows kept interest rates in the US much lower than they otherwise would have been (and demand for loans correspondingly higher), fueling both the inflation of capital assets and consumer spending. As a result of these flows China and the US were responsible for 45–60 percent of all global growth in the period immediately prior to the "Great Recession," with the US absorbing an astounding 70 percent of the net capital flow in the world economy (Westra 2012, pp. 19–20).

From the standpoint of capital, neoliberalism was a tremendous success. Profit levels significantly recovered in the US. While levels of growth did not reach those of the post-WWII "golden age," they were comparable to previous periods of expansion (McNally 2010; Duménil and Lévy 2011). The value of financial assets in general trended steeply upwards for decades. Trade and foreign direct investment exploded, facilitating unprecedented growth rates in East Asia. US capitalism, in brief, had found a way to lead the world market forward from the overaccumulation crisis of the 1970s without having to undergo a massive destruction of excess productive capacity or a massive devaluation of capital.

Some features of US neoliberalism could be imitated elsewhere. Capital's on-going war against labor intensified in many other regions as well. Countries controlling their own currency (Japan, China, United Kingdom [UK]) also created immense amounts of credit money. Speculative bubbles in equity and housing markets erupted in numerous other regions. And growing imbalances between surplus and deficit regions stimulated growth elsewhere, as the dynamic connecting Germany and the European Union (EU) periphery graphically illustrated (Lapavitsas *et al.* 2012). Nonetheless, it makes little sense to speak of a US "variety" of capitalism that other regions could emulate. Only a region with the "exorbitant privilege" of a national currency functioning as world money could expand credit money on such a vast scale for such an extended period, while simultaneously enjoying an unprecedented flow of capital inflows receiving relatively low rates of return. It follows that no other region could expand debt-fueled speculative bubbles and domestic consumption on the same scale. And no other region has possessed a Central Bank serving as the de facto central banker of the world, with an unparalleled ability to determine where the horrors of financial crisis would fall with full force and where they would be alleviated (Toussaint 1999).

Financialization enabled the US to maintain its central position in the world market. But many have insisted this came at the cost of a "hollowing out" of the "real" economy. Wall Street's support for highly leveraged mergers and acquisitions intensified the desire of CEOs to keep their companies' share prices elevated, and thereby reduce the risk of being the target of a hostile take-over (and increase the chances of being the one taking over). Focusing on quarterly returns was the best way to elevate share prices, and "offshoring" production to China and other low-wage regions allowed many firms to maintain high quarterly returns (Davis 2009). The long-term implications of offshoring could be overlooked when low value-added parts of the production chain were lost. But the hollowing out imposed by the financial sector eventually eroded high-value production as well, symbolized by the emergence of an unprecedented US trade deficit in advanced-technology products.[8]

The narrative presented in this section has followed the arc Marx discerned in the history of previous leading regions: a phase of commercial and industrial advantages, followed by the loss of these advantages and a turn to financial activities. After the implosion of financialization in the "Great Recession" US capitalism now seems poised to complete the last phase of this narrative arc: extended decline, perhaps followed by China's emergence as the next hegemonic power (Arrighi 2009).

This story is not without plausibility. But it overlooks aspects of US capitalism that should not be disregarded.

Part 2

Technological change is both the main weapon in inter-capital competition and the key factor underlying relative surplus value, the dimension of the capital/wage labor relation most crucial to the reproduction of capital (Marx 1976, pp. 431–38; Smith 2010). After World War II the US unquestionably possessed the world's most effective national innovation system. While government funding accounted for roughly two-thirds of all R&D expenditures, corporate labs also engaged in long-term research generating a stream of significant innovations. That changed when the large oligopolies that dominated national markets began to face price competition from Japanese and European capitals, along with increasing pressure from Wall Street to maintain quarterly earnings. Private-sector funding of R&D actually increased in response. Industry R&D expenditures in constant terms increased two and a half times between 1992 and 2002, rising to two-thirds of total R&D spending in the US (National Research Council 2012, p. 134). But corporate labs abandoned long-term R&D, concentrating almost exclusively on projects promising a commercial advantage in the relatively short term.[9]

These developments potentially generated a profound problem. Basic research was still funded by the government (along with long-term projects of interest to the military). As just noted, the private sector was more than willing to fund projects with foreseeable commercializable results in the short term. But long-term civilian R&D was in great danger of falling in a "valley of death" between basic research and development. If it did, the technological dynamism of US capitalism would soon erode.

For all its rhetoric regarding the "magic of the marketplace" the Reagan administration recognized market failure when it saw it. It began to offer federal labs and publicly funded university labs various carrots and sticks to undertake the long-term R&D US capitals needed, but did not wish to undertake themselves. New programs were developed to provide start-ups with the necessary resources to develop innovations prior to the "proof of concept" required by venture capitalists. These and other forms of "public-private partnerships" have granted US capitals tremendous competitive advantages in the world market.[10]

Apple is perhaps the paradigmatic example. It "offshores" manufacturing, and the import of assembled iPads/iPods/iPhones adds to the US trade deficit with China. Apple, however, appropriates an inordinate share (around 30 percent) of their final sale price. Statistics regarding the US trade deficit in high-tech goods are therefore quite misleading, since they render the privileged place of firms like Apple in cross-border production and distribution chains invisible.[11] The biggest source of Apple's advantages is its insertion in the US national innovation system. Twelve core technical innovations are incorporated in "i" products; all twelve were the fruit of publically funded research and development (Mazzucato 2013).

By all relevant measures the US still has the best funded and most effective national innovation system in the globe *despite the rise of neoliberal financialization*. In 2010 the US accounted for 32.8 percent of global R&D spending, more than all of Europe combined (24.8 percent), and far more than either China (12 percent) or Japan (11.8 percent) (National Research Council 2012, p. 18). Unlike the earlier cases of Venice, Holland, and England the rise of financialization in the US did *not* come at the cost of leadership of the most technologically dynamic sectors of the world market (Panitch and Gindin 2012, pp. 288–89).

After the global slowdown of the 1970s the US alone was able both to place itself at the center of neoliberal financialization *and* to establish an unsurpassed national innovation system. Other regions could at most hope to do one (the UK) or the other (Germany, Japan). This unique combination may well continue to give US capitalism relative advantages in the world market, calling into question the narrative of decline.

The continued advantages of financialization for US capitals can ironically best be appreciated through appreciating the limits of financialization. While the explosion of credit money helped capital go forward from the slowdown of the 1970s, it did not resolve underlying overaccumulation problems. In fact, financialization exacerbated these difficulties by supporting the rise of new centers of accumulation.[12] With mutation of the "Great Recession" into today's "contained depression" the long-deferred threat of a massive destruction of excess capacity has returned to haunt the world market. "Zombie" banks and corporations have been kept alive through low interest rates and other forms of government support; at some point rates will rise and support will be curtailed. Many units of capital incapable of operating as proper units of capital (that is, as vampires, not zombies) will then go under. As always, the question will then be who will bear the brunt of devaluation and who will be spared.

It should go without saying that in the absence of radicalized mass social movements the greatest costs will be imposed on those who do not own and control capital, whether in a brutal and immediate fashion (the option of the right), or in a somewhat less brutal and somewhat more drawn-out manner (the "progressive" agenda, in effect). What else can be said?

In general, countries with extensive surpluses are in a position to displace devaluations to deficit regions, with Germany's relationship to debtor regions in the euro zone forming the paradigmatic case. As a deficit region itself, the US is not in this position. As long as the dollar plays the role of world money, however, US capitals can be protected from devaluation through infusions of central bank liquidity to a greater extent and for a longer period than other capitals in the world market, displacing a significant portion of the costs of devaluation elsewhere.[13]

This may be a path forward. But is it really a path forward for US *capitalism*? Has the fifty trillion dollars of debt in the US economy led to a mutation of capitalism into something quite different? A brief digression on this provocative hypothesis will set the stage for the remainder of this section.

For Marx, money in capitalism is the form of value, the objective measure of the extent to which privately undertaken (concrete) labor is socially necessary (abstract) labor. The essential connection between value and money is loosened with corporate bonds, stocks, and other financial assets. While these assets are commodities with a money price, they do not themselves have a value. They are *fictitious capital,* granting holders a claim on future returns generated by the use of the real assets represented by the stock or bond. In speculative bubbles the prices of these financial assets lose contact with any reasonable estimation of future earnings. In Marx's day if a critical mass of lenders and investors feared this point was approaching (or had been reached) a flight to gold would commence, restoring the tie between value and (commodity) money. This mechanism no longer operates in a world of pure fiat money. This would seem to allow credit money to eventually grow to the point where the tie between value and money has been irrevocably broken. If this were the case, a defining feature of capitalism would no longer hold, implying that capitalism has mutated into some different sort of beast. This conclusion appears to be reinforced by the fact that the creation of many trillions of dollars of credit money has been so thoroughly and obviously dependent on the state.[14] Does this not undermine the public/private distinction upon which capitalism is supposedly based?

I believe the tie between money and value has *not* been cut. It does, however, operate in a new way. Credit money created in the US today is not merely part of a strategy for buying time while the costs of devaluation fall elsewhere. Nor is it simply a manifestation of delusion and fraud, although they are unquestionably part of the story too. Credit money must also be conceptualized as a promise that the national innovation system will generate a stream of commercializable innovations in the future. This promise is in effect a "prevalidation" that the privately undertaken labor associated with US capitals will be socially validated in the future through the successful commercialization of innovations generated within the US national innovation system. The greater the explosion of credit money in the US through quantitative easing and other measures, the further the promise extends in time.[15] This is a *capitalist* project, albeit one that could not be pursued on this scale in any previous period of world history. It essentially involves the state, but the state has *always* been a feature of capitalism's concrete historical development.[16]

What are the prospects of this project?

Prominent specialists in technology studies believe that the national innovation system in place in the US today will *not* be adequate in the coming period. The present system – federally funded basic research, medium-to-long-term R&D within "public-private partnerships," and corporate funding of innovations promising commercializable results in the near term – has fostered extensive interdisciplinary collaborations of scientists and technologists. But scientific and technological workers engaged in manufacturing have been largely excluded from the formal and informal networks of collaboration due to the extensive "offshoring" of manufacturing. In contrast, the main competitors of US capitals are associated with national innovation systems incorporating extensive feedback from manufacturing in all stages of the innovation process. Over time national innovation systems with strong feedback loops connecting upstream R&D with the insights of those who daily confront scientific and technological issues in manufacturing will tend to be more effective than systems lacking this feedback. Experts fear that this flaw will have pernicious long-term consequences, as US firms with the capacity to manufacture innovative products disappear (Berger 2013; National Research Council 2012).

Three developments suggest that this structural weakness is being overcome. First, the differential in labor costs between the US and the main beneficiary of offshoring, China, is rapidly declining. As it shrinks the relative importance of other factors increases, including transportation costs, the difficulty of adapting to rapidly changing domestic markets when manufacturing has been "offshored," the need to protect intellectual property – and the contribution of manufacturing to scientific-technical innovation emphasized above. As the relative import of these factors increases, much manufacturing investment by US capitals will return ("reshoring"), or not leave in the first place (Sirkin *et al.* 2011).

Advances in automation technologies will reinforce this trend. Machine intelligence and the physical dexterity of robots and other forms of automated equipment are rapidly increasing as costs rapidly decline. Further, major technical advances and cost declines can be expected to result from the vast expenditures of public funds on R&D for drones and land-based robots for the military, along with the extensive technical insights emerging from their deployment.[17] Manufacturing will not move offshore to take advantage of low wages when labor costs are a vanishing percentage of total investment (Brynjolfsson and McAfee 2012).

A third factor concerns the so-called "internet of things" (Chui *et al.* 2010). In recent years manufacturing has not been the part of the production and distribution chain where the greatest "value" could be extracted. This will change as sensory receptors are attached to every material input and every machine in the manufacturing process, with the resulting data effectively processed by advanced algorithms. Knowledge of inventory, the workings of the supply chain, and manufacturing operations will be available in unprecedented detail. Firms mobilizing this knowledge effectively to make continuous and precise adjustments to manufacturing lines in real time will have a significant competitive advantage in both cost and quality of output. They will also be well positioned to undertake successful innovations in materials, machinery, and product design. Manufacturing, in short, is rapidly becoming an important site of value extraction, undermining the economic case for offshoring.

Specialists in technology policy hold that appropriate public policies are required to ensure that manufacturing is reincorporated within the US national innovation system.[18] If we assume for the sake of argument that the requisite policies will be forthcoming, an extremely strong case can be made that the United States is likely to retain competitive advantages in the world market in the coming historical period. A few specific examples must suffice.

The "internet of things" is only one example of innovations associated with the concept of "Big Data," where US capitals have an immense head start (Manyika *et al.* 2011). These innovations will further *mass customization* in numerous sectors. Suppose, for example, pharmaceutical firms are able to construct data bases including extensive information regarding chemical compounds, the known effects of various combinations, and the genetic make-up and medical histories of individuals. It should be possible for a sophisticated algorithm to predict what particular combination of compounds is likely to be of most benefit to a particular patient with a particular genetic make-up and medical history. Consumers and insurance companies would surely be willing to pay a premium for medicines promising to be more effective in particular cases than drugs aimed at the mythical statistically average patient.

The most familiar example of Big Data in everyday life is the collection of data about consumer behavior and the use of algorithms as prediction engines, generating probability estimates of the likelihood of a consumer's future behavior from correlations with the behavior of relevantly similar individuals. "Collaborative filtering" technologies enable Amazon to predict with ever-improving accuracy the books customers might be interested in, Google to predict the results sought by those undertaking internet searches, and Netflix to predict the movies their customers might like to see. With the right algorithms, data banks on users collected at websites can be effectively used to mass customize advertising to the individuals most likely to respond with purchases. Sale of this data to marketers has proven to be a tremendous source of revenue in the internet age.[19]

US capitals also appear to derive considerable competitive advantages from the mobilization of networks through social media. Commodities do not have value unless they have use-value. The social psychological processes in which brand identity and the personal identity of users are intertwined can be extended and intensified within social media networks. These processes can thereby extend and intensify the perceived use-values of commodities (Willmott 2010). The US units of capital that most effectively monitor and shape social media networks therefore have an advantage in valorization processes over other capitals in the world market.

Another potential "game changing" technology concerns the energy sector – and every sector that uses energy. Until recently the United States has been a major importer of energy. Thanks to contemporary developments in drilling technology ("fracking") the US is now poised to become an energy exporter, greatly improving its trade balance. Even more importantly, energy costs have been lowered. The 51 percent annual increase in shale gas production in the US, for example, has lowered costs of natural gas by two-thirds (Lund *et al.* 2013, p. 7). Cost reductions of this magnitude will give US firms a competitive advantage in coming years vis-à-vis regions in the world economy devoting significant revenues to importing energy.

Needless to say, the future remains uncertain. But it does appear that there are good reasons to reject the narrative of inevitable US decline relative to other centers of accumulation. The relative advantages neoliberal financialization provides to US capitalism have not been eroded. As long as the dollar remains the major form of world money, the US will remain in a unique position to create credit money protecting its capitals from waves of devaluation in the global economy. And the US possesses the national innovation system in the strongest position to make good the promise that a critical mass of credit money created today will be valorized tomorrow and the day after.[20] Most importantly, the US is absolutely unique in being able to combine both advantages simultaneously.

The future of US capitalism, however, does not depend simply on its relative advantages. The world economy is not an aggregate of separate national economies. It is a higher-order complex whole, with emergent properties of its own. The future prospects of US capitalism must be considered in the context of this higher-order unity.

Part 3

Multiple rounds of quantitative easing have contained deflationary tendencies in the US thus far. That is not the same as removing these tendencies, and they have not been so well contained in other regions. There are numerous reasons to hold that deflationary tendencies will be exacerbated in the world market in coming years.

Technological changes in capitalism have always generated a surplus population, "surplus," that is, to the needs of capital. In previous periods, however, this aspect of capital accumulation has largely been displaced from the "center" of the world market to the periphery (Patnaik 1997). This will no longer be the case. Automation may contribute to a renaissance of US manufacturing, but as it does so it will also increase the "surplus population" substantively in absolute and relative terms, both in the US and the global economy as a whole.[21] This in itself generates a powerful deflationary tendency, which is then reinforced by the relentless pressure on real wages a growing surplus population imposes. Capital has numerous disciplinary mechanisms to control a growing surplus population; they may or may not prove successful. But its only effective mechanism to check the deflationary bias created by a growing surplus population is a vast expansion of household debt, and that card has already been played. How much will a competitive advantage in productivity matter when the growing gap between productivity advances and real wages in the world economy becomes an ever-greater chasm? How much will a competitive advantage in the technologies of mass customization matter in a world market where the mass customer base has been eroded? In the world economy as a whole there is an irresolvable tension between the drive to automate and the need to reproduce the capital/wage labor relationship. We appear to be approaching the period when this tension reaches a breaking point (fulfilling the prediction Marx made in his discussion of the "the general intellect" in the *Grundrisse*; Marx 1987, p. 92).[22]

A strong deflationary bias can be discerned in inter-capital relations no less than in the capital/wage labor relation. The US may continue to possess the single most effective national innovation system in the globe. But in capitalism the relevant issue is not simply who has a competitive advantage in innovation, but how long surplus profits can be appropriated from successful innovations. The days when the US had the only effective national innovation system are long over. As a result there has been a tremendous compression of the length of time high profits can be appropriated from superior technologies.

Today four countries spend over 3 percent of their Gross Domestic Product on research and development, and another six devote over 2 percent of their annual economic output on R&D (*The Economist* 2011, p. 97). The US has slipped from first in the world ranking of research intensity (measured by the ratio of R&D spending to GDP) to eighth (OECD 2011, p. 76). Other nations also provide relatively extensive public and private funding for scientific-technical training, have government procurement policies guaranteeing markets for innovative products, implement generous public policies encouraging private sector investment in technological change (e.g. accelerated depreciation of fixed capital embodying advanced technologies), and have financial sectors capable of allocating credit rapidly to start-ups operating close to the technological frontier.[23]

In use-value terms this is a recipe for continued technological dynamism. In value terms things are much more complicated. There are a sufficient number of effective national innovation systems to ensure that the time US capitals can enjoy a monopoly on innovations is greatly compressed. The moment a cluster of innovations with great commercial potential emerges a plethora of extensive research expenditures, tax breaks, other direct and indirect subsidies, and allocations of credit, will be mobilized in a number of other regions more or less simultaneously. The period when high profits can be won as a result of technological advantages therefore tends to shorten. The period when the commercialization of new innovations spurs a high rate of investment is condensed as well, as serious overcapacity problems quickly arise in innovating sectors. A new "golden age" of capitalism with high rates of investment, economic growth, and real wages gains over an extended period is not likely in these circumstances in the US (or anywhere else, for that matter).

Of course the tendency for the period when high profits can be appropriated from innovations to shorten can be checked if intellectual property rights are granted and enforced. The extension in scope and enforcement of intellectual property rights has accordingly been a defining feature of US-led globalization in recent decades. This has allowed individual corporations with extensive portfolios of intellectual property (like Apple) to enjoy their own "golden age." But the very extension in scope and enforcement of intellectual property rights that furthers valorization on the level of particular firms hampers the future prospects of valorization on the level of the "knowledge economy" as a whole in a number of ways that include the following:

- the costs of acquiring necessary inputs into the production of new information goods are raised;
- ever-more resources must be devoted to unproductive legal expenditures defending contested claims;
- ever-greater efforts must be spent to design around existing intellectual property claims, generating systematic inefficiencies in scientific-technological research;
- firms are more able to claim rights to innovations even when they have no intention of developing them, but simply wish to block competitors from profitable opportunities;
- the greater the monopoly profits from intellectual rights, the greater incentive established firms have to use their considerable economic and political power to hamper breakthroughs threatening that monopoly; and
- large companies are in the best position to meet infringement suits with counter-suits, negotiate favorable cross-licensing agreements, and so on; as a result they are increasingly able to subordinate small innovating companies in emerging sectors, choking economic dynamism.

Individual companies associated with effective national innovation systems undoubtedly benefit from intellectual property rights. US capitals – associated with the most effective national innovation system of all – benefit most of all. But the extension of intellectual property rights is likely to reinforce, rather than reverse, the deflationary tendencies in the world market. As these tendencies become more entrenched, whatever advantages US capitalism may possess relative to other regions will not be the most important factor determining its future prospects.

Finally, no consideration of the coming era in world history should conclude without at least mentioning environmental concerns, even if no adequate treatment can be provided here. A strong consensus has emerged among scientists that the boundaries within which environmental conditions have fluctuated over the last 10,000 years have either been surpassed or are in the process of being surpassed as a result of human activity.[24] If these processes are not reversed, greater environmental instability is likely to result, affecting the future prospects of US capitalism far more than any relative advantages US capitals may happen to possess.

All systems of producing and distributing goods and services use natural resources and generate wastes. Capitalism, however, accelerates these processes into hyper-drive. Firms are forced by competitive pressures to attempt to appropriate as much profit as possible as fast as possible by producing, transporting, and selling as many commodities as possible as fast as possible. The accelerated temporality of valorization processes inevitably comes into tension with the temporality of replenishing natural resources and processing wastes. More specifically, natural resources tend to be extracted at a faster rate than ecosystems can replenish them, and wastes tend to be generated at a faster rate than ecosystems can absorb them (Marx 1976, p. 638; Foster *et al.* 2010, Introduction; Albritton, Chapter 6). Eventually, a tipping point will be reached past which the degeneration of natural conditions exceed the "planetary boundaries" within which human history has unfolded. Particular units of capital can prosper from "disaster capitalism" for a period (Klein 2008). Over time, however, the prospects for the capitalist world market as a whole – and of the leading region within it – are dire.[25]

How is capitalism responding to this existential threat? Untold trillions have been devoted to propping up the global financial system, pushing environmental funding aside. In the face of the increasing threat of devaluation firms have been focusing their scientific-technological research ever more on projects with immediate commercial potential, whatever the long-term environmental consequences (cf. the fracking technologies and technologies for intensifying consumerism, hailed by business consultants as "game changers" for the US economy). Oil companies, whose estimated 2,795 gigatons of fossil-fuel reserves are worth approximately *$20 trillion*, are using every last bit of their immense political influence to valorize every last every drop of oil, even though what they own is five times more than what can be burned safely (McKibben 2013). And in a world of excess capacity those firms that do develop superior technologies from an environmental point of view are not especially inclined to share them at low cost with competitors. Their future hopes of valorization rest on the productive capacity of competitors being destroyed, not improved.

Substitutes for exhausted natural resources will continue to be found; new ways of producing that use fewer natural resources and generate fewer wastes will be discovered; and new techniques for processing wastes into non-harmful or useable substances will be introduced. Nonetheless, there are good reasons to renounce the faith that a "technological fix" will save us. As the nineteenth-century economist Jevons pointed out, the technologies of the first industrial revolution became more "sustainable" over time, as the amount of coal used per unit of output decreased. Nonetheless, the aggregate amount of coal burned continued to increase. The paradox is easily explained: the growth of total output overwhelmed the reduction of coal per unit of output. The "grow or die!" imperative reigns more extensively and intensively now than it did then; across the globe units of capital that do not accumulate at as fast a rate as competitors necessarily tend to be taken over, pushed to the margins, or destroyed. As long as this is the case the "Jevons paradox" will frustrate the hope for a technological fix (Foster 1999, Chapter 9).

Finally, the proliferation of reasonably effective national innovation systems discussed above is relevant here as well. The time high profits can be won from innovations will tend to be compressed for green technologies too; there will be no future "golden age" of capitalism set off by investment in green technologies. The level of investment in these technologies (and the associated "built environments" required for their optimal use) will therefore not come remotely close to what is required.

Scientific and technological advances in capitalism have been associated with *greater* economic insecurity in global economy, *more intense* structural coercion of workers, *less* access to the material preconditions for human flourishing, and a *growing* environmental threat to the viability of contemporary human societies. Capitalism has outlived whatever historical justification it may once have claimed. From this perspective the question whether US capitalism possesses relative advantages over other "varieties of capitalism" is a completely secondary matter.

Acknowledgments

I would like to thank Dan Krier and Forrest Perry for their very helpful feedback.

Notes

1 When more efficient producers enter a sector, it can be a rational response for established firms to remain operating for a number of reasons. Their workforce and managerial staff have sector-specific skills. They have already made fixed capital investments, and if they continue operating they may hope to obtain at least the average rate of profit on their variable costs (raw materials, wages, etc.). There may

be important relationships with suppliers, distributors, and local governments that would be difficult to reproduce were they to shift production to a different sector. And they may hope to make innovations in the future allowing them to leapfrog over their competitors. See Reuten 1991, Brenner 2006.

2 The relative advantages of US capitalism and the geopolitical/military power of the US state presuppose and reinforce each other. Unfortunately, space limitations prevent discussion of the latter here (see Westra 2012; Panitch and Gindin 2012).

3 The destruction of capital that did occur in the recessions of the 1970s and early 1980s should not be downplayed. But there was no "'slaughter of capital values' on a scale sufficient to end [overcapacity and overproduction]" (Desai 2013, pp. 24–25).

4 According to Mohun, the ratio of money surplus value to the wages of productive labor increased by about 40 percent (Mohun 2009, p. 1028; see Moody 2007).

5 In 1981 the debt of the private sector in the US equaled 123 percent of GDP; by the end of 2008 it had reached 290 percent. Corporate debt increased from 53 percent of GDP to 76 percent and household debt jumped from 48 percent to 100 percent. But the financial sector's debt increased fivefold, from 22 percent of GDP to 117 percent (Roubini and Mihm 2010, p. 83).

6 "From 2000 to 2007, the US ran a cumulative current-account deficit of roughly $5.5 trillion, with nearly symmetrical offsetting increases in reserves in China and Japan" (Volcker 2012; see Duncan 2012; and, especially, Westra 2012.)

7 Regions enjoying trade surpluses had other reasons to increase dollar reserves. Dollars are necessary for the purchase of oil and weapons in international markets. Dollars have provided a fairly secure store of value in an increasingly turbulent global economy. And the greater the reserves of world money held by a nation's Central Bank, the more protected its national economy is from sudden stampedes of capital outflows – and from the need to turn to the IMF and its onerous structural adjustment programs to recover from such stampedes.

8 The US trade deficit in advanced-technology products reached $99 billion in 2011 (National Research Council 20).

9 Seventy percent of private expenditure is now devoted to product development, and roughly another 20 percent to applied research (National Research Council 2012, p. 46).

10 An analysis *R&D Magazine*'s annual awards suggests that roughly two-thirds of the most important (non-classified) innovations in the last decades have emerged from private/public partnerships (Block and Keller 2011).

11 It is worth noting that an estimated 90 percent of China's trade surplus is in pro-cessing trade (trade in goods assembled in China from imported parts and materials) generated by multinational corporations and foreign joint ventures (National Research Council 2012, p. 219).

12 One measure of persisting overaccumulation is the clear downward trend of non-financial investment in the world market as a whole, despite the astounding growth of investment in China and other regions (Harman 2010, pp. 231 ff., 282). Another is the way more credit money has been needed over time to generate a given increment of GDP growth (Duncan 2012, p. 49).

13 If "unorthodox" Central Bank policies lead to a devaluation of the dollar that enables US capitals to capture export markets, so much the better from the Federal Reserve's standpoint.

14 In 2007 the Federal Reserve held around $900b of assets. By the middle of 2009 its balance sheet showed $2.3–2.4 trillion of assets (Roubini and Mihm 2010, p. 153). The figure at the end of 2013 was over $3 trillion (*The Economist* 2013, p. 113).

15 This tendency of temporal expansion is the inverse of the tendency of capitalism to compress time discussed in the following section. Both tendencies hold simultaneously.

16 Marx's comprehensive systematic ordering of the essential determinations of the capitalist mode of production was always meant to include a Book on the State (Smith 2009, Chapter 6).

17 Unfortunately, limitation of space prevents a general discussion of the immense role of the military in US capitalism.

18 Reports commissioned by M.I.T. and the National Research Council advocate increased spending on scientific-technical education, a transformed curriculum emphasizing science and mathematics, an expansion of technical training programs on the junior college level, various tax breaks and financial incentives to manufacturers, etc. See Berger 2013, National Research Council 2012.

19 A recent McKinsey report predicts $325 billion will be added annually to US GDP from big data analytics in retail and manufacturing by 2020 (Manyika *et al.* 2011).

20 In the US 17.4 percent of R&D spending is devoted to basic research; 22.3 percent to applied research and development (that is, to R&D with medium-to-long term commercial application) and 60.3 percent to R&D development, focused on short-term results. For the sake of comparison, the proportions in China are 4.7, 12.6, and 82.7, respectively (National Research Council 2012, p. 205). Everything else being equal, the former distribution of R&D funds is far more likely to generate a stream of significant future innovations. (And everything else is *not* equal; the US is responsible for more than two and a half times the global spending on R&D of China.) The pattern of allocation of R&D in China also helps explain why China holds only 1 percent of global patents (filed in leading patent offices outside the home country), despite accounting for 11 percent of global R&D.

21 Wage labor will hardly disappear. Some tasks will remain extremely difficult and costly to automate in the foreseeable future, others will prove impossible to ever automate. But the number of tasks machine intelligence can accomplish more reliably and cheaply than humans, and the range of tasks that can *only* be accomplished by machines, can both be expected to increase greatly across a wide range of sectors. The most dynamic sectors of the world market in the remainder of the twenty-first century are not likely to be able to absorb the labor displaced in older sectors as effectively as the factories of the twentieth century absorbed rural labor displaced by the mechanization of agriculture.

22 Theorists concerned with the social effects of automation typically call for a basic income grant (e.g. Ford 2009). But a level of basic income large enough to counteract the growing gap between the rate of increase of productivity and the rate of increase of real wages will almost surely prove incompatible with the capital/wage labor relation, based as it is on the compulsion of the latter to submit to the former.

23 It should not be forgotten, however, that effective national innovation systems are extremely costly. Only a relatively few regions can afford to establish them. This is a major factor explaining uneven development in the world economy, that is, the ability of leading centers of accumulation to reproduce their advantages (Shaikh 2007; Smith 2010; Westra 2012).

24 The boundaries concern climate change, ocean acidification, nitrogen and phosphorus cycles, global freshwater use, land use, biodiversity loss, and chemical pollution (Rockström *et al.* 2009).

25 Rockström *et al.* hold that if the upper-range of projections of global warming were to occur, it "would threaten the ecological life-support systems that have developed in the later Quaternary environment, and would *severely challenge the viability of contemporary human societies*" (Rockström *et al.* 2009, p. 473, emphasis added).

References

Albritton, R. (2009) *Let Them Eat Junk: How Capitalism Creates Hunger and Obesity* (New York: Pluto).

Arrighi, G. (2009) *Adam Smith in Beijing: Lineages of the 21st Century* (New York: Verso).

Berger, S. with the MIT Task Force of Production and Innovation (2013) *Making in America: From Innovation to Market* (Cambridge, MA: MIT Press).

Block, F. and M. R. Keller (2011) "Where do Innovations Come From?" in F. Block and M.R. Keller (eds) *State of Innovation: The U.S. Government's Role in Technology Development* (Boulder, CO: Paradigm Publishers, pp. 154–73).

Brenner, R. (2006) *The Economics of Global Turbulence* (New York: Verso).

Brynjolfsson, E. and A. McAfee (2012) *Race Against the Machine: How the Digital Revolution is Accelerating Innovation, Driving Productivity, and Irreversibly Transforming Employment and the Economy* (Digital Frontier Press).

Chui, M., M. Löffler and R. Roberts (2010) *The Internet of Things* (New York: McKinsey Quarterly).

Davis, G. (2009) *Managed by Markets: How Finance Re-Shaped America* (Oxford: Oxford University Press).

Desai, R. (2013) *Geopolitical Economy: After US Hegemony, Globalization and Empire* (London: Pluto).

Duménil, G. and D. Lévy (2011) *The Crisis of Neoliberalism* (Cambridge, MA: Harvard University Press).

Duncan, R. (2012) *The New Depression* (Hoboken, NJ: Wiley).

The Economist (2011) "R&D Spending," October. 1: 97.

——(2013) "The Federal Reserve at 100," December. 21: 113.

Ford, M. (2009) *The Lights in the Tunnel: Automation, Accelerating Technology, and the Economy of the Future* (Wayne, PA: Acculant Publishing).

Foster, J. B. (1999) *The Vulnerable Planet* (New York: Monthly Review Press).

Foster, J. B., B. Clark and R. York (2010) *The Ecological Rift: Capitalism's War on Earth* (New York: Monthly Review Press).

Harmon, C. (2010) *Zombie Capitalism* (Chicago, IL: Haymarket).

Klein, N. (2008) *The Shock Doctrine: The Rise of Disaster Capitalism* (New York: Picador).

Lapavitsas, C., *et al.* (2012) *Crisis in the Euro Zone* (New York: Verso).

Lund, S., J. Manyika, S. Nyquist, L. Mendonca and S. Ramaswamy (2013) *Game Changers: Five Opportunities for US Growth and Renewal* (New York: McKinsey Global Institute).

Manyika, J., M. Chui, B. Brown, J. Bughin, R. Dobbs, C. Roxburgh and A. Hung Byers (2011) *Big data: The next frontier for innovation, competition, and productivity* (New York: McKinsey Global Institute).

Marx, K. (1976) *Capital, Volume I* (New York: Penguin Books).

——(1987) *Economic Manuscripts of 1857–58* [the *Grundrisse*, conclusion] in Karl Marx and Frederick Engels, *Collected Works: Volume 29* (New York: International Publishers).

Mazzucato, M. (2013) *The Entrepreneurial State: Debunking Public vs. Private Sector Myths* (London: Anthem Press).

McKibben, B. (2013) "The Great Carbon Bubble: Why The Fossil Fuel Industry Fights So Hard," *TomDispatch* website, February 7. Available at: www.tomdispatch.com/post/175499/ [accessed September 23, 2014].

McNally, D. (2010) *Global Slump* (Oakland, CA: PM Press).

Mohun, S. (2009) "Aggregate Capital Productivity in the US Economy, 1964–2001," *Cambridge Journal of Economics*, 33(5): 1023–46.

Moody, K. (2007) *US Labor in Trouble and Transition: The Failure of Reform from Above, the Promise of Revival from Below* (New York: Verso).

National Research Council (2012) *Rising to the Challenge: U.S. Innovation Policy for the Global Economy* (Washington, DC: The National Academies Press).

OECD (2011) *Science, Technology and Industry Scorecard 2010* (Paris: Organization for Economic Co-operation and Development).

Panitch, L. and S. Gindin (2012) *The Making of Global Capitalism* (New York: Verso).

Patnaik, P. (1997) *Accumulation and Stability Under Capitalism* (Oxford: Clarendon Press).

Reuten, G. (1991) "Accumulation of Capital and the Foundation of the Tendency of the Rate of Profit to Fall," *Cambridge Journal of Economics*, 15(1): 79–93.

Rockström, J., *et al.* (2009) "A Safe Operating Space for Humanity," *Nature*, September 24: 472–75.

Roubini, N. and S. Mihm (2010) *Crisis Economics: A Crash Course in the Future of Finance* (New York: Penguin).

Shaikh, A. (2007) "Globalization and the Myth of Free Trade," in A. Shaikh (ed) *Globalization and the Myths of Free Trade: History, Theory, and Empirical Evidence* (New York: Routledge, pp. 50–68).

Sirkin, H., M. Zinser and D. Hohner (2011) *Made in America, Again* (Boston, MA: Boston Consulting Group).

Smith, T. (2009) *Globalisation: A Systematic Marxian Account* (Chicago, IL: Haymarket Books).

——(2010) "Technological Change in Capitalism: Some Marxian Themes," *The Cambridge Journal of Economics*, 34(1): 203–12.

Toporowski, J. (2000) *The End of Finance: The Theory of Capital Market Inflation, Financial Derivatives and Pension Fund Capitalism* (New York: Routledge).

Toussaint, E. (1999) *Your Money or Your Life! The Tyranny of Global Finance* (London: Pluto).

Volcker, P. (2012) "Is Global Financial Reform Possible?" *Project Syndicate* website, June 4. Available at: www.project-syndicate.org/commentary/is-global-financial-reform-possible [accessed September 23, 2014].

Westra, R. (2012) *The Evil Axis of Finance* (Atlanta, GA: Clarity Press).

Willmott, H. (2010) "Creating 'value' beyond the point of production: branding, financialization and market capitalization," *Organization*, 17(5): 517–42.

6 The transformations of Italian capitalism in the global financial crisis

Grant Amyot

Introduction

The global financial crisis hit Italian capitalism particularly hard because Italy's economy had been losing ground for several years before the crisis broke out in 2008. So seriously did Italy suffer that some of the basic economic institutions underwent significant change, including labor market and collective bargaining rules, corporate finance and governance, and the welfare state. While the varieties of capitalism approach as elaborated by Hall and Soskice (2001) and others depends on the implicit premise that institutions are durable and resistant to change, this case study demonstrates that in fact the institutions of capitalism are a product of class struggle and capitalist strategies to maximize profit within a set of constraints, which include the following aspects: the balance of class power, the given institutional framework, the opportunities offered within the international capitalist economy, and the capital already sunk in plant, equipment, and other factors of production. At the turn of the century, Italy's capitalism most closely resembled the co-ordinated market economies (CMEs) of Germany and other smaller northern European states, albeit with several peculiar characteristics. After nearly a decade of stagnation and the financial crisis, Italian capitalists were able to exploit economic globalization and their heightened class power to bring about significant changes in the country's basic economic institutions. These were, however, not as radical in practice as they appeared at first glance, and preserved several features of the CME. In fact, they strikingly paralleled similar changes that had already altered the original CME model in Germany. In both countries, a combination of international economic pressures and internal tensions within the existing institutional framework allowed capital to alter the basic rules in its favor. These changes produced a temporary upsurge in exports and growth in Germany from the early 2000s. It remains to be seen whether they will do the same in Italy, which has historically followed the German example but with less success (Procacci 1970).

This chapter aims to demonstrate that the institutional rules of the economy are more flexible than argued by the varieties of capitalism approach, and that they change in response to the relative power of the major classes, in the context of the basic facts of production and profitability. The first section of this chapter is a brief discussion and "immanent" critique of the varieties of capitalism (VoC) approach. In the second, we situate Italy before the financial crisis within our reworked version of this framework. The third section briefly highlights the crisis of performance the Italian economy has experienced in the twenty-first century, as a prelude to the fourth, which outlines the principal changes in its institutional structure over the past five years. In the fifth section, we summarize our findings and what they suggest needs to be revised in the VoC approach.

The Varieties of Capitalism approach

The core thesis of the varieties of capitalism approach is that capitalism can function according to different sets of institutional rules, and that the liberal market economy (LME) variety, as found in the USA and the UK, for instance, is not the only one which can be successful in terms of growth and overall welfare. It seeks to distinguish between models of capitalism on the basis of a set of key characteristics, notably the sources of corporate finance, wage-setting institutions, and the welfare state, as well as vocational training, inter-corporate relations, and, more contentiously, the political system. The principal alternative model to the LME is the co-ordinated market economy, typified by Germany and a number of smaller European states. The various features of each model are held to be functionally related: hence in the LME stock markets are the principal source of corporate finance, which leads firms to take a short-term view of profitability; this makes them put a premium on flexibility, so that they are unwilling to enter into long-term agreements with workers or unions, or to invest large sums in multi-year product development projects. In CMEs firms are classically more dependent on bank financing, and capable of undertaking longer-term planning as a result. They seek stability in labor relations, and hence participate in national or sectoral collective bargaining; they also support welfare policies that maintain their labor force even through periods of unemployment or personal misfortune so that it will continue to be available when needed.

This perspective has been subjected to numerous critiques (e.g. Kesting and Nielsen 2008). On the most general level, it comes close to functionalism in its contention that the various features of each model fit together into a coherent and potentially successful whole. Hall and Soskice's language has a basis in rational choice assumptions, i.e., that certain institutions are chosen as the most efficient way of addressing the co-ordination problems of firms, given the institutional context. Each variety is held to have its particular institutional advantages. Certainly the approach appears economistic in its focus, and does not account in the first instance for political conflict or distributional struggle, though in later work Hall and Thelen have argued that the institutional rules of an economy are the subject of continual conflicts around their interpretation or modification (2009). More generally, like all neo-institutionalist approaches, the varieties of capitalism approach has been criticized for the assumption of institutional continuity, and its inability to account for change; this has been addressed by authors such as Streeck and Thelen, who argue that institutions can change through processes such as layering and displacement, without however incorporating the sources of change in their theory (2005).

More specifically, critics have questioned whether the reality of contemporary capitalism corresponds closely enough to ideal types such as the LME and CME for the classification to be useful. Hall and Soskice themselves recognize that there may well be mixed or hybrid cases, such as the Mediterranean states of Europe (2001, p. 21), while other authors such as Vivien Schmidt, following Zysman and others, propose a third type, the state-led market economy (SME) (Schmidt 2002; Zysman 1983). Other suggested types include the Mixed Market Economy (MME), and others located outside Western Europe and North America, such as the Dependent Market Economy (DME) in Eastern Europe (Nölke and Vliegenthart 2009; Molina and Rhodes 2007). Alternatively, it has been suggested that the VoC perspective is not only economistic, ignoring ideology as well as gender, race and other key differences in the work force, but focused too narrowly on manufacturing industries, leaving services and the public sector largely outside its purview. And it may analyze economies at the wrong level – the national rather than the sectoral.

Our criticism of the VoC approach starts from Marx's theory of capitalism in general. He saw capitalism as a mode of production driven by its particular laws of motion and, as a result, prone to crisis tendencies. Different strategies of accumulation can be deployed to attempt to overcome these tendencies and ensure continued growth (Jessop 2008, Ch. 1). In *Capital*, vol. 3, Marx mentioned several ways in which the tendency of the rate of profit to fall could be countered, including foreign trade, the cheapening of constant capital, depressing wages, etc. (1966, pp. 232–40). In the early twenty-first century, the major cause of the fall of the rate of profit is the overaccumulation of capital (Kliman 2012; cf. Piketty 2014). The varieties of capitalism approach, to the extent that this typology is a genuine distinction that finds some reflection in empirical reality, represent different strategies of accumulation, which stem from the national histories and the current opportunities of capital in various states. Indeed, Rudolf Hilferding's classic Marxist work, *Finance Capital* (1981), has not received due acknowledgment from the authors of the VoC approach – his "finance capital," which he differentiated from the English, or Anglo-Saxon, variety, is clearly the ancestor of the CME.

If we situate the observations of the VoC approach within this broader framework, we note that for the CMEs, the collective bargaining system has proved useful in restraining wage increases and hence promoting the international competitiveness of economies such as Germany's. In this context, the role of the central bank (before 1999 the Bundesbank, and since, if in a different way, the ECB) in enforcing wage restraint with the threat of recession-inducing interest rate increases deserves to be considered as one of the key features of the CME; it is responsible, to a significant extent, for its success as a model of capitalism in the later twentieth century.[1] This, combined with Germany's advantages in the production of high-quality manufactured goods, ensured continued export growth and the accumulation of large profits from foreign trade. Overaccumulation, however, was the result. In the last twenty years, Germany's political economy has deviated considerably from the original CME model, as globalization and the pressures of reunification have shifted the balance of power in favor of capital. The largest firms can finance themselves out of retained earnings, and are less dependent on the banks, while the banks have become more international and reduced their involvement with domestic manufacturing firms; traditional centralized bargaining has given way to plant-level accords that have allowed firms to contain labor costs; and welfare state provision has been cut back (Streeck 2009; Jackson and Sorge 2012).

In the United States, the central capitalist economy, changes in the world economy and the domestic political scene have changed the nature of its liberal market economy (LME) as well. Political power has shifted to the financial sector, which has ensured the passage of legislation reducing regulation, which in turn has increased its profitability. While finance plays a larger role in the LME in any case, given the importance of the financial markets in co-ordinating firm decisions, the USA and other LMEs have seen an increase in the weight of the financial sector; this had a major role in causing the global financial crisis.

While the VoC approach has recognized other models of capitalism, some of which are not functional to growth or capital accumulation,[2] this recognition conflicts with the rational choice elements of the approach, which sees firms choosing the most promising strategies within a given institutional context. In fact, such models are under-theorized in the VoC literature. To understand them we must recognize the variety of roles that political institutions can play in shaping the economy. Where these institutions are open to firms' political power and influence, they may pursue an accumulation strategy consisting of rent-seeking behavior, securing protected markets, state subsidies, or other non-market advantages. Indeed protected, monopolistic situations, when available, are always preferred by firms to the rigors of market competition, and rent-seeking tendencies are strong in all capitalist economies. In some countries rent-seeking coalitions are dominant, and create a vicious circle that is very difficult to exit, as the favored economic interests become entwined with the leading political forces (Acemoglu and Robinson 2012, pp. 364–67). This "model" of capitalism might be seen as the degenerated version of the state-led variety identified by some authors, whose exemplar is France in the post-World War II period. However, the "rentier" model is not co-ordinated by the state as a central authority – favored treatment is accorded as a function of the political power of different firms and industries. These actors are the propulsive forces of the economy, rather than the state; but the availability of a rent-seeking strategy does influence their behavior.

The Italian "variety" of capitalism

In their seminal "Introduction to Varieties of Capitalism," Hall and Soskice allude very briefly to the countries that occupy "more ambiguous positions" in the CME-LME typology, and suggest they may constitute a "Mediterranean" variety of capitalism, characterized by large agrarian sectors and a history of state intervention that allows certain kinds of "non-market co-ordination in the sphere of corporate finance but more liberal arrangements in the sphere of labor relations" (2001, pp. 21, 35–36). Italy is among these "Mediterranean" states. This classification suggests that the French "state-led" variety of capitalism may be a relevant comparator for Italy. Vincent Della Sala has also noted the poor performance of the Italian economy in recent years, and described it as "dysfunctional state capitalism" (2004). Molina and Rhodes (2007), as noted above, call Italy and Spain "Mixed Market Economies," characterized by sharp differences between regions and between large and small firms, fragmented interest associations, and a significant state role. Schmidt and Gualmini group Italy, along with most of Hall and Soskice's Mediterranean states (France, Spain, Portugal, and Greece), in the category of "state-influenced market economies" (SMEs) (Gualmini and Schmidt 2013). On the other hand, I have argued that to characterize the Italian economy as "state-led" is misleading because the state has not had a unified and coherent policy for growth or development (Amyot 2004, p. 79). While it has undoubtedly played a significant role in the economy, that role cannot be described as a leading one, and, what is important for the present discussion, it has not even played the central role in co-ordination of economic activity. The state has offered some rent-seeking opportunities that have influenced firms' strategies, but they have not dominated their strategy of accumulation. Instead of a form of state-led capitalism, and even less of the market-led LME variety, I argued that Italy has a variant of the "Rhenish," or CME, model, albeit with several peculiar characteristics such as the source of corporate finance (2004, p. 80).

This parallel between Italy and Germany can be demonstrated for the period up to the early 2000s. A discussion of changes since then will follow in the next section. While the authors using the VoC approach fail in general to situate their models in the international economy, this is a necessary first step. As Bellofiore, Garibaldo, and Halevi have argued, Germany has pursued a "neomercantilist" policy, prioritizing the accumulation of trade surpluses; Italy has adopted in turn "a weak form of neomercantilism, which in the past depended on real currency devaluations" (2011, p. 137). This was the strategy pursued during and after the "economic miracle" of the 1950s, and as long as devaluation was possible, the country was generally able to show trade surpluses. Its strengths did not lay only its traditional high-quality consumer goods, but also machinery and equipment, as well as some of the Fordist mass-production industries (Amyot 2004, Table 5.4, p. 84).

This similarity in accumulation strategy was matched by economic institutions that were in many respects analogous, if not identical, to those of Germany. As in Germany, control of major Italian firms was in the hands of large "blockholders" who were immune to takeover bids. In Italy, typical devices used to retain control were pyramided companies ("Chinese boxes"), syndicates of large allied shareholders, and issuing classes of shares with different voting rights. Often even the largest firms were family-controlled (e.g. Fiat, controlled by the Agnellis). As a result, there was no market for corporate control in Italy, and stock market capitalization remained extraordinarily low until quite recently (see Table 6.1). More than half of the firms listed on the Milan exchange were under the majority control of a single owner (Deeg 2005a, p. 185). At the same time, bank finance has not been as important as in Germany: commercial banks were not permitted to engage in long-term lending or to buy shares in industrial companies. Most banks were under state ownership until the 1990s, but they did not exercise a directing role – much of their capital was invested in government debt, and they lacked the expertise to play the same role as German banks in guiding the firms they lent to. A few medium- and long-term credit banks were an exception to this pattern, especially Mediobanca, which, under Enrico Cuccia, played a central role in Italian capitalism. Cuccia, however, saw his as a support role for the large industrial firms of the so-called "good salon" (Fiat, Pirelli, Falck, Bonomi, etc.), most of which were under family control. Mediobanca was owned by three state-owned banks, but Cuccia always pursued his own policy – a good illustration of the absence of state direction despite a large formal state presence in the economy. The result was, as Deeg writes, that "Most big companies faced little control/monitoring from either banks or the stock market" (2005b, p. 527). Indeed, their dependence on bank loans was relatively limited by 2001 (see Table 6.1) – they used retained earnings or bond issues to finance a large part of their activity. On the other hand, the small and medium firms that are so significant in Italy remain largely dependent on the banks for capital. But at the level of large companies, the dominance of blockholding owners, acting with few constraints, rather than banks or markets, was in the end one of the dysfunctional elements of the Italian model – ill-considered

Table 6.1 Data on financial systems (percentages of GDP), 2001

Country	a) Bank loans to private sector	b) Stock market capitalization	c) b/a
Germany	117	64	0.55
Italy	77	60	0.78
France	85	100	1.18
UK	132	170	1.29
USA	42	146	3.48

investments, such as Fiat's diversification and its alliance with General Motors, were often the result.

While the state did not play a directing role in the economy, its influence was nonetheless important in sustaining the rentier tendencies in Italian capitalism. For instance, Silvio Berlusconi, who remains Italy's richest man, owes much of his fortune to the licenses he obtained for his three television channels, which dominate the private sector of Italian broadcasting. His connections with the major political forces of the time were crucial to his success.

From major firms like Fiat to small companies, corruption has been an important way of securing profits (Griseri *et al.* 1997). While the Tangentopoli investigation of the early 1990s lifted the lid on a vast network of corrupt practices, it by no means put an end to them (Nelken 1996). One of the most insidious forms of corrupt behavior is tax evasion, which has diverted, by most estimates, over €200 billion from the treasury (*Economist* 2013). Tax evasion does not signify a strong state because it is a covert form of subsidy to those firms that are successful evaders. The state has also acted to protect some major Italian firms from take-over by foreign investors.

In 2005, Berlusconi's government favored groups of Italian investors over foreign banks that wanted to take over two significant Italian banks, the Banca Nazionale del Lavoro and the Banca Antonveneta (Messori 2006). Similarly, in 2008 he campaigned in the general election to keep Alitalia, the state airline, Italian, and once elected organized a consortium of private investors to take it up, rather than accept Air France's bid for the company. It is estimated that this exercise in economic nationalism (which also aimed at electoral advantage in the North, where Malpensa airport risked being downgraded) cost the treasury ca. €4 billion in subsidies and other costs (Amyot 2009). Fiat also received a considerable amount of state aid under numerous headings, including subsidies for the construction of plants in the South and for research, protection from Japanese competition (thanks to a 1955 trade agreement), and favorable tax treatment. In purely quantitative terms, the aid it received was second only to that of the major French firms (Germano 2011, Table 2, p. 285). In this and other instances, political influence led to economic advantage for favored capitalists, but it was advanced without the state's formulating an industrial policy or attempting to direct the sector's development. In terms of the VoC approach, the state was not performing a co-ordinating role in the economy. Rather it seconded the decisions of the major firms. At most, the state influenced their decisions by making available subsidies and supports, altering the firms' calculations when choosing between alternative strategies.

In its industrial relations as well Italy in the post-war period followed the continental, rather than the Anglo-Saxon, model of collective bargaining: collective agreements were bargained at the industry level, and applied to all employers in the sector independent of union presence. However, unlike Germany, Italy's unions were divided along political lines into three main national confederations. This division made bargaining more difficult and weakened labor until the "Hot Autumn" of 1969. Although strengthened by this upsurge in militancy, thanks to their divisions, the unions were not capable, like their German counterparts, of providing the centralized control over bargaining that allowed German firms to control their wage costs and thus penetrate export markets. In the 1980s, an employers' reaction beat back many union gains, but wage inflation remained a problem, in large part because of cost-of-living indexation. In the early 1990s, however, as Italy prepared to enter the euro, this pattern changed: with the encouragement and mediation of the technocratic Prime Minister Carlo Azeglio Ciampi, unions and the employers' associations reached the "July accord" of 1993. It provided a new framework for collective bargaining, in which industry-level contracts set base wage increases in the light of the expected level of inflation. Plant-level bargaining was regulated in this framework, and was intended to provide for bonuses linked to productivity and local conditions. This accord appeared to inaugurate a system of industrial relations quite similar to those of the CMEs; the method of "concertation" between the "social partners" was extended to other policy issues, including pension reform and taxation. Though some businesses rebelled, the large firms, like Fiat, accepted the method of concertation at the national level, while at the same time seeking to control labor costs as stringently as possible in their own factories.

The Italian welfare state, too, was designed on the "continental" pattern typical of Germany and some of the other CMEs. Once again, it displayed certain differences. Its benefits were more unequally distributed, and pensions accounted for an exceptionally large share of spending, but it played the same income-preserving function as the other continental systems, while offering remarkably little for the younger unemployed and the indigent.

In summary as the twenty-first century opened, Italy's economy resembled the CME model more than any other, but with several particular features. First, major firms obtained much of their capital through self-financing and bond issues, and when they sought loans from the banks, the latter did not exercise close supervision over them. In addition, state supports and positions of monopolistic privilege were available, and they altered the strategies of some of the firms. Second, the division of the union movement into three confederations impeded the smooth functioning of the industrial relations system. Third, the welfare state was more unequal and less comprehensive in its coverage. In addition, there was a large gap between large companies and small and medium firms, on the one hand, and between North and South, on the other.

Crisis of performance in the 2000s

In the early 2000s, coinciding with its entry into the euro in January 1999, Italy entered a new phase of development, characterized by relative stagnation. The strategy of growth of Italian capitalism, based on an export orientation and fuelled by devaluation, was now no longer practicable. Italy enjoyed a uniquely poor record, the only OECD country to experience a fall in real per capita GDP from 2000 to 2011.[3] Labor income stagnated. The balance of trade turned negative in 2005 (see Table 6.2):

Table 6.2 Italian trade balance (goods and services), 1997–2008

Percentage of GDP	
1997	4.0
1998	3.4
1999	2.1
2000	1.0
2001	1.4
2002	1.0
2003	0.5
2004	0.7
2005	−0.1
2006	−0.8
2007	−0.3
2008	−0.8

These figures confirm the weakness of Italy's "neomercantilism." Italy's major firms also went through a period of serious crisis. For example, by 2004 Fiat was in dire straits, thanks to the failure of its "world car," which aimed to penetrate emerging markets, and (because?) of its alliance with General Motors. Berlusconi's government did little to improve the situation. The "Biagi law" of 2003 liberalized employment contracts to some extent, but its practical effect was limited. This led to a crisis of confidence in the accumulation strategy as followed hitherto. The global financial crisis accelerated this already developing crisis, and prompted changes that, while they appeared to move Italy closer to the Anglo-Saxon LME model, were in fact similar to those that had already occurred in Germany.

The emergence of a new model?

The lead in institutional innovation was taken by Fiat. As we have seen, it had been a major beneficiary of state support, but in the early 1990s that support began to rapidly diminish. Two major factors were involved: the large government debt and the Maastricht criteria for entry into the euro, which limited the amount of public money available; and the EU's general prohibition on state aid to industry. In addition to the failure to develop successful new models, Fiat in the early 2000s was suffering from ill-considered management decisions such as the GM alliance and diversification into the financial and other sectors. Furthermore, Berlusconi's center-right government was not well-disposed towards Fiat, as its major components, including Berlusconi's own Forza Italia and the Northern League, were more oriented to small and medium industry (Germano 2011).

When nearly on the verge of bankruptcy, Fiat appointed a new president, the Italo-Canadian Sergio Marchionne, in 2004. Marchionne determined that Fiat could not remain centered on the Italian domestic market. He predicted that only a few very large automobile companies, perhaps five or six, would be able to survive in the new, globalized marketplace, and for that reason Fiat needed to expand its overseas operations and seek foreign alliances or mergers. As the previous levels of state aid were no longer available in any case, Fiat needed to be able to grow and be profitable on its own on the world stage.

While Marchionne had already decided to change Fiat's strategy, the financial crisis provided both the stimulus and the opportunity for him to accelerate his plans. On the corporate front, the near-bankruptcy of Chrysler in the United States gave Fiat the opportunity to acquire an interest in the Big Three auto makers with a minimum of cash outlay: Fiat's technology and patents were the consideration for a 20 percent share in the company, while the American government contributed $6.5 billion. From April 2009, when it thus rescued Chrysler, till January, 2014 Fiat gradually increased its share until it owned the whole of the American company, as sales and profits recovered. The final 41.5 percent was purchased from the UAW's benefit fund, Veba, for a total of $4.3 billion (Griseri 2014a). The takeover of Chrysler was followed very quickly by the fusion of the two auto companies into FCA (Fiat Chrysler Automobiles). The new company set up its corporate head-quarters in Amsterdam and its domicile for tax purposes in London, and prepared to issue shares on the New York stock exchange, with a secondary market in Milan. In March 2014 the last Fiat shareholders' meeting was held in Turin. The reorganization created much brooding in Italy, as the country was seeing the departure of its leading private company, a "national champion" that had benefitted from a great deal of state support in the past.

The new company was breaking out of the closed world of Italian capital-ism, and seeking to finance itself on the principal financial market of the Anglo-Saxon world. These developments appeared on the surface to mark a shift to the LME model of corporate finance, with a greater reliance on open markets. In fact, Marchionne and the Agnelli family aimed to preserve the peculiar Italian model of the self-sufficient firm, free from conditioning by either the financial markets or the banks, and now no longer beholden to the state (Sivini 2013). A guiding principle of Marchionne's financial strategy has been to limit investments to those that can be covered from the firm's cash reserves (self-financing). This has led him to seek bargains such as Chrysler, and to use state incentives wherever possible to reduce the cost of new plants (e.g. in Serbia, for the new factory in Kragujevac). In the case of the final 41.5 percent of Chrysler, only $1.75 billion was cash, paid from Fiat's reserves. The balance consisted of an extraordinary dividend paid by Chrysler itself, and a series of deferred payments to Chrysler workers, linked to productivity (Griseri 2014a). The objective was to preserve the capital of the Agnelli family, the largest shareholder of Fiat, by a cautious and parsimonious investment strategy, while expanding the company to meet the new conditions of global competition.

The Agnellis also aimed to maintain control of the new company. The acquisition of 100 percent ownership of Chrysler was achieved, it was emphasized, without increasing the capitalization of Fiat. And, significantly, the headquarters of the new FCA was established in the Netherlands, where the law permits controlling shareholders to give extra votes to their shares: this is an anti-takeover device that is not available in Italy, and it will allow the Agnelli family, with less than 30 percent of the shares in the company, to retain control of it (Griseri 2014b). In other words, far from becoming an American-style "public company," FCA will be dominated by a major blockholder, in keeping with the established Italian (and CME) pattern of corporate governance.

In the areas of ownership and corporate finance, despite the passage of Fiat to the international stage and the adoption of new, more aggressive business strategies, there has not been a fundamental alteration. The firm used the opportunities afforded by globalization to assure its survival in an increasingly competitive industry and also to escape the institutional limits of Italian law and to further secure the Agnelli family's control.

In the field of industrial relations, the crisis has also led to major changes, again spearheaded by Fiat. During the years of stagnation in the early 2000s, the system inaugurated in 1993 had already fallen into disrepair. When Berlusconi returned to office in 2001 as the head of a right-wing coalition, the practice of concertation was partly abandoned and the system of wage bargaining began to unravel, as divisions reappeared between the union confederations. In 2009, a new framework for bargaining was agreed between Confindustria, the employers' association, and only two of the three union confederations. This revised accord reflected the weakness of the unions. It seemed that the Italian system might follow the pattern of short-lived social pacts reached in other states that were preparing to join the euro (Rhodes 2001).

As part of his new, global strategy, Marchionne compared the productivity of the Italian plants to those in other countries. He often cited the statistic that Fiat's Brazilian plant was able to produce 730,000 cars with 9,400 workers, while the 22,000 workers in Italy turned out only 650,000, and one-third as many workers produced the same number in Poland (Berta 2011, p. 17). One of the reasons for this difference was that the Italian plants were under-utilized, working at 50 percent capacity. Marchionne's short-term strategy was to compete on costs, rather than introduce new models. He therefore determined that the efficiency and productivity of the Italian plants had to be brought in line with the other factories in the group, and that required a flexible labor force. He introduced the same management methods, first World Class Manufacturing (WCM) in 2005, then Ergo-UAS in 2008, as Fiat had adopted at its other plants.

In 2010 Marchionne presented a longer-term five-year investment plan, in which he envisaged spending €20 billion in Italy on a new plant to double the number of vehicles produced. The logic behind this was that the Italian plants, already in existence but underutilized, offered the fastest route to expanding production: they would specialize in higher-end makes and models, which would allow for higher wages and the costs of transportation to foreign markets. But in order to make these investments, Marchionne stated that he required labor flexibility.

The battle occurred at Fiat's Alfa Romeo plant at Pomigliano d'Arco, near Naples. While promising €700 million in investments, Marchionne demanded that the workers accept a radically different contract, which provided for eighteen shifts a week instead of ten, required more overtime work, reduced the mid-day break from 40 to 30 minutes, introduced disciplinary sanctions for absenteeism, and forbade strikes that interfered with planned overtime. This sort of demand was similar to the concession bargaining he had engaged in with the UAW in the United States. However, in Italy there was more resistance. The metalworkers' unions, affiliated with two of the three major national confederations (CISL and UIL), agreed to Marchionne's demands, while the FIOM, affiliated to the more radical CGIL, refused. Among its arguments was that the prohibition on strikes violated the constitutional guarantee of the right to strike. In a ratification vote held on June 22, 63.3 percent of the workers at the plant accepted the new contract signed by the two unions. They were heavily influenced by the company's threat that the planned investment would be made elsewhere, outside Italy, if they refused, and their plant would be left without work. The result, however, was not the overwhelming acceptance that the company had expected, and the FIOM was able to claim a kind of moral victory in the face of Marchionne's heavy-handed tactics. Upon the ratification of the accord, Fiat, in accordance with the provisions of the 1970 Statute of Workers' Rights, excluded the FIOM from the plant stewards' council at Pomigliano, on the grounds that it had not signed the contract. This deprived the FIOM of numerous rights to operate in the factory and communicate with its members. Fiat was particularly concerned that the contract be enforceable, and that the unions would allow it to back up the no-strike clause with penalties; hence it did not want the FIOM involved in its administration (Germano 2011; Berta 2011).

A similar contract was signed at the major Turinese plant, Mirafiori, and ratified in December by 54 percent of the employees, including only a very slight majority of blue-collar workers. This result further encouraged the FIOM in its opposition to Marchionne. Confindustria was also discomfited by Marchionne's break with tradition, because his contracts modified elements of the national metalworkers' contract, signed by the Confindustria's metalworking branch, Federmeccanica. In other words, Fiat was introducing the Anglo-Saxon model of industrial relations, in which all bargaining is at the plant level; in Italy plant-level agreements had long existed and were given recognition and a specific role in the July 1993 accords, but the national contract of the industry took precedence. The legal device Marchionne employed to legitimize his new contracts was to establish two new companies to run the plants. These companies were not members of Federmeccanica, and hence were not bound by the national metalworkers' contract (Berta 2011).

At the same time, Confindustria and the three union confederations were working on a reform of the framework for negotiation, and on June 28, 2011 they reached an agreement (Ichino 2011). This strengthened the legal force of plant-level contracts, making them enforceable vis-à-vis all workers if they were supported by a majority, and expanded the scope for plant-level bargaining, allowing plant contracts that provided less favorable treatment for workers than the industry contract where the situation demanded it. It thereby satisfied some of Fiat's demands. However, the agreement did not go far enough for Marchionne, as the national contract still took precedence and plant-level bargaining took place within that framework, and it recognized that, while contracts could bind unions not to engage in strikes while they were in force, the individual workers retained the right to strike guaranteed by the constitution. Moreover, the Pomigliano and Mirafiori contracts were not covered by the new accord as they had been concluded before it came into effect. Therefore on June 30, Marchionne announced that Fiat would leave Confindustria on January 1, 2012 (*La Repubblica* 2011).

This move significantly altered the landscape of Italian industrial relations. Fiat had been the dominant member of Confindustria until the twenty-first century, and remained its most important one. But it now broke with the system of national bargaining, impatient with the slow evolution of the Italian system of industrial relations. The rest of Confindustria continued to bargain with the three confederations, and in January 2014 reached another agreement that further specified the framework established in 2011, and elaborated in 2013. In the conclusion of national contracts, the weight of the union confederations would be based half on their dues-paying membership, and half on their share of votes for the stewards' councils (RSU), which would be elected by proportional representation. All unions with over 5 percent support, established by this criterion, would be allowed to participate in bargaining, and contracts would be valid and enforceable if approved by unions with over 50 percent support and then by a majority of workers in a ratification vote (Del Conte 2014).

Fiat's departure seemed to indicate the beginning of a fragmentation of Italian industrial relations. And while the VoC approach suggests a functional connection between corporate ownership and finance, on the one hand, and industrial relations institutions, on the other, Marchionne's action broke this link, as ownership remained in the hands of the Agnelli family, while industrial relations moved towards the LME model. But despite their differences, Fiat and the firms remaining in Confindustria were moving in a similar direction, which Germany, the principal CME, had already embarked on twenty years before. In response to the burdens of reunification and the threat of firms to move production to nearby Eastern European countries, the

German unions had decided to take advantage of the flexibility of their industrial relations system and permit plant-level agreements that established worse pay or conditions than those provided in the national contracts (Dustmann *et al.* 2014). This was indeed the only way to preserve some East German factories. In addition, the number of workers covered by the national agreements fell. In other European states, including Italy, change was not as easy, as national framework agreements and legal rules entrenched the national level of bargaining. For instance, the principle that the national contract was valid in all workplaces, whether the employer had signed it or not (*erga omnes*) (Dustmann *et al.* 2014, 183). The accords of 2011 and 2013 represented a belated catching-up with German practice. At the same time, Fiat was forced to go back on some of its more extreme steps. While the courts upheld the Pomigliano and Mirafiori agreements, they ruled Marchionne's exclusion of the FIOM from the stewards' council was unconstitutional (Corte Costituzionale 2013). In this the courts simply registered the success of the FIOM's campaign of resistance, which did not prevent Marchionne from imposing his contracts, but did require him to accept the presence of the left-wing union in the factory. The new industrial relations system is thus the product of a new balance of class forces, in which capital has been reinforced by the possibilities of offshoring offered by globalization, and in Italy the unions have been weakened by political divisions, but in which the workers, represented by the FIOM and the CGIL, retain a capacity to resist and avoided total defeat.

The financial crisis had serious repercussions for Italy's government, as well. By 2011, the sovereign debt crisis that had hit Greece, Portugal, and Ireland, forcing them to obtain bail-outs from other EU member states and the IMF, had led investors to demand higher interest rates from Italy as well. While its government deficit was moderate, its total public debt was a cause for concern. The failure of Silvio Berlusconi's government to take sufficiently decisive steps, in the eyes of the bond markets and the EU, particularly the Germans, eventually led to his resignation in November 2011, and his replacement by a technocratic government led by Mario Monti, a former EU Commissioner. Monti's government undertook measures demanded by the EU to stabilize Italy's public finances and reform its economy in a neoliberal direction – the same type of package imposed on the three bailed-out countries. One of Monti's most controversial measures was the "reform" of labor law, which, among other measures, amended Article 18 of the Statute of Workers' Rights. This is the article which allowed workers to appeal firings to the courts, and, if the dismissal was found unjustified, be reinstated to their jobs. Neoliberal theory holds that this sort of protective measure reduces labor market flexibility and discourages employers from hiring, while employers contend that it increases the costs and uncertainty associated with firing workers. While not all CMEs have this sort of protective labor market regime, it is consistent with the general tendency in CMEs to preserve the skilled labor force, and is certainly incompatible with the LME model.

In the end, the new version of Article 18 passed by the Monti government changed less than its proponents expected, and increased rather than reduced the uncertainty for employers surrounding dismissals. The new law replaced the remedy of reinstatement with monetary damages equal to twelve to twenty-four months' wages, with the exception of dismissals due to discrimination, offences for which the collective agreement prescribes a lesser penalty, and cases where the alleged facts on which the dismissal was based are not true. The courts, interpreting the new law, expanded the third exception to cover most disciplinary firings that they considered unjustified, while typically imposing monetary damages where the alleged reasons were economic (Del Conte 2014). This solution is, in fact, similar to the regime in Germany, where judges have the discretion to order either reinstatement or damages. (Ironically, the representatives of the EU, who were acting to implement the German prescription for indebted states, had pressed Italy to adopt a neo-liberal solution that excluded the possibility of reinstatement.) We can interpret this result as the product of institutional resistance to radical changes in basic norms of the existing system – as an example of the stickiness of institutions. But the court decisions also reflected the level of opposition to the new law, again spearheaded by the CGIL.

The Monti government also undertook a significant reform of the welfare state, another distinguishing feature of the varieties of capitalism. With respect to pensions, which represent by far the largest share of Italian welfare expenditure, the reform aimed to make the pension system sustainable and restore intergenerational equity. To that end, it accelerated the timetable for raising the retirement age for women in the private sector, so that it would equal that of men by 2018 (going from 60 to 66 years and 7 months); it also radically raised the length of service required for a "seniority" pension from 40 years or the "96 factor" (the sum of age and length of service) to 42 years and 5 months for men, and 41 years and 5 months for women, with an actuarial reduction for the years left before the pensioner's normal retirement age (Mania 2011). These changes significantly reduced the possibilities for early retirement, leaving many more older workers in the position of having to remain in the labor market for as long as six more years (in spite of the record high levels of youth unemployment). This was particularly devastating for those who had left their jobs or planned to do so, and as a result of the sudden increase in the age of retirement, found themselves without an income.

Monti's welfare minister, Elsa Fornero, aimed to cushion the greater ease of firing under Article 18 with a more comprehensive unemployment insurance scheme. The new scheme covered a slightly larger share of private sector workers (81 percent instead of 63 percent), but reduced the benefit period to twelve months (eighteen for those over 55) from the much longer periods available under the previous schemes (Santelli 2012). Like the pension reform, this restricted the period for which benefits were payable, thereby increasing the pool of available labor. While these two reforms had a rationalizing intent they also, in reducing coverage, moved the welfare system closer to the Anglo-Saxon "liberal welfare state." But this movement was only moderate, and, as in other spheres, paralleled earlier developments in Germany, where one of the most controversial changes introduced by the Schröder government limited unemployment benefits to one year, and where pension reforms had also raised the retirement age (to 67).

Conclusions

We have seen that the changes in the institutions of Italian capitalism over the past five years, in response to the impact of the global financial crisis, are in many respects parallel to the evolution of the German version of CME since reunification. In the field of corporate finance, the largest German firms had become, thanks to their profitability, less dependent on the banks and more able to finance themselves. The Italian firms were already more independent thus *de facto* less subject to bank monitoring. But in the crisis the power of the controlling blocks was confirmed and dependence on the state was reduced. In industrial relations, plant-level bargaining, whether inside or out-side the national contracts, has been strengthened, and may now derogate from the provisions of the national agreement. This has been a crucial element in maintaining the competitiveness of German industry in the past twenty years. The regime of employment protection was brought much closer to Germany's, and "reforms" of the pension and unemployment insurance systems also echoed changes German governments had introduced in the first decade of the twenty-first century.

While very significant, these changes still represent an evolution of the CME model, rather than its abandonment in favor of an LME. While many capitalists are theoretically committed to a thoroughgoing neoliberalism, in practice they do not adhere to the pure doctrine – for instance, on the issue of corporate governance and open markets for corporate control, they frequently defend family or blockholder dominance. And they cannot simply implement their preferences, as economic institutions are the product of a balance of political forces, especially the major social classes. Changes in the structure of the economy, particularly the international situation of the firm and the country, may give one class a reason to seek change and may augment its power to alter the institutions. But change can occur only through a process of political struggle.

Notes

1 Soskice (2007). But this is not included as a feature of the CME model in the classic statement of the VoC approach, Hall and Soskice's "An Introduction to Varieties of Capitalism" (2001) or in any of the other standard presentations of the framework.

2 Molina and Rhodes, for instance, argue that Spain's and Italy's Mixed Market Economies are particularly diverse, both territorially and in terms of firm size, with strong but fragmented interest groups. The state plays an important role in

attempting to co-ordinate these different interests, but they admit that stagnation and sclerosis are possible. See Molina and Rhodes (2007).
3 OECD (2014). The fall was 0.1 percent p.a. on average, versus gains of 1.2 percent p.a. for Germany and the UK, 0.6 for the USA, and 0.5 percent for France.

References

Acemoglu, D. and J. Robinson (2012) *Why Nations Fail* (New York: Crown Business).
Amyot, G. (2004) *Business, the State, and Economic Policy: The case of Italy* (London: Routledge).
——(2009) "La privatizzazione di Alitalia," in G. Baldini and A. Cento Bull (eds) *Politica in Italia: Edizione 2009* (Bologna: Il Mulino).
Bellofiore, R., F. Garibaldo and J. Halevi (2011) "The Global Crisis and the Crisis of European Neomercantilism," in L. Panitch (ed.) *Socialist Register 2011* (London: Merlin).
Berta, G. (2011) "La Fiat e la crisi delle relazioni industriali," *Economia & Lavoro*, XLV, 2.
Corte Costituzionale (2013) *Constitutional Court decision 231/2013*, available at: www. cortecostituzionale.it [accessed May 18, 2014].
Deeg, R. (2005a) "Change from Within: German and Italian Finance in the 1990s," in Streek, W. and K. Thelen (eds) *Beyond Continuity* (Oxford: Oxford University Press).
——(2005b) "Remaking Italian Capitalism? The politics of corporate governance reform," *West European Politics*, 28(3).
Del Conte, M. (2012) "Il nuovo Articolo 18 ... " October 30, available at: www.lavoce. info [accessed May 14, 2014].
——(2014) "Sindacati alla conta di quanti lavoratori rappresentano," January 14, available at: www.lavoce.info [accessed May 14, 2014].
Della Sala, V. (2004) "The Italian Model of Capitalism," *Journal of European Public Policy*, 11(6).
Dustmann, C., B. Fitzenberger, U. Schönberg and A. Spitz-Oener (2014) "From Sick Man of Europe to Economic Superstar: Germany's Resurgent Economy," *Journal of Economic Perspectives*, 28(1).
The Economist (2013) "Big Government Meets Big Data," January 8.
Germano, L. (2011) "Fiat ancora un interesse privilegiato? L'evoluzione delle politiche governative per il settore auto," *Rivista Italiana di Politiche Pubbliche*, 2.
Griseri, P. (2014a) "Tutta la Chrysler nelle mani Fiat," *La Repubblica*, January 2.
——(2014b) "Fiat Chrysler Automobiles: sede in Olanda, fisco inglese, e quotazione a New York," *La Repubblica*, January 29.
Griseri, P., M. Novelli and M. Travaglio (1997) *Il processo. Storia segreta dell'inchiesta Fiat tra guerre, tangenti, e fondi neri* (Rome: Editori Riuniti).
Gualmini, E., and V. Schmidt (2013) "The political sources of Italy's economic problems: Between opportunistic political leadership and pragmatic, technocratic leadership," *Comparative European Politics*, 11(3).
Hall, P., and D. Soskice (2001) "An Introduction to Varieties of Capitalism," in P. Hall and D. Soskice (eds) *Varieties of Capitalism: the Institutional Foundations of Comparative Advantage* (Oxford: Oxford University Press).
——and K. Thelen (2009) "Institutional Change in Varieties of Capitalism," *Socio-Economic Review*, 7(1).

Hilferding, R. (1981 [1910]) *Finance Capital: A Study of the Latest Phase of Capitalist Development* (London: Routledge and Kegan Paul).

Ichino, P. (2011) "Si volta pagina nel rapport sindacati-imprese," June 29, available at: www.lavoce.info [accessed May 14, 2014].

Jackson, G. and A. Sorge (2012) "The Trajectory of Institutional Change in Germany, 1979–2009," *Journal of European Public Policy*, 19(8).

Jessop, B. (2008) *State Power: A Strategic-Relational Approach* (Cambridge: Polity).

Kesting, S. and K. Nielsen (2008) "Varieties of Capitalism: Theoretical Critique and Empirical Observations," in W. Eisner and G. Hanappi (eds) *Varieties of Capitalism and New Institutional Deals* (Cheltenham: Edward Elgar).

Kliman, A. (2012) *The Failure of Capitalist Production: Underlying Causes of the Great Recession* (London: Pluto).

La Repubblica (2011) "Marchionne: 'Lasceremo Confindustria," June 30.

Mania, R. (2011) "Pensioni, uomini via dal lavoro a 42 anni, fino a sei anni di attesa obbligata," *La Repubblica*, December 5.

Marx, K. (1966) *Capital*, vol. III (London: Lawrence and Wishart).

Messori, M. (2006) "The Bank Takeover Bills and the Role of the Bank of Italy," in G. Amyot and L. Verzichelli (eds) *The End of the Berlusconi Era?* vol. 21 of *Italian Politics: A Review* (New York: Berghahn).

Molina, O. and M. Rhodes (2007) "The Political Economy of Adjustment in Mixed Market Economies: Spain and Italy," in B. Hancké, M. Rhodes and M. Thatcher (eds) *Beyond Varieties of Capitalism* (Oxford: Oxford University Press).

Nelken, D. (1996) "A Legal Revolution? The Judges and Tangentopoli," in Gundle, S. and S. Parker (eds) *The New Italian Republic* (New York: Routledge).

Nölke, A. and A. Vliegenthart (2009) "Enlarging the Varieties of Capitalism," *World Politics*, 61(4).

OECD (2014) *Economic Outlook Database*, available at: http://dx.doi.org/10.178/888932791609 [accessed May 14, 2014].

Piketty, T. (2014) *Capital in the 21st Century* (Cambridge, MA: Harvard University Press).

Procacci, G. (1970) *History of the Italian People* (London: Weidenfeld and Nicholson).

Rhodes, M. (2001) "The Political Economy of Social Pacts: 'Competitive Corporatism' and European Welfare State Reform," in P. Pierson (ed.) *The New Politics of the Welfare State* (Oxford: Oxford University Press).

Santelli, F. (2012) "Aiuti a chi perde il lavoro, indennità per 160 mila persone in più," *La Repubblica*, June 17.

Schmidt, V. (2002) *The Futures of European Capitalism* (Oxford: Oxford University Press).

Sivini, G. (2013) *Compagni di rendite: Marchionne e gli Agnelli* (Viterbo: Nuovi Equilibri).

Soskice, D. (2007) "Macroeconomics and Varieties of Capitalism," in B. Hancké, M. Rhodes and M. Thatcher (eds) *Beyond Varieties of Capitalism* (Oxford: Oxford University Press).

Streeck, W. (2009) *Re-forming Capitalism: Institutional Change in the German Political Economy* (Oxford: Oxford University Press).

——and K. Thelen (2005) "Introduction: Institutional Change in Advanced Political Economies," in W. Streeck and K. Thelen (eds) *Beyond Continuity: Institutional Change in Advanced Political Economies* (Oxford: Oxford University Press).

Zysman, J. (1983) *Governments, Markets, and Growth: Financial Systems and the Politics of Industrial Change* (Ithaca, NY: Cornell University Press).

7 Germany and the crisis
Steady as she goes?

Ian Bruff

Introduction: the mask of "success"

This chapter critically discusses Germany in order to question its international profile of stability and strong economic performance. This is important because, as noted by the EuroMemo Group (2014, p. 9), German GDP is only 3 percent above its 2007 level. Within the European Union (EU) only Malta, Poland, Slovakia, and Sweden have recovered at a faster rate from the so-called Great Recession, which on the surface justifies the aforementioned international profile. Nevertheless, it shows how far expectations have fallen when any growth at all is viewed positively. Furthermore, it highlights the long-lasting power of notions of a German "model," i.e. as an exemplar for others to follow, which survived even the period from the mid-1990s to the mid-2000s, when low growth and high unemployment were the norm.

This combination of relatively good economic performance and the potent symbolism of the phrase *Modell Deutschland* mask three key weaknesses at the heart of the German political economy. Each weakness is a consequence of the substantial neoliberalization that Germany has undergone from the 1990s onwards, a process which is rooted in the changing spatial constitution of German capital. They are the following: (i) an intensification of Germany's dependence on exports; (ii) the imbrication of the financial sector with global and Eurozone crises; and (iii) a more volatile system of political representation. Although clearly not of the order witnessed in countries such as Greece and Spain, these manifestations of crisis indicate that the current period is potentially transformative for all of Europe, and not just for the so-called PIIGS.

The neoliberalizing of the German political economy, and the weaknesses that this has produced, poses many challenges for the dominant literatures on capitalist diversity – be it the paradigmatic Varieties of Capitalism (VoC) framework or the broader, yet still institutionalist, Comparative Capitalisms (CC) approaches. The German "model" has often been central to these literatures, but apart from a few exceptions the contributions take institutions as the starting point for research. The result is a narrow and unsatisfactory framework, because it entails the redefinition of "capitalism" as "the economy" and its reduction to a mere external constraint or contextual factor. This is significant because "it focuses research agendas on the specific political and social conditions across the globe, leaving 'the economy' relatively untouched" (Bruff and Hartmann 2014, p. 74). Instead, we ought to acknowledge that although "institutions are of considerable importance for how capitalist societies evolve ... such institutions are clearly also grounded in capitalist conditions of existence" (Bruff 2011, p. 482). Crucially, this enables us to foreground what critical political economy approaches believe should be central to our analysis: the contradictions, inequalities, and conflicts which define and characterize capitalism (Bruff and Ebenau 2014). In the case of Germany, the advantages of this richer analytical framework can be demonstrated via an investigation of the profound implications of the changing spatial constitution of German capital.

The chapter is structured as follows. After a critical overview of the institutions-centered debates on the German political economy, I outline how the spatial constitution of German capital has evolved in recent decades. The consequences of this are then discussed, and I examine the cases of export dependence, financial crises, and political representation. Finally, I conclude with brief reflections on the broader implications of my argument.

CC Debates about the German "Model"

There are common points of reference across the CC debates on what comprised the "traditional" German model, even if the emphasis has differed according to the author and/or the particular strand of the literatures. These common points include the following: long-term, bank-based investment in manufacturing as opposed to short-term, equity-based notions of "shareholder value"; social partnership between employers and unions in the workplace and between the social partners and the state in policy-making processes; a relatively equal society in socioeconomic terms, with a comparatively narrow spread of wage levels and a reasonably comprehensive welfare state; and a stable political system dominated by two "catch-all" parties (the Christian and social democrats) which represent a broad range of social groups (for example, see Katzenstein 1989; Streeck 1997; Thelen 2004). Most fundamentally, though, is the agreement that "this was certainly a capitalist market economy ... [but] richly organised and densely regulated by a vast variety of institutions" (Streeck 1997, p. 239). Hence Germany was often viewed as an alternative to the more lightly regulated Anglo-Saxon "model," which exhibits comparable levels of economic performance but scores considerably less well on issues such as skill levels, product quality, socioeconomic inequality, welfare, and the role of organized labor (Albert 1993; Hutton 1995).

However, the economic warning signs in the 1980s became much more prominent in the 1990s, when low growth and high unemployment led Germany to lag significantly behind comparator countries. There was no consensus, during or since, about the role of German unification in the economic malaise, even if all considered it to have been important. Examples here include the increased level of government taxation and spending related to the need to upgrade eastern Germany's infrastructure, and the damage inflicted by Chancellor Kohl's imposition of a 1:1 exchange rate between the West and East German marks, which quickly produced rapid deindustrialization and mass unemployment in the uncompetitive East. Although these developments were clearly important, it was notable that even those who focused on the significance of unification ultimately argued that the failure to overcome the difficulties was due to the inability of the institutional environment to adapt sufficiently well to the new era (Carlin and Soskice 1997).

Hence the growing debate about the viability of the German "model" focused on the pressure exerted by economic under-performance and the seemingly greater ability of "Anglo-Saxon" countries such as the US and the UK to adapt more successfully to an increasingly globalized world (compare and contrast Streeck 1997; Harding and Paterson 2000; Manow and Seils 2000; Dyson 2001). Inevitably, there were varying degrees of optimism and pessimism on this question, but a common theme was that Germany's "social" institutions "needed" to be reformed, with institutions regulating labor markets, welfare programs, and industrial relations viewed as central to any successful response. Therefore, the key issue for the CC literatures was how much Germany wanted to reform itself, with labor market flexibilization, welfare retrenchment, and the reduction of trade union power – all of which tacitly endorsed a broadly neoliberal set of policy and institutional prescriptions – being central to many contributions (cf. Bruff 2008b). This reflected broader CC debates (e.g. Scharpf and Schmidt 2000a, 2000b), which were dominated by the assumption that institutions which upheld the "social" elements of the given political economy needed to be responsive to new challenges if they were to ensure that an alternative to the Anglo-Saxon "model" could still exist – which meant, in an irony lost on most authors, that they would become less "social" as a result.

Therefore, what mattered to these literatures were policies and regulations, not broader developments in capitalism. In consequence, capitalism was acknowledged only in the form of a globalizing "economic environment" or as a more pronounced set of "external constraints" on various actors and institutions – not, as I would advocate, as a mode of production that needs to be critically analyzed and critiqued. This lack of enquiry into "the economy" meant that the higher levels of German growth in the 2005–08 period and the relatively good recovery in the 2010-period, combined with gradually falling unemployment, were simplistically interpreted as signalling the "comeback" of *Modell Deutschland*. CC scholars acknowledged that the common points of reference mentioned at the start of this section had evolved, but nevertheless argued that they were still recognizable compared to the past. Therefore, Germany's renewed economic strength had not come at the expense of its "social" institutions: instead, they had ultimately proved responsive to new challenges (see, among others, Hassel 2012; Reisenbichler and Morgan 2012; Rinne and Zimmerman 2012; Eichhorst forthcoming). Although some notable exceptions did not concur with this positive assessment (Streeck 2009), they remained wedded to an institutionalist paradigm and thus to the neglect of "the economy."

We are therefore left with no option but to take the alternative path that was outlined in the introduction. And, as the rest of this chapter will show, through taking this path we can see clearly how developments in Germany over the past few decades are not rooted in institutional evolution but in the changing spatial constitution of German capital. This, unlike in the CC literatures, enables "the economy" to be incorporated into our analytical approach rather than kept separate from institutions.

The changing spatial constitution of German capital

There were numerous continuities in German capitalism across different historical periods – for example, from Empire to Weimar to National Socialism to West German Republic. This is because Germany's transition to capitalism left it with a particular insertion into the world economy. Notably, German territory contained specific locales which often provided for the most propitious conditions for capital accumulation in the world capital goods industries (van der Wurff 1993). One key consequence was the tendency for industrial fractions of capital to prevail over finance fractions, leading to a long-lasting equation of strong industrial performance with strong overall economic performance (Coates 2000, pp. 176–77). As such, after 1949 the West German political economy was characterized by a highly competitive manufacturing exports sector, and this record has often been invoked in wider discourses about *Modell Deutschland.*

However, from the 1970s onwards the advantages of producing in West Germany were increasingly challenged by lower-cost competitor countries, especially in East Asia. Although this began to impact negatively on economic growth and unemployment in the 1980s, it was not until the 1990s when real shifts began to occur. There was a substantial withdrawal of investment from German territory as industrial fractions of capital became less territorially constrained. In particular, the opening of spatially proximate markets in Central and Eastern Europe provided the means for lower-cost production in "nearshore" locations (Berndt 2010), which in turn meant that German unification *was* significant, but more because of its part in a broader process of social change. This growing transnationalization, whereby lower-value parts of the production process are hived off to cheaper locations and the remaining production in Germany is accomplished by a shrinking workforce, became more notable over the years. Hence, even before finance fractions became increasingly important in the neoliberalization of the German political economy, *Modell Deutschland* was being hollowed out from the inside.

As already noted, finance was historically subordinate to, and interwoven with, industrial fractions of capital, giving it a national and bank-based profile as opposed to the international and equity-based profile one could see in the UK (Coates 2000, pp. 167–77). Several consequences flowed from this, including the following: the emphasis on long-term strategy over short-term returns on investment; the close relationships between banks and the firms they provided credit to, which extended to the former having seats on the company board; and, via the same bank often providing credit for a number of firms in the same region and/or sector, significant levels of cross-shareholding across these firms. This gave rise to a relatively localized spatial constitution of German finance capital.

During the 1990s, there was a growing reorientation of larger banks towards global equity markets as they sought either to realize profits on money lent to firms based anywhere in the world, or to engage in more speculative activities related to generating returns on derivatives and other financial instruments. Larger German firms were not strongly affected as they also increasingly focused on global equity markets. More damagingly smaller, localized companies experienced growing difficulties in gaining access to credit, meaning that the fruits of any economic growth have been increasingly distributed towards internationalized corporations (cf. Grahl and Teague 2004, pp. 563–64). This destabilization of traditional links between banks and companies also manifested itself in the weakening or elimination of cross-shareholdings across different firms – a process accelerated by the 2000 abolition of taxation on the sale of such assets. Hence the growing attention paid to Germany's shift towards short-term "shareholder value," and away from long-term "patient capital" orientations (Dörre 2001; Sablowski 2008).

CC scholars are not wrong when pointing out that the German political economy has not fully transformed from a nationally-oriented, bank-based form of capitalism to an internationalized, finance-based model (Lütz and Eberle 2008; Thelen 2009; Deeg 2010; Jackson and Sorge 2012). However, the changing spatial constitution of German capital did produce a marked shift in the conditions in which the German political economy evolved. Over time, this shift led to the emergence of new forms of social compromise which were considerably more unequal than in the postwar period and thus at odds with the imagery of *Modell Deutschland*. It also helped produce the crisis tendencies which the mask of success is currently concealing. These two developments take up the rest of this chapter.

New, more unequal forms of class-based social compromise

The social compromises forged in the postwar period were not intrinsically just. Günter Minnerup (1976) pointed out that, during the 1950s, high economic growth and falling unemployment masked the longer-than-average working hours and the lower-than-average wage levels at the core of the *Wirtschaftswunder*. Moreover, the legally mandated reintroduction of Works

Councils in the early 1950s was seen by some in the labor movement as an attempt to neuter union power through the explicit tying of the workforce to company fortunes (Upchurch *et al.* 2009, pp. 62–63). Therefore, we must always be aware that German unions have sometimes sought to protect their interests by agreeing to painful restructuring which maintains their presence in the sector, especially in manufacturing. Nevertheless, although radical forms of laborism were discouraged by the *Mitbestimmung* (co-determination) system, so was union weakness, with (for example) collective bargaining becoming an integral part of the politico-economic landscape. This strategic position for organized labor within the German political economy was augmented by increasingly high levels of capital investment and the emergence of an extensive welfare state. As a result, the values and practices now commonly associated with *Modell Deutschland* were in place by the early 1970s, and of a more egalitarian flavor than what emerged in the 1990s and 2000s.

The changing spatial constitution of German capital had a direct impact on capital-labor relations within Germany. The growing possibilities for investment to be exported to lower-cost locations led to a constant squeeze on unions – not least because it was now easier for employers to threaten to relocate in order to extract concessions (Bieler 2006, pp. 59–67, 78–79). For example, there was a growing tendency for companies to assert the need for hardship clauses, which exchanged job guarantees for little or no wage compensation (either in total or per hour) and thus for, at best, stagnant real incomes. Over time, such clauses became the norm rather than the exception, with them frequently being invoked even if the company was not struggling (Seifert and Massa-Wirth 2005). In other words, increasingly built into the fabric of production relations was the undermining of social partnership between employers and unions, especially when bargaining on wages and conditions of employment (Pickshaus *et al.* 2003). Therefore, the continued presence of corporatist institutions within Germany should not be taken to mean – as posited by many in the CC literatures – that we should acknowledge "the lengths to which most employers have been willing to go to manage new pressures for flexibility within traditional institutions" (Thelen 2001, p. 85). The increasing desire to *transform* these institutions is neglected in such analyses.

In addition, there was the rising tendency of large firms to shift employment to subcontractors in the name of a more short-term, shareholder-oriented approach to running a capitalist enterprise. This enabled employers "to maintain a commitment to sectoral agreements for their core workforces, while simultaneously weakening them by moving some jobs out of the sector" (Doellgast and Greer 2007, p. 71). In consequence, there was a recalibration and stratification of institutional relationships within Germany, preserving traditional arrangements in some respects but also predicating their continued viability on practices which embodied more unequal relations of power. Key examples here include the growing roles for temporary work agencies in recruitment strategies and for "opening clauses" in collective bargaining agreements (which allowed companies to deviate below the minimum set by the sector-wide wage structure). These developments all exerted downward pressure on labor costs, especially at the lower end. In the process, real wages were stagnant across the two decades after unification and fell during the 2000s (Lapavitsas *et al.* 2012, Ch. 3; Lehndorff 2012, p. 86).

Unsurprisingly, employers were increasingly in favor of transforming the German "model" more generally. For instance, in the mid-1990s the employers' associations instigated the *Standortdebatte* which was, on the surface, a dialogue about Germany's attractiveness for investment in times of economic difficulties, but in fact was "one of the major political catalysts through which neoliberal policies have been mobilised in post-unification Germany" (Brenner 2000, p. 320). The rhetoric "was designed to de-legitimise the post-war consensus, questioning labour market regulation, the scope of the welfare state, and tax levels in light of the purported need to render the country an attractive site for investment and production" (Menz 2005, p. 199). And here we see a curious alignment between German employers and the CC literatures on the German "model": both stressed the need for "social" institutions to respond to new challenges, and both placed the blame for any perceived hold-up in the reform process on allegedly recalcitrant trade unions and supposedly outdated welfare programs (see for example Streeck and Hassel 2003). This, more than anything else, highlights the poverty of approaches which stress the normative superiority of "social" models of capitalism while simultaneously delivering analyses which critique precisely these "social" elements.

With employers attempting to turn into reality the transformation of German capitalism that they sought (Kinderman 2005), there was a growing likelihood that any future reforms would be both neoliberal in nature and exclusionary of unions in the decision-making process (Upchurch *et al.* 2009, p. 69). This is what came to pass in 2003 with the "Agenda 2010" package, which covered many policy areas and institutional arrangements and were driven forward by the "progressive" social democrat-green governing coalition. The reforms were a wide-ranging and comprehensive attempt to significantly further and deepen the neoliberalizing trends discussed above, and restructuring of pensions, taxation, health, education, craft professions and shopping hours were part of the legislative program (for more, see Bruff 2010). The most notorious measure was the abolition of unemployment assistance (known as Hartz IV), but the centerpiece welfare and labor market reforms were broader still. Indeed, via the conscious mobilization of welfare programs and labor market regulations towards new ends, Agenda 2010 explicitly connected the increased disciplining of labor within the workplace to a growing emphasis on the "right" to work rather than to welfare.

A key consequence was that the regulations governing the labor market came to mirror the new practices in the workplace that were noted earlier. These regulations include the following: much shorter government training programs for the unemployed, which were combined with stricter rules on the job offers that could be refused; the removal of regulations on temporary

agency work in order to promote its expansion; the abolition of social security contributions for employees earning less than €400 a month; and the
introduction of a sliding scale of increasing contributions for jobs that earned
between €400 and €800 (for more, see Bruff 2008a, pp. 148–50). While "core"
jobs remained quite well protected, the changes encouraged the growth of
low-wage and/or irregular employment outside the legal framework governing
full-time and/or permanent employees. This made it possible, in a four-year
period, for a loss of more than one million "first-class" jobs to be exchanged
for a similar rise in the number of "second-class" posts (Benoit 2006), and for
the number of low-wage workers to rise from 4.3 million in 1998 to 6.6 million
in 2008 (Kulish 2010). Inevitably, the promotion of atypical and low-wage work
proved to have a serious impact on socioeconomic inequality through the
"strengthening [of] labour market segmentation along specific lines" (Giesecke
2009, p. 642). Indeed, up to the onset of global crisis in 2008, income inequality
and poverty had risen faster since 2000 than in any other OECD country,
surpassing the EU average in the process (Lehndorff 2011, p. 345).

To summarize this section, it is clear that Germany has forged new forms
of class-based social compromise that are considerably more unequal than in
the past. However, the neoliberalizing of the German political economy has
not been without consequence.

Consequences

Numerous illustrative examples could be given, but here I focus on three of
the most important. Space constraint permits little more than a general
overview, but the discussion below should be viewed in light of the above.

Consequence 1: intensification of export dependence

Wolfgang Streeck's classic article on the German "model" argued that Germany
faced a "socioeconomic tightrope walk" if it were to maintain *Modell
Deutschland* as traditionally conceived (1997, pp. 245–47). However, his contention that one of the conditions for successfully remaining on the tightrope – sufficiently large global markets for quality-competitive goods – was in
hindsight too narrowly drawn. This occurred because he assumed – as, in all
fairness to Streeck, did everyone else – that the German political economy
had "barred itself from serving price-competitive markets" (ibid., pp. 245–46).
As we have seen already, it was precisely during this period, the mid-1990s,
that a decisive turn was made towards lower labor costs and shorter-term
planning horizons (cf. Ryner 2003). The introduction of the euro in 1999
aided this process – sharing the new single currency with numerous economically weaker countries meant that the euro was not as strong as the old
German mark. Combined with the shift towards stronger price competitiveness, this enabled Germany's current account, from a position of balance at
the end of the century, to grow to a surplus of more than 6 percent of GDP

by 2007 and largely remain at this level since then. While strong export performance is generally viewed as a positive economic indicator, for Germany it masks two key underlying weaknesses. I consider financial issues in the next sub-section; for now, I will focus on the broader implications for the German "model."

As Lapavitsas *et al.* (2012, p. 21) outline, "Germany has [from the mid-1990s] been marked by low growth, flat investment, stagnant consumption, rising saving, and falling household debt … The only source of dynamism has been exports." This can be explained by the aforementioned new tightrope walk, whereby a greater share of domestic investment than in the past is deployed in lower-value, lower-wage activities, and flat real wages and rising inequality encouraged deficient private demand and higher savings. In addition, apart from brief rises in the government budget deficit in the early 2000s and again in the immediate aftermath of the collapse of Lehman Brothers, public consumption has provided little support for economic growth. This was compounded by the "debt brake" constitutional amendment passed in January 2009 with the support of all political parties apart from the Left Party, which required progress to be made towards a permanently balanced budget from 2016 onwards.

In consequence, Germany's recent economic performance has been largely driven by its huge current account surplus, and future growth will be similarly dependent on exports (the value of which is now more than 50 percent of German GDP). Although Germany was known prior to the 1990s for its competitiveness, this was backed up by higher levels of domestic investment, growing private consumption, and a more discretionary role for government. Nowadays, all of its eggs have been placed in the "exports" basket, with a significant proportion of *both* economic growth in the 2001–07 and post-2009 periods *and* the 5 percent fall in GDP in 2009 explained in this way (cf. Guerrieri and Esposito 2012, p. 537). Moreover, the austerity policies advocated for the rest of the Eurozone by Germany and, more broadly, the Troika (the European Central Bank [ECB], the European Commission, and the International Monetary Fund), makes it likely that the sources of continued export success will be narrower than was the case in the 2000s. German exports to Eurozone countries were flat across the 2008–13 period, with significant growth largely recorded where the country in question did not pursue austerity policies, or at least not to the same extent (for example, Australia, China, India, Russia, the US) (Statistisches Bundesamt 2013, p. 407).

As a result, although Germany's export profile is diversifying, with exports to transition and developing economies growing from 18.5 percent of the total in 2005 to 26.1 percent in 2012 (UNCTAD 2013, p. 62), it is also dependent on a few key markets for continued success. This begs the question of what would happen should one or more of these markets run into trouble. Given the current (April 2014) nerves about the state of the Chinese economy and especially the large rise in private sector debt in China, and about the potential impact of the end to America's quantitative easing program, this question may be answered sooner than we think. And even if it is not, it is likely that the German political economy will remain in a state of intense export dependence.

Consequence II: imbrication of finance capital with global and Eurozone crises

Much attention has been paid to the role played by "Anglo-Saxon" financial institutions in the run-up to the global crisis, and to the limited regulatory constraints placed on them since 2008 by seemingly intimidated American and British governments. This is understandable, given the way in which the implosion of the American sub-prime market catalyzed such a violent chain reaction across the globe in 2007–08, culminating in the collapse of Lehman Brothers and the massive bailouts and recapitalizations of heavily indebted banks. However, the powerful critiques articulated by German political elites of what they viewed as irresponsible and immoral lending practices in the finance sector, coupled with Germany's attitude towards the sovereign debt crises experienced by several Eurozone countries, have masked the deep intertwining of German financial institutions with global and Eurozone crises.

German financial institutions were far from alone in participating enthusiastically in the global casino prior to 2008. This could be observed in August 2007, when the ECB suddenly injected almost €100bn into the Eurozone interbank market in order to maintain liquidity. This surprise move was the first sign of how much the cross-border claims of European banks had risen in the 2000s, taking advantage of the aforementioned internationalization strategies plus the new and large euro-denominated market in Europe (Lapavitsas *et al.* 2012, pp. 44–46). As a result, European banks were badly exposed in two ways by the late 2000s: to the fall-out from the implosion of the American sub-prime market; and to the coming storm within the Eurozone. German banks were strongly implicated in both. Regarding the former, Cafruny and Ryner (2012, p. 42) report that in 2008 "German banks had the largest leverage rates among OECD countries ... [and by] the end of 2009 European banks were estimated to hold more than US$1 trillion in toxic assets, more than two-thirds of which were held by German banks." Turning to the latter, although banks headquartered in other countries (such as France and Austria) were also badly exposed in peripheral Eurozone states, German banks were in a more acute position because of a higher concentration of their activities in market-sensitive financial assets such as derivatives. Moreover, this extended even to public *Landesbanken* – normally seen as the embodiment of the traditional German approach to banking, yet some (such as the Westdeutsche Landesbank) were forced to close or be dissolved into the "bad banks" which were created to deal with toxic assets of little worth.

Another factor that made German banks stand out was their connection to German current account surpluses. As many have argued, the integration into one single currency area of economies at different levels of development and with dissimilar economic structures was likely to produce divergent outcomes on the current account, with some countries persistently in surplus and others consistently in deficit. This is the case whether one views varying levels of competitiveness as key to the process, or "catch-up" development which leaves poorer, higher-growth countries as net importers of capital due to the greater returns on investment that could be generated compared to richer, lower-growth countries (compare here Lapavitsas et al. 2012 with Milios and Sotiropoulos 2010). German banks were central to the process of "dependent financialization" in countries with current account deficits that needed financing (Becker *et al.* 2015 forthcoming, p. 7), because huge current account surpluses were available to them for recycling/investing in apparently high-return parts of the Eurozone. In the 2000s, such countries included contemporary pariahs like Greece and Spain. Although there were different modes of debt-backed growth in these countries, the outcome was the same – the emergence of the Eurozone crisis in 2009–10 as these investments appeared increasingly toxic. The subsequent sharp contraction of some of these economies goes some way to explaining why German banks in 2014 remain highly leveraged (in the case of the beleaguered Deutsche Bank, to a greater degree than Lehman Brothers before it collapsed).

This is why Germany is so keen for no Eurozone country to default on its debts. Otherwise, the house of cards, starting with German banks, could collapse, triggering an economic meltdown dwarfing the so-called Great Recession after 2007. It is also why the relentless focus of the German political elite has been on servicing the *public* debt in countries such as Greece and Spain rather than the *private* debt held by European banks (cf. Demirović and Sabloswki 2011). Otherwise, it would become clear that the recapitalization of German banks and the orderly write-downs of their debt are just as much a German as a Greek question. This is not to absolve the Eurozone's institutional architecture from any criticism, for it is deeply neoliberal and flawed. But it is clear that the neoliberalizing of the German political economy is strongly implicated in the "asymmetrically linked [and] uneven processes of development" which are at the heart of the Eurozone crisis (Becker *et al.* 2015 forthcoming, p. 1). As a result, unless there are drastic changes in how the Eurozone operates it is likely that Germany will remain imbricated in global and especially Eurozone crises in the coming years.

Consequence III: a more volatile system of political representation

The victory for the Christian democrats in the September 2013 elections was largely interpreted as a resounding triumph for Angela Merkel's leadership. Indeed, on first glance the results were impressive. Compared to 2009 the CDU-CSU bloc increased its share of the national vote by 8 percent to 42 percent, meaning that it would be the dominant component of any government which emerged out of the elections. However, the overall score for the center–right alliance – traditionally the CDU-CSU and the Free Democrats – actually fell from 48 percent to 46 percent. The FDP's disastrous performance was rooted in the generally negative view of its role in the 2009–13 government, but there were two different reasons for this perception. The first was the more general dissatisfaction with what was seen as ministerial incompetence and unnecessary clashes with the CDU-CSU. The second was more specific, but no less important – disillusionment among a small but significant section of German society with the failure of the FDP to implement no more than token aspects of its explicitly neoliberal election manifesto. As such, we should not be surprised that the center–right alliance lost ground compared to 2009, for it was driven by organizational *and* ideological discord from the beginning of its term in office. Putting this back together for the 2013 campaign would always have been an uphill task. Ultimately it led to the FDP's first failure in its history to enter Parliament (parties need 5 percent of the vote, and the FDP won 4.8 percent).

One of the ironies of the situation is that, during the Agenda 2010 debates, Merkel explicitly aligned the CDU-CSU with neoliberalism, declaring that Agenda 2010 did not go far enough. However, this approach almost snatched defeat from the jaws of victory at the 2005 elections. After being well ahead in opinion polls the CDU-CSU was only just the largest party. Consequently, and against expectations, the result did not deliver a majority for the CDU-CSU/FDP alliance and was thus interpreted as a popular rejection of further restructuring. Subsequent to this, Merkel backtracked on her enthusiasm for neoliberalism and sought to reclaim the traditional mantle of the Christian democrats as a "catch-all" party which represented a broad swathe of social groups. As a result, there has been a subtle shift in coalitional strategizing, with Grand Coalitions between the CDU-CSU and the social democratic SPD no longer seen as a strictly exceptional scenario. Prior to 2005, in post-war (West) German history this had only happened from 1966–69, when the first serious economic slowdown after 1949 catalyzed a rise in support for far-right parties. Nevertheless, by 2017 Germany will have been governed for eight of the previous twelve years by a Grand Coalition. Of course, these governments have overwhelming strength in Parliament because they are comprised of the two largest parties, but this is also indicative of a growing volatility in the system of political representation.

In order to consider the latter we need to start with the formation of the Left Party (*Die Linke*) in 2007. It combined "an alliance of former SPD members, various trade union officials and left-wing intellectuals" in western Germany who were disillusioned with the SPD in the wake of Agenda 2010, with the Party of Democratic Socialism (PDS), which was largely confined to the old East Germany because of its roots in the pre-1990 communist party" (Nachtwey and Spier 2007, p. 143). Standing for election as an alliance, these two groups won almost 9 percent of the vote in 2005, enabling *Die Linke* to become firmly established as a national Left alternative to the politics of Agenda 2010 and to neoliberalism more generally (Solty 2008, pp. 17–26). Solty argues that this rise to prominence shifted political discourse to the left, and it was possible to see how "the theme of 'social injustice' has become, for the moment at least, a national argument" (Anderson 2009, p. 24).

More recently, there was the formation of *Alternative für Deutschland* in 2013. AfD is an anti-euro, though not necessarily anti-EU, party, and has sought to build on the strong unease felt by many Germans about the bailouts of countries such as Greece. For instance, its policy proposals include abolishing the euro and ensuring that all transfers of sovereignty from Germany to the EU are subject to the outcome of a referendum rather than just of a parliamentary vote. The AfD did not enter the *Bundestag* in the 2013 elections, but another 0.3 percent of the popular vote would have been enough for it to have crossed the 5 percent hurdle into Parliament. Furthermore, although it is unclear how the party will fare in the future, it is significant that it tapped into the disillusionment felt by some of those who voted FDP in 2009 (Krouwel *et al.* 2013). In other words, the CDU-CSU did benefit to an extent from the FDP's collapse, but Merkel's post-2005 move to the center ground has left behind some of the social groups benefiting from, or attracted to, neoliberalism.

In summary, when taking a longer historical view one can observe that the two "catch-all" parties, the Christian and social democrats, will never again come close to taking 90 percent of the popular vote between them, as was the case in the 1970s. Instead, it is clear that a multi-party system is here to stay. To an extent, this is welcome as it increases the choices for voters when they peruse the ballot paper. However, in practice it means that two developments are at play – the growing fragmentation and polarization of the system of political representation, and the increased likelihood of Grand Coalitions being formed out of necessity rather than due to exceptional circumstances. As can probably be inferred, these two developments can potentially feed off each other.

This is not intended to paint a doomsday scenario, whereby Germany returns to the days of the Weimar Republic. Instead, the aim here has been to point out that a focus on Merkel's leadership misleads us; instead, she and her party were forced onto the center ground partly by forces from the left, and this in turn has created opportunities for forces from the right to make gains (the FDP in 2009, the AfD in 2013). Merkel's outstanding skills as a negotiator and as a tactician are recognized by many when considering the Eurozone crisis, but acknowledged by fewer people when it comes to domestic politics. After all, she has been Chancellor for almost a decade, and during this period the CDU-CSU bloc has clearly been the most popular political party. Nevertheless, we must conclude that, in addition to an intensified export dependence and the imbrication of German finance with global and Eurozone crises, the neoliberalizing of the German political economy has helped produce a more volatile system of political representation.

Conclusion

In this chapter, I have sought to problematize Germany's current status as a beacon of stability and strong economic performance. This is a tricky balancing act, for the German political economy is clearly in better shape than many, especially in the Eurozone. Nevertheless, careful analysis reveals how the changing spatial constitution of German capital has had the following consequences: the dependence on exports for any kind of economic growth; the imbrication with financial crises at the global and European scales; and the more volatile system of political representation. This does not mean that Germany will inevitably plunge into systemic and transformative turmoil in the future, and nor, even if it does, would it be possible to guess when this would happen. But as things stand now, Germany's trajectory over the last two decades has left it with pathologies which are being neglected. Moreover, such neglect makes it increasingly difficult to deal with these pathologies should they become manifest in more visible and damaging ways.

The broader implications of my argument are in line with how this chapter was introduced. That is, for a richer, more holistic and more appropriate analysis of "models" of capitalism to be possible, we need to foreground the contradictions, inequalities, and conflicts which define and characterize capitalism. Nevertheless, I do not advocate the replacement of the mainstream worldview with a "critical" orthodoxy which simply imposes a new paradigm upon the field, not least because the best examples of CC scholarship provide important insights into institutional practices that are sometimes neglected by critical political economy researchers (for example, see Becker 2009). Therefore, at its best the term "critical political economy" covers a wide range of alternative approaches that could be mobilized for the study of capitalist diversity (Bruff *et al.* 2013; Bruff and Ebenau 2014; Ebenau *et al.* 2015 forthcoming). Embracing this pluralism is key to furthering our understanding of capitalism more broadly and capitalist diversity more specifically.

Acknowledgments

Thanks to Richard Westra for inviting me to write this chapter. On the chapter itself, I am grateful to the following (in alphabetical order) for feedback on earlier drafts and, more generally, for conversations about the German political economy: Andreas Bieler, Matthias Ebenau, Alexander Gallas, Laura Horn, Peter Humphreys, Johannes Jäger, Jeremy Leaman, Christian May, Clare Murray, Gareth Price-Thomas, Magnus Ryner, and Brigitte Young. Thanks also to the German trade unions IG Metall and Ver.di, which invited me to present at their workshop "Europe Step by Step" in July 2013 in Manchester, where some of the above arguments were articulated for the first time.

References

Albert, M. (1993) *Capitalism against Capitalism* (London: Whurr).
Anderson, P. (2009) "A New Germany?" *New Left Review*, 2(57): 5–40.
Becker, J., J. Jäger and R. Weissenbacher (2015) "Uneven and Dependent Development in Europe: The Crisis and its Implications," in J. Jäger and E. Springler (eds)

Asymmetric Crisis in Europe and Possible Futures: Critical Political Economy and Post-Keynesian Perspectives (Abingdon: Routledge, forthcoming).

Becker, U. (2009) *Open Varieties of Capitalism: Continuity, Change and Performances* (Basingstoke: Palgrave Macmillan).

Benoit, B. (2006) "Germany's Labour Market Develops a Second Tier," *Financial Times*, October 26.

Berndt, C. (2010) "Methodological Nationalism and Territorial Capitalism: Mobile Labour and the Challenges to the 'German Model,'" in S. McGrath-Champ, A. Herod and A. Rainnie (eds) *Handbook of Employment and Society: Working Space* (London: Edward Elgar, pp. 290–308).

Bieler, A. (2006) *The Struggle for a Social Europe: Trade Unions and EMU in Times of Global Restructuring* (Manchester: Manchester University Press).

Brenner, N. (2000) "Building 'Euro-regions': Locational Politics and the Political Geography of Neoliberalism in Post-unification Germany," *European Urban and Regional Studies*, 7(4): 319–45.

Bruff, I. (2008a) *Culture and Consensus in European Varieties of Capitalism: A 'Common Sense' Analysis* (Basingstoke: Palgrave Macmillan).

——(2008b) "Germany's Shift from the Alliance for Jobs to Agenda 2010: The Role of Transnationalizing German Capital," *Debatte*, 16(3): 273–89.

——(2010) "Germany's Agenda 2010 Reforms: Passive Revolution at the Crossroads," *Capital & Class*, 34(1): 409–28.

——(2011) "What about the Elephant in the Room? Varieties of Capitalism, Varieties in Capitalism," *New Political Economy*, 16(4): 481–500.

Bruff, I. and M. Ebenau (2014) "Critical Political Economy and the Critique of Comparative Capitalisms Scholarship on Capitalist Diversity," *Capital & Class*, 38 (1): 3–15.

Bruff, I. and E. Hartmann (2014) "Neo-pluralist Political Science, Economic Sociology and the Conceptual Foundations of the Comparative Capitalisms Literatures," *Capital & Class*, 38(1): 73–85.

Bruff I., M. Ebenau, C. May and A. Nölke (eds) (2013) *Vergleichende Kapitalismusforschung: Stand, Perspektiven, Kritik* (Münster: Westfälisches Dampfboot).

Cafruny, A. and M. Ryner (2012) "The Global Financial Crisis and the European Union: The Irrelevance of Integration Theory and the Pertinence of Critical Political Economy," in P. Nousios, H. Overbeek and A. Tsolakis (eds) *Globalisation and European Integration: Critical Approaches to Regional Order and International Relations* (Abingdon: Routledge, pp. 32–50).

Carlin, W. and D. Soskice (1997) "Shocks to the System: The German Political Economy under Stress," *National Institute Economic Review*, 159(1): 57–76.

Coates, D. (2000) *Models of Capitalism: Growth and Stagnation in the Modern Era.* (Cambridge: Polity).

Crouch, C. and W. Streeck (eds) (1997) *Political Economy of Modern Capitalism: Mapping Convergence and Diversity* (London: Sage).

Deeg, R. (2010) "Industry and Finance in Germany since Unification," *German Politics & Society*, 28(2): 116–29.

Demirović, A. and T. Sablowski (2011) "Finanzdominierte Akkumulation und die Krise in Europa," *Prokla*, 42(1): 77–106.

Doellgast, V. and I Greer (2007) "Vertical Disintegration and the Disorganisation of German Industrial Relations," *British Journal of Industrial Relations*, 45(1): 55–76.

Dörre, K. (2001) "Das Deutsche Produktionsmodell unter dem Druck des Shareholder Value," *Kölner Zeitschrift für Soziologie und Sozialpsychologie*, 53(4): 675–704.

Dyson, K. (2001) "The German Model Revisited: From Schmidt to Schröder," *German Politics*, 10(2): 135–54.

Ebenau, M., I. Bruff and C. May (eds) (2015) *New Directions in Comparative Capitalisms Research: Critical and Global Perspectives* (London: Palgrave Macmillan).

Eichhorst, W. (forthcoming) "The Unexpected Appearance of a New German Model," *British Journal of Industrial Relations*.

EuroMemo Group (2014) *EuroMemorandum 2014: The Deepening Divisions in Europe and the Need for a Radical Alternative to EU Policies*. Available at: www.euromemo. eu/euromemorandum/euromemorandum_2014/index.html [accessed April 2, 2014].

Giesecke, J. (2009) "Socio-economic Risks of Atypical Employment Relationships: Evidence from the German Labour Market," *European Sociological Review*, 25(6): 629–46.

Grahl, J. and P. Teague (2004) "'The German model in danger," *Industrial Relations Journal*, 35(6): 557–73.

Guerrieri, P. and P. Esposito (2012) "Intra-European Imbalances, Adjustment, and Growth in the Eurozone," *Oxford Review of Economic Policy*, 28(3): 532–50.

Harding, R. and W. E. Paterson (eds) (2000) *The Future of the German Economy: An End to the Miracle?* (Manchester: Manchester University Press).

Hassel, A. (2012) "The Paradox of Liberalization: Understanding Dualism and the Recovery of the German Political Economy," *British Journal of Industrial Relations*, 52(1): 57–81.

Hutton, W. (1995) *The State We're In* (London: Cape).

Jackson, G. and A. Sorge (2012) "The Trajectory of Institutional Change in Germany, 1979–2009," *Journal of European Public Policy*, 19(8): 1146–67.

Katzenstein, P. J. (ed.) (1989) *Industry and Politics in West Germany: Toward the Third Republic* (Ithaca, NY: Cornell University Press).

Kinderman, D. (2005) "Pressure from Without, Subversion from Within: The Two-pronged German Employer Offensive," *Comparative European Politics*, 3(4): 432–63.

Krouwel, A., T. Eckert and Y. Kutiyski (2013) "The Polarisation of the German Party System in the 2013 Elections and the Disappearance of the FDP Explain the Country's Tortuous Coalition Negotiations," *EUROPP blog*, November 7. Available at: http://blogs.lse.ac.uk/europpblog/2013/11/07/the-polarisation-of-the-german-party-system-in-the-2013-elections-and-the-disappearance-of-the-fdp-explains-the-countrys-tortuous-coalition-negotiations [accessed March 28, 2014].

Kulish, N. (2010) "German Identity, Long Dormant, Reasserts Itself," *International Herald Tribune*, September 10.

Lapavitsas, C., *et al.* (2012) *Crisis in the Eurozone* (London: Verso).

Lehndorff, S. (2011) "Before the Crisis, in the Crisis, and Beyond: The Upheaval of Collective Bargaining in Germany," *Transfer*, 17(3): 341–54.

——(2012) "German Capitalism and the European Crisis: Part of the Solution or Part of the Problem?" in S. Lehndorff (ed.) *A Triumph of Failed Ideas: European Models of Capitalism in the Crisis* (Brussels: European Trade Union Institute, pp. 79–102).

Lütz, S. and D. Eberle (2008) "Varieties of Change in German Capitalism: Transforming the Rules of Corporate Control," *New Political Economy*, 13(4): 377–95.

Manow P. and E. Seils (2000) "Adjusting Badly: The German Welfare State, Structural Change, and the Open Economy," in F. W. Scharpf and V. A. Schmidt (eds)

Welfare and Work in the Open Economy. Vol. II: Diverse Responses to Common Challenges (Oxford: Oxford University Press, pp. 264–307).

Menz, G. (2005) "Old Bottles – New Wine: The New Dynamics of Industrial Relations," *German Politics*, 14(2): 196–207.

Milios, J. and D. P. Sotiropoulos (2010) "Crisis of Greece or Crisis of the Euro? A View from the European Periphery," *Journal of Balkan and Near Eastern Studies*, 12 (3): 223–40.

Minnerup, G. (1976) "West Germany since the War," *New Left Review*, 1(99): 3–44.

Nachtwey, O. and T. Spier (2007) "Political Opportunity Structures and the Success of the German Left Party in 2005," *Debatte*, 15(2): 123–54.

Pickshaus, K., H. Schmitthenner and H. J. Urban (eds) (2003) *Arbeiten ohne Ende: Neue Arbeitsverhältnisse und gewerkschaftliche Arbeitspolitik* (Hamburg: VSA).

Reisenbichler, A. and K. Morgan (2012) "From 'Sick Man' to 'Miracle': Explaining the Robustness of the German Labor Market During and After the Financial Crisis 2008–9," *Politics & Society*, 40(4): 549–79.

Rinne, U. and K. F. Zimmerman (2012) "Another Economic Miracle? The German Labor Market and the Great Recession," *IZA Journal of Labor Policy*, 1(3): 1–21.

Ryner, M. (2003) "Disciplinary Neo-liberalism, Regionalization and the Social Market in German Restructuring," in A. W. Cafruny, and M. Ryner (eds) *A Ruined Fortress? Neoliberal Hegemony and Transformation in Europe* (Lanham, MD: Rowman & Littlefield, pp. 201–27).

Sablowski, T. (2008) "Towards the Americanization of European Finance? The Case of Finance-led Accumulation in Germany," in L. Panitch, and M. Konings (eds) *American Empire and the Political Economy of Global Finance* (Basingstoke: Palgrave Macmillan, pp. 135–58).

Scharpf, F. W. and V. A. Schmidt (eds) (2000a) *Welfare and Work in the Open Economy. Vol. 1: From Vulnerability to Competitiveness* (Oxford: Oxford University Press).

——(eds) (2000b) *Welfare and Work in the Open Economy. Vol. II: Diverse Responses to Common Challenges* (Oxford: Oxford University Press).

Seifert, H. and H. Massa-Wirth (2005) "Pacts for Employment and Competitiveness in Germany," *Industrial Relations Journal*, 36(3): 217–40.

Solty, I. (2008) "The Historic Significance of the New German Left Party," *Socialism and Democracy*, 22(1): 1–34.

Statistisches Bundesamt (2013) *Statistisches Jahrbuch* (Wiesbaden: Statistisches Bundesamt).

Streeck, W. (1997) "German Capitalism: Does It Exist? Can It Survive?" *New Political Economy*, 2(2): 237–56.

——(2009) *Re-forming Capitalism: Institutional Change in the German Political Economy* (Oxford: Oxford University Press).

Streeck, W. and A. Hassel (2003) "The Crumbling Pillars of Social Partnership," *West European Politics*, 26(4): 101–24.

Thelen, K. (2001) "Varieties of Labor Politics in Developed Democracies," in P.A. Hall, and D. Soskice (eds) *Varieties of Capitalism: The Institutional Foundations of Comparative Advantage* (Oxford: Oxford University Press, pp. 71–103).

——(2004) *How Institutions Evolve: The Political Economy of Skills in Germany, Britain, the United States, and Japan* (Cambridge: Cambridge University Press).

——(2009) "Institutional Change in Advanced Political Economies," *British Journal of Industrial Relations*, 47(3): 471–98.

United Nations Conference on Trade and Development (2013) *UNCTAD Handbook of Stastistics, 2013* (New York and Geneva: United Nations).

Upchurch, M., G. Taylor and A. Mathers (2009) *The Crisis of Social Democratic Trade Unionism in Western Europe: The Search for Alternatives* (Farnham: Ashgate).

van der Wurff, R. (1993) "Neo-liberalism in Germany? The 'Wende' in perspective," in H. Overbeek (ed.) *Restructuring Hegemony in the Global Political Economy: the Rise of Transnational Neo-Liberalism in the 1990s* (London: Routledge, pp. 162–87).

8 The Japanese model dismantled in the multiple crises

Makoto Itoh

Introduction: characteristics of the past Japanese model

Japanese capitalism was recognized until the end of 1980s as the most efficient, ideal model in the world to be emulated by other countries.

The model was formed in the post-World War II recovery process and
greatly contributed to Japan's "miraculous" high economic growth for more
than two decades until 1973. The annual average real GDP growth rate in
Japan was 9.2 percent in twenty-two years since 1951.

The core of the Japanese model was characterized by a stable style of labor
management, which rested on lifelong employment (until about 55–60 years
old as an age limitation), seniority wage escalation system, and company-
based trade unions among big businesses. It helped growing firms to procure
increasing numbers of experienced workers, while promoting their loyalty and
corporative attitudes within firms.

Four conditions were also indispensable for the core of the Japanese model
to maintain rapid expansion.

First, availability of additional wage-workers existed in local agricultural
villages. By mobilizing wage-workers, the total number of Japanese wage-
workers increased by almost 20 million from 14.2 million in 1950 to 33.8
million in 1970. Most of them could easily adapt to new technologies, because
of the steadily rising level of education at the time. While the foregoing conditions continued to hold, Japanese manufacturing industries could maintain
an increase in real wages by a factor of 2.29 during the 1955–70 period, lower
than the increase in labor productivity by a factor of 3.99 in the same period.

Second, a wide range of industrial technologies were available mainly from
the US. By utilizing them, production and consumption of various consumer
durables of increasingly higher quality became generalized in Japan, eventually transforming the country into an automobile society. At the same time,
Japan became a high energy-consuming economy, particularly of oil. The
proportion of (mostly imported) oil reached 77.6 percent of total energy
consumption in 1973.

Third, an increased supply of cheap oil, below $2 US per barrel, was con-
tinuously available as a result of the expansion of the oil supply mainly from

the Middle East. Dollar prices of other imported primary products, such as iron ore, wood, cotton, and corn also remained low until the late 1960s.

Fourth, under the stable Bretton Woods international monetary system, a fixed exchange rate at ¥360 (yen) per US dollar, which initially worked against Japanese exporting industries, turned more and more favorable for them as their productivity and competitive edge strengthened.

In addition to these four conditions, the Japanese model of high economic growth continued with another noteworthy characteristic – growth dependent mainly on its domestic market thus keeping a relatively low rate of export dependency (export/GNP), to around 10 percent. It helped form a more egalitarian society, as it was commonly said that the entire Japanese population of 100 million was becoming middle class. Though such a statement was certainly exaggerated, it was really an exceptional period in Japan's long history where substantial improvement in the economic conditions of most rural areas was equal to those in urban areas due to positive effects of land reform after the war, price support for agricultural products (especially rice), and rising wage income from supplementary side jobs.

Together with an increasing consumer demand in urban wage-workers and investment demand, the rise of demand in rural agricultural families formed an element of the Japanese type of Fordist regime of accumulation (à la French Regulation approach) to generate domestic effective demand necessary to absorb expanding supply.

The Japanese model of high economic growth became untenable when the four conditions above began to deteriorate by the beginning of the 1970s.

As a result of the over-accumulation of capital in relation to easily available working population, the balance between demand and supply in the Japanese labor market became favorable towards workers similar to other advanced economies. The negotiating power of trade unions was thus strengthened. Nominal wages in Japanese manufacturing rose by 63 percent in 1970–73, enabling a 31 percent rise in real wages, more than the rise in productivity.

Simultaneously, the limit of the elastic supply of primary products was surpassed by rapid increase in demand in the world market, and caused a sharp rise in the prices of primary products. The first oil shock that quadrupled the price of crude oil was not an isolated event. Japanese terms of trade worsened by 32 percent between 1970 and 1974. Combined with the rise in real wages, this surely squeezed the profit rate in Japan as well as in other advanced countries.

Dominant US industrial technologies that produced a variety of electrical appliances and cars in large-scale factories were generalized across the advanced capitalist world by the end of 1960s allowing German and Japanese rivals to eventually catch up to and even surpass US manufacturing prowess. The Bretton Woods international monetary system rested on the US promise of stable convertibility of its dollars into gold. When the US's trade surplus became negative, Bretton Woods became untenable and broke down through repeated dollar crises. The resultant shift of the world monetary system to the system of floating exchange rates removed the international constraint of the supply of currency and credit for most of the advanced economies and induced vicious inflation along with rising prices of primary products and wages. Thus the inflationary crisis in 1973–75 initiated stagflation (stagnation with inflation) and a further series of repeated crises and prolonged period of restructuring in the world and Japan.

Keynesianism turned out to be ineffective at solving such inflationary crises. It was thus abandoned and, in major advanced economies by the beginning of the 1980s, replaced by neoliberal ideas about the effectiveness of market principles.

At the same time, information technologies (IT) became broadly introduced and increasingly sophisticated as a material ground for the restructuring of capitalist economies in many aspects (see Itoh 2000).

At the beginning of such a process of change and shift in the US toward neoliberal policies, at least until the end of 1980s, the Japanese model seemed to show its superior adaptability and strength. The Japanese annual average real economic growth rate in 1974–90 was 4.2 percent, higher than most advanced economies by 1–2 percent, although it declined to less than half of the previous growth rate until 1973. Despite the first and second oil shocks and the heavy pressure of the soaring yen from 360 yen a dollar in 1971 to 145 yen a dollar in 1990, Japanese manufacturing industries recovered and maintained trade surpluses, and continued to increase employment. Japanese average GDP per person became higher than that of the US in 1987, and gave the impression of "Japan as number one" in the world.

The core of the Japanese model of capitalism in corporative labor management was globally regarded as the strength of Japanese economy, facilitating streamlining of wage costs by means of factory automation (FA) and office automation (OA). The internationally competitive power of Japanese manufactured cars and other machineries owed much to lower failure rates in many products which was also due to loyal and diligent attitudes among Japanese workers.

The model dismantled through multiple crises

The annual real economic growth rate of Japan between 1991–2011 markedly declined to 0.9 percent from 4.2 percent between 1974 and 1990 (it had been 9.2 percent until 1973). This period is called the "lost two decades" for the Japanese economy. It demonstrates a failure of neoliberal restructuring to realize a desirably "rational and efficient" economic order predicated upon deregulated competitive market principles. A fundamental trend in restructuring capitalism since the inflationary crisis at the beginning of 1970s in Japan, as well as in many other advanced economies, has been in reforming and expanding a flexibly available cheaper labor force for capitalist firms in a competitive market.

In Marx's crisis theory, such a trend characterizes the phase of depression after cyclical crisis in the form of reformation of an "industrial reserve army" through strengthened competitive pressure to promote innovation with a rise in the composition of capital so as to reduce the portion of variable capital (to be invested in employment). Such a trend in our age of neoliberalism was very much prolonged and extended both domestically and at a global scale for decades to form a sort of super-long wave depression, containing multiple bubbles and crises.

In Japan, the seemingly successful decade of the 1980s ironically initiated such a trend by dismantling the previous model of Japanese capitalism.

Under the heavy pressure of depression, due to inflationary crises caused by the first and second oil shock, Japanese firms endeavored to "rationalize" (cut down) wage costs by IT automation technologies both in factories and offices. The Japanese model of company-based trade unions did not resist the introduction of new technologies in work places and helped to maintain Japan's industrial global competitive power despite the appreciation of the yen.

Both FA and OA enabled mobilization of more and more cheaper casual female part-timers into a wide range of work places. As the Japanese model of company-based trade unions used to organize mostly male regular workers, the combined casualization and feminization of the labor market weakened the social position of trade unions by reducing their organization rate from 35.4 percent in 1970 to 25.9 percent in 1989.

In addition, the privatization of three state-owned enterprises in 1985 – Japan National Railways (JNR), Nippon Telegraph and Telephone Public Corporation (NTT), and the Japan Tobacco and Salt Public Corporation – was a typical neoliberal policy which dealt a heavy blow against traditionally militant trade unions in the public sector.

All these changes resulted in a continuous trend that depressed consumer demand due to stagnant real wages despite rising labor productivity due to means of IT rationalization in most of the work places. Industrial capitalist enterprises slowed down or tended to avoid large-scaled investment in plant and equipment and became self-financed. In the meanwhile, the traditionally high propensity to save among Japanese households did not fall by much. Consequently, idle money capital increased in banks and other financial institutions and was easily mobilized for speculative financial trading.

Thus occasional recovery of the Japanese economy from continuously depressed effective demand required speculative bubbles in the stock exchange and real estate markets either domestically, like toward the end of 1980s, or internationally, like bubble booms that facilitated Japanese exports preceding the Asian crisis in 1987, the US new economy crisis in 2001, or the subprime crisis in 2007. Transformation and dismantling of the previous Japanese model was consistently promoted after the 1980s through such economic recoveries resting on bubbles and the crises after they burst.

In the "lost two decades" after the burst of a huge bubble in the Japanese economy, a series of structural changes followed the changes initiated in the 1980s.

Feminization of market labor was conspicuous. The proportion of female against male employees increased from 49 percent or less than one half in

1973, to 64 percent or nearly two-thirds in 1996, to 74 percent or almost three-quarters in 2010. A large number of female workers, over one-half of them in 2011, were in lowly paid casual jobs; many simply hired on a part-time basis. Such casualization with feminization of the labor market was clearly enabled by FA and OA, and was promoted also by global competitive pressures from lower wages in Asian and other developing countries where more and more of the Japanese multi-national firms shifted their factories and offices.

Multi-nationalization of Japanese manufacturing firms was accelerated by further appreciation of the yen to 79.75 yen a dollar in 1994, due to the NAFTA-induced monetary crisis, from 145 yen in 1990. Thus Japanese manufacturing firms could no longer continue to increase domestic employment. In fact, Japanese manufacturing firms began to reduce the absolute number of employees in the secondary (manufacturing) industry by more than 30 percent from 1993 to 2010. The proportion of employees in tertiary (service) industries grew from about 50 percent in 1973, to 60 percent in 1995 to more than 70 percent in 2010, showing rapid industrial hollowing out.

Along with the foregoing dramatic change in the configuration of Japan's economy, casualization of male workers also occurred, and by 2010 the proportion of casual employment in total male employment also increased to over 20 percent. The deregulation of labor laws in the 1990s facilitated the casualization of labor by legitimizing casualization in more and wider areas. In total nearly one-third of Japan's employees are now in unstable and lowly paid casual jobs. While housewives became wage earners often in lowly paid casual jobs, the reproduction of labor-power required the work of both adult family members, as the value of labor-power was also simultaneously reduced; a trend Marx (1867) had observed back in the earlier epoch of capitalism he studied. Trade unions could not effectively fight against such trends as their organization rate declined further to around 18 percent.

Thus, the core of the previous model of Japanese capitalism in stable corporative-labor management was largely dismantled under neoliberal restructuring. Real wages evidenced no rise despite increases in labor productivity, unlike the past Fordist regime of accumulation where real wages tended to rise in tandem with productivity. The gap was utilized not for the welfare of workers, but to cope with economic crises and pressure of appreciation of the yen for capitalist firms.

A relatively egalitarian economic order in the past, the Japanese model radically reversed into a widely unequal order. The ratio of income disparity between the top 20 percent of households against the lowest 20 percent greatly increased to more than a factor of 10. According to Tachibanaki (1998), Japan's Gini coefficient before tax rose from 0.349 to 0.439 during 1980–92. Japan's Gini coefficient became greater than in the US, which is a notoriously unequal society among advanced economies.

Although, in the process of neoliberal globalization of capitalism, advanced economies more or less experienced a similar trend toward a wider disparity among households as well as stagnant or even deteriorating real wages for the majority of workers, the Japanese case displayed a remarkable reversal from the previous egalitarian corporative model of growth. Through the prolonged deflationary "lost two decades" since the 1990s, even regular workers in Japanese big businesses could not expect a raise in real wages in spite of increases in physical labor productivity. Even their employment became insecure in the face of repetitive crises.

As casualization of labor extended to include male workers, the increase of the working-poor became a social problem. In 2002 the number of households below the level of income qualifying (as a legal possibility actually difficult to realize) them to receive public assistance (in the social security system) rose to 11.05 million or 22.3 percent of the total households, in which households having any employed members (namely working poor households) numbered 6.2 million. Although recipients of social security support had increased to 2.13 million by 2012, it is estimated that they are just 15–20 percent of the number of households that substantially need to receive public support at their actual income level (Itoh 2013).

Feminization of the labor market mobilized masses of women to workplaces without social arrangements (either by the state or companies) to facilitate marriage, childbirth, and child raising and, together with severe working conditions, caused a sharp decline in the birth rate per woman in Japan from 2.05 in 1973 to 1.26 in 2005. As a result, total population in Japan began to decrease from 128 million in 2008, and is estimated to be halved by the end of this century. Thus we are witnessing a rapidly aging society with fewer children. The average number of the working population of 20–64 years old who must socially support an aged person beyond 65 years old declined from 7.7 in 1975 to 2.6 persons in 2010. It will soon become below 2 persons after 2020.

Such a demographic trend is depressing for the future of economic life, as pension schemes will inevitably be cut back and, simultaneously, the burden of maintaining a pension scheme will fall on the shoulders of the working population.

The cost of maintaining a certain level of welfare policies (such as social security, public health insurance, and pension schemes) in a rapidly aging society, as well as repetitive public expenditures as emergency economic policies in the face of stagnant tax income through the continuously depressed decades, increased public debt. Paradoxically, although neoliberalism in Japan started initially by stressing the necessity to resolve the state budget crisis at the beginning of the 1980s, public debt did not decrease but continuously increased under neoliberal governments. The ratio of long-term state debt against GDP rose from 38.3 percent in 1980 to 75.6 percent in 1997. The ratio of total public debt including local governments to GDP was over 100 percent already by 1997, much beyond the same ratios in most of the other advanced countries. It reached 200 percent in 2010, and is still moving up beyond 210 percent in 2012.

The public budget crisis thus deepened. Neoliberal inspired reductions of the highest marginal income tax rate from 70 percent before 1986 to 40 percent, and of the corporate tax rate from 43.3 percent before 1984 to 30 percent after 1990, in combination with the reduction of inheritance tax in favor of the wealthy class of persons and capitalist firms, were political factors that worsened the debt crisis. In contrast, the introduction of a consumer tax of 3 percent in 1989, increased to 5 percent in 1997, hit the mass of working people and socially weaker persons. However, it could not be utilized effectively enough to solve the Japanese debt crisis of the state.

Generating such contrasting impacts of tax reforms, the deepening public budget crisis under neoliberalism was clearly an important factor that shifted the economic burden more to the majority of working people, and spread a sense of disillusion regarding the role of the state, in the face of real economic difficulties in their lives. The prolonged depression of domestic consumer demand in Japan has surely been related to such uneasy conditions of the majority of working people.

In sum, the Japanese model of capitalism under neoliberalism has been formed by dismantling and reversing the old model in the era of high economic growth.

The remarkably high economic growth was turned into a continuously stagnant economy with almost zero growth. The egalitarian and stable socio-economic trend with corporative relations between workers and capitalists in a sort of Fordist regime changed into a widely uneven and unstable economic model with an increasing number of working-poor. Even simple reproduction of the population became impossible due to the declining birth rate. The public budget crisis continuously deepened much more than most of the other advanced economies in comparison to the relatively sound state budget in the old Japanese model.

Tentative attempt with a new social democracy

The subprime financial crisis that occurred after the speculative housing boom in the US surfaced in 2007 turned into a world economic crisis after the failure of Lehman Brothers, a big investment bank. It spread to European banks and other financial institutions because they bought and held a large part of US mortgage backed securities (MBS) sold abroad. It was thus natural to see that the Euro crisis occurred in the process of the world crisis.

In comparison, Japanese banks and other financial institutions were relatively immune from the wave of crisis and remained stable, as they tended to avoid risky speculative securities after the process of mergers and restructuring among them in the lost two decades following the collapse of the huge bubble in Japan. Nevertheless, Japanese real GDP declined to negative 1.0 percent in 2008 and further to negative 5.5 percent in 2009, wider than in the US or in the Euro area. A riddle remained as to why the Japanese real economy suffered most among the three major advanced economies, while maintaining a relatively stable financial sector in the process of global crisis originating from the financial system.

The riddle must be deciphered from the nature of the economic recovery preceding the crisis. Although the Japanese government was proud of "the historically longest economic recovery" since 2002, the general public used to call it a recovery without actual feeling effects of such. In fact the real growth rate in Japan remained weak, usually below 2 percent a year (excepting 2.3 percent in 2003) with continuously stagnant domestic demand. As a result, Japanese recovery during the period between 2002 and 2007 substantially depended on the growth of export demand by 81 percent, while domestic consumer demand grew by only 0.9 percent in these years.

By expanding exports, most of the Japanese corporations could increase their earnings. Total current profit of Japanese corporations went up from 33.3 trillion yen in 2002 to 60.5 trillion yen in 2007, or by 82 percent. Toyota earned a record amount of current profit of 2.2 trillion yen both in 2006 and 2007.

In contrast to such an increase in profit, however, the average nominal salary per worker continuously fell from 351 thousand yen a month in 2001 to 330 thousand yen in 2007. Thus the labor share (labor costs/value added) in Japanese corporations also declined from 75.1 percent in 2001 to 69.3 percent in 2006.

These contrasting trends in corporate earnings and wages clearly demonstrate that such a basic tendency in a capitalist economy typically occurs in Japan under neoliberalism. Related with a series of other socio-economic problems such as industrial hollowing out, casualization and feminization of the market labor, a rapidly aging society that is experiencing depopulation, increasing inequality in income distribution, and a deepening public budget crisis, even in the recovery phase since 2002, the Japanese economy was characterized by structural fragility and stagnant domestic demand. Consequently, when the leading factor in the expansion of exports was largely reduced in the global subprime crisis beginning in the US, that ended the US consumer boom, which had been based on inflating value of housing, the Japanese economy was substantially damaged.

The subprime world economic crisis showed the failure of the neoliberal path to restructuring not just in US capitalism as its driving center, but also in Japan with its own specific features.

The political changes that occurred in 2009 in the US and in Japan to Democratic Party (DP) governments revealed the general public's expectation of "change." Following President Obama's so-called New Deal policies – green recovery and other contemporary social democratic policies including public health insurance reform – the Japanese Democratic Party government initially tried similar New Deal type policies. As a whole, new policies were called "from concrete to human beings."

For instance, an eco-point system was implemented to give purchasers of more energy-efficient models of home electric appliances, cars, or houses, certain sums of vouchers to be used in local shops in order to encourage the demand and supply of ecological goods in line with green recovery policies.

Another example of Japanese new social democratic policy was child allowance. This allowance distributed 13 thousand yen monthly per child below the age of 15 with a plan to increase it twice in order to mitigate the sharp decline in the number of children. Since this child allowance was given unconditionally, i.e., without a means test, the policy was broadly regarded as an initial test case for basic income in Japan. In effect, the Japanese average birth rate per woman actually recovered a little from 1.26 in 2005 to 1.39 in 2011–12.

Although conventional Keynesian reflationary policy in the form of public construction was repeated during Japan's lost two decades as emergency economic policy, costing a hundred trillion yen in total, it was not successful. The multiplier effect was reduced as long as automated heavy constructing machinery reduced the employment effect. A change of type of reflationary policy "from concrete to human beings" such as new child allowance and eco-point system was attractive and encouraged the Japanese majority to expect a more reliable path for the future.

Therefore the new policy clearly worked effectively to revive domestic consumer demand, and helped to restore Japan's real economic growth rate by 9 percent from negative 5.5 percent in 2009 to 4.5 percent in 2010. In the US the growth rate also increased by 5.5 percent to 2.4 percent in 2010. Against the general neoliberal view that social democratic reflationary national economic policies became ineffective in globalized economies, these experiences provided powerfully opposing evidence. Similarly they demonstrated against the conventional Keynesian belief in the reflationary effect of public construction or military spending; instead public support for human welfare as well as an ecologically friendly future must be much more promising as economic recovery policies in our age.

However, once the acute economic crisis was over, DP governments both in the USA and Japan were pushed to tone down the progressive social democratic policies by neoliberal pressure from business circles and opposition political parties under the pretext of worsened budget crisis of the state. In Japan the eco-point system was mostly closed down toward the end of 2010 as initially planned, and the child allowance was going to be amended and reduced for the next fiscal year. Thus the general expectation for 2011 was another slowdown of the Japanese economy.

Then the great earthquake and giant Tsunami that rocked Japan on March 11th, 2011 and the resulting disastrous accident at the Fukushima atomic power plant affected directly Japan's North-Eastern areas and indirectly the entire Japanese economy. The impact of the Euro crisis, beginning in Greece and followed in the summer of the same year as a sort of afterbirth of the subprime world crisis, also hit the Japanese economy especially its exporting industries due to relatively appreciated yen rates. Under such multiple shocks and crises, the Japanese economy experienced another fall in its real growth rate below zero to minus 0.8 percent in 2011.

Although the Japanese growth rate recovered to around 2 percent in 2012, it was still feeble and unstable due to political friction with China over the Senkaku islands in the East China Sea. The government was shaken by the difficulty of reconstructing devastated areas, and could not answer to the demand made by many citizens for an anti-nuclear energy policy consistent with extension of a green recovery strategy.

These situations dealt a heavy blow to the Democratic Party government in a form of disappointment among many people and induced its defeat in the general election for the House of Representatives in December 2012 followed by the restoration of the Liberal Democratic Party (LDP) government.

Thus, the attempt to restructure a twenty-first-century model of social democracy after the failure of neoliberal capitalism did not last long in Japan.

Why? On the one hand, unlike the New Deal in the 1930s, New Deal in our age in the US and Japan failed to set up a new type of Wagner Act, so as to re-strengthen cooperative workers' trade unions and other cooperative social organizations as a social ground to support its governance.

On the other hand, global financial capital survived in major advanced countries and still retained a strong material basis for neoliberalism. Although the subprime world crisis signified the immanent self-destructive contradictions within the hypertrophied speculative global system of financialized capitalism, the system was not abolished but rather maintained by the effects of rescue operations by the states for banks and other financial institutions. International attempts to reduce the risk of banks and other financial institutions failing in the future were limited mainly to regulations that required safer preparation and increases of reserves did not reform the existing neoliberal framework for global capitalism itself. Against this background, and without more powerful social organization to support them, tentative attempts at renewed social democratic economic policies were difficult to maintain in Japan (as well as in the US and Euro zone) after an acute phase of crisis due to renewed pressures from the domestic business circle and from international pro-business political coordination.

Is Abenomics a reliable model?

The set of economic policies which the premier Shinzō Abe and his LDP cabinet have implemented since 2013 is called Abenomics. Abenomics aims at revival of the Japanese economy from deflationary stagnation, and is composed of the following "three arrows": mobile fiscal policy, bold monetary policy, and a growth strategy to induce private investment.

The first arrow of fiscal policy began with a large-scale 2012 supplementary budget of 10.3 trillion yen, followed by the historically largest 92.6 trillion yen fiscal budget of 2013. The fiscal budget of 2014 is further increased to 96 trillion yen. In those budgets, expenditure on public works is continuously expanded, together with military (defense) spending, clearly exhibiting the conservative color of the cabinet. In contrast, social security aid, public support for child allowance, as well as for senior persons' medical costs are reduced. Thus it is generally characterized as an economic recovery policy that invests in "concrete" rather than human beings, or a return to the old LDP tradition by reversing the previous DP government's social democratic stance.

In April 2014 the consumption tax was raised to 8 percent from 5 percent, and the plan is to raise it further to 10 percent in the next year. At the same time, corporate tax was reduced.

Evidently business-centered expansionary fiscal and tax policies must increase the burden of cumulative public debt by placing it on the shoulders of the Japanese working class and the more vulnerable persons like aged pensioners.

The second arrow of monetary policy started when the government forced the Bank of Japan (BOJ) to establish an inflation target of 2 percent per year. The newly appointed governor of the BOJ, H. Kuroda, announced an increase in base-money which commercial banks have in a form of reserve balance at BOJ through a large-scaled purchasing operation. The balance of Japanese banks' base-money is planned to expand to 138 trillion yen (already a historically highest proportion against GDP, beyond the proportion in the US or Euro zone) to 270 trillion yen. Under the current reserve deposit system, the due balance of deposits which commercial banks should have in BOJ is around 6–7 trillion yen. Base-money supplied beyond this amount must be in idle funds used for lending.

It is dubious, however, whether such a large volume of idle loanable funds can be sufficiently lent out to industrial business activity and successfully solve continuous deflation. Already in the lost two decades, in Japanese financial markets, the interest rate was lowered nearly to zero, without a substantial effect on the revival of the real economy. Contemporary Keynesian advisors to Abenomics seem to believe that the effect of an increase in the supply of base money cause a fall in the exchange rate of yen (in accordance with the quantity theory of money) in favor of exporting industries, and (combined with the announcement effect of the inflation target) to induce a general expectation for inflation, and a rise in share prices in the stock exchange market (Hamada 2013; Iwata 2013).

Initially Abenomics's monetary policy impressed foreign and domestic speculative investors on their expectation for yen rate fall and share price rise from November 2012 when the policy was announced for the general election in the next month. Especially from April 2013 when the BOJ began to ease the supply of money, the Japanese Nikkei average share price rose sharply to 15627 yen in May 2013 from 8665 yen in the middle of November 2012 (about 80 percent), and the yen weakened against the dollar to 103 yen per dollar from less than 80 yen, a change of around 30 percent. The fall in the yen rate actually worked well to facilitate and restore the profits of Japanese exporting companies, as they had previously suffered from the appreciation of the yen against the dollar and Euro during the subprime and Euro crisis.

Though such a fall in the yen probably includes also a sort of normalization effect on the part of the dollar and Euro after an acute crisis, we have to admit that the monetary policy of Abenomics impelled the yen to fall in rapid order.

Facilitated by export expansion, and combined with increased trade in domestic real estate and consumer durables markets by purchasers intending to avoid the rise in consumer tax planned for the next year, the real growth rate in the Japanese economy for the first two quarters of 2013 was pushed up above 4 percent in the annual term. However, the effects of Abenomics faltered after the summer as yen exchange rates no longer continue to fall. Japan's real economic growth rate in annual terms declined to 0.9 percent and further to 0.7 percent in the third and fourth quarter of 2013. GDP deflator as a price index still remains deflationary, far from the inflation target of 2 percent, reflecting the stagnant wage income and domestic consumer demand as a whole.

In addition, most private economic research institutes and economists predict a considerable negative impact of the increase in consumer tax from April 2014 on real growth rate (such as by minus 5 percent in the annual term), including reaction to moved up purchases of houses and consumer durables in order to avoid the tax increase in advance.

Thus, the effects of the first and second arrows of Abenomics in Keynesian types of fiscal and monetary policies are not sure or reliable, though they have short-term speculative impact. The resulting achievements do not seem to be superior to those of the emergency economic policies in the two "lost" decades.

The third arrow represented growth strategies to induce private investment, and was expected to propose promising new ideas beyond conventional Keynesian policies in the past. However, in the process of planning them within the cabinet or in a council for industrial competitive power, arguments do not seem to successfully propose attractive fresh ideas for new industrial growth paths. Bureaucrats and politicians tend to argue for protection of the vested interests of particular industries and are apt to neglect the stability and welfare of working class people. The third arrow is not popular but rather disappointing to the general public. And there is growing international perception that the growth strategy of Abenomics is stalling. Nevertheless a key point in the growth strategies of Abenomics lies in further deregulation of employment so as to help capitalist firms to utilize more casual workers by revising employment insurance schemes, and encouraging a limited term employment system, so as to strengthen the competitive powers of Japanese industries. This represents the neoliberal capitalist-firms-centered character of Abenomics.

The same neoliberal character of Abenomics is also shown in positive attitudes to join the Trans Pacific Partnership (TPP) negotiations to set up a free market zone with the US and the other twelve countries that excludes China and many other Asian countries. TPP is also in accord with the interests of big exporting businesses and would add to the competitive pressures on the working conditions of the majority of employees and also sacrifice Japanese agriculture as well as rural areas, food security, and the social health insurance system by opening free markets for US big businesses under protection of Investors and State Dispute (ISD) codes. TPP may also work to suffocate economic cooperation with China and other Asian non-member countries.

Thus Abenomics could not and will not be able to present a reliable path for the recovery of the Japanese economy. It is not founded upon synthetic analyses of structural causes of multiple crises and difficulties, which have forced continuous Japanese economic decay under neoliberalism. Actually it basically accedes to the neoliberal belief in competitive market principles, especially in the field of employment relations, so as to assist capitalist firms in utilizing flexible and cheaper casual workers. So long as wage income is thus generally repressed along with neoliberal inspired cuts to social security, the difficulties of the working poor and other new forms of poverty must worsen, as well as increasing instability of economic life of all working class people.

Keynesian-like fiscal and monetary policies in the first and second arrows of Abenomics, just as the repeated past Japanese emergency economic policies since 1980s, are thus combined with continuous neoliberal labor market policies, so as to form a theoretically inconsistent, peculiar, and unfair policy mix. In the view of the European and American left against neoliberal austerity policies, occasionally Japanese contemporary Keynesian policies are favorably referred (e.g. Boyer 2013; Harvey 2011). However, we have to note that Keynesian policy devices are actually utilizable not only in the social democratic political vein, but also in combination with conservative neoliberalism one-sidedly in favor of business interests and wealthier people. This must be a new historical experience on the varieties of capitalism in our age, though it may surely be against Keynes' (1936) original intensions that favored the economic interests of working class people.

However, the Japanese variety of capitalism with such a policy mix, as shown clearly in Abenomics, after multiple crises, cannot be a considered a trustworthy model for the future. As we have seen, Abenomics's effects are limited to recovery and economic growth only for the first half of a year after initial implementation. Reaction to a rise in consumer tax and the risk of cumulative public debt worry the majority of Japanese workers and socially weaker people because they are the ones who will shoulder the increasing public burden, instability, and economic difficulties.

Alternative strategies required

As we have seen, the Japanese model of capitalism with egalitarian tendencies and high economic growth was dismantled in the 1980s under neoliberalism. The resulting decline of Japanese capitalism with almost continuous zero growth rates through the lost two decades characterized by multiple crises, deepening budget crisis of the state, increased inequality and instability in a rapidly aging society, is difficult to resolve and leaves most working people with a sense of dismay for the future.

Although the Democratic Party managed to galvanize the public and was successful during the short period after the subprime financial crisis, it could not establish a new model of capitalism. The socio-economic basis of neoliberalism in the regime of globally financialized capitalism survived the crisis. The devastation brought by the huge earthquake, tsunami, and the Euro crisis as an after-birth of subprime financial crisis against the Japanese economy, shook the DP and gave way to the restoration of a conservative LDP government. Thus neoliberalism was revived as Abenomics that favored globalized big businesses in the form of a peculiar policy mix including Keynesian devices.

In this regard, Japan's historical experience is not a model to be followed by other capitalist countries, although it is still occasionally referred to as such in the Western world, especially from the point of view of working class people. The twenty-first-century models of social democracy and socialism should be rebuilt against neoliberal austerity policies for the future of working people in the world as well as in Japan.

In retrospect, twentieth-century models of social democracy, including the past Japanese model in the era of high economic growth, was formed through competition against the twentieth-century model of socialism represented by the USSR. The collapse of Soviet-style socialism strengthened neoliberalism's dismantling of the egalitarian social democratic models of capitalism. Although the orthodox Soviet-type of socialism tended to criticize social democracy as revisionism unable to overcome capitalism, we should reflect also that twentieth-century models of both social democracy and socialism had similar egalitarian goals in favor of working class people and a similar statist tendency in common, and co-existed mutually as rivals by strengthening each other.

We now need to ask the following question: In order to remodel social democracy and socialism against neoliberalism, what kinds of alternative strategies are desirable and required? A series of promising possibilities seem to be, in my view, represented by recent attempts by Democratic Party governments both in the US and Japan. I shall explain in the following four points below (see also Itoh 2014).

First, not only in order to overcome neoliberalism, but also to prepare a desirable future of socialism described as an "association of free individuals" (Marx 1867), twenty-first-century models of socialism, unlike twentieth-century models, should not reject but cooperate with new forms of social democracy at least in the advanced countries. There probably are differences of opinion on this matter among Marxian socialist political economists in the world. This point still seems worth further arguments not in order to divide, but to try to understand different stances, seeking cooperation as far and broadly as possible.

Second, green recovery must be one of the pillars for twenty-first-century targets for both socialism and social democracy. It can easily gather popular support of an increasing number of people in the world who are concerned with and want effective action against the deepening ecological crisis. Ecological issues are clearly not at all solvable by unregulated, neoliberal capitalism. Twentieth-century models of socialism and social democracy also generally neglected this problem. From our recent disastrous experience of the nuclear power plant accident at Fukushima, green recovery strategies should extend to an energy policy of breaking with nuclear power generation.

Third, basic income (BI) is another possibility as an alternative strategy against neoliberalism. In Japan the new type of child allowance was welcomed as an initial attempt to introduce a germ of BI without a means test. It is generally argued that BI can overcome the deadlock of inefficient and dysfunctional bureaucracies facing increasing numbers of working poor, single mothers, and isolated elderly persons. Also for twenty-first-century models of socialism, BI may serve as a desirable policy device to guarantee individual economic freedom (Parijs 1995). In so far as twenty-first-century models of socialism are based upon public ownership of the major means of production and are often combined with (socialized) markets, these models need to incorporate social security systems sufficiently beyond the narrow limitations in capitalism. (This remark should be applied to China, so long as her Communist Party government insists on constructing a socialist market economy). Just as O. Lange (1936–37) conceived of a kind of BI in his classic model of market socialism, based upon the public ownership of means of production, all members of society are qualified to receive a social dividend unconditionally.

Fourth, traditional social democracy and twentieth-century models of socialism tended to rely on the universal interest of organized workers in the form of trade unions, and the redistributing and regulating social functions of nation states. As we are witnessing the weakening of the socio-economic power of both trade unions and states with the globalization of capitalism, we need to recognize varieties of socially cooperative organizations such as workers' cooperatives, NGOs, and NPOs among others as subjects driving social change. For many of them, local communities are more important grass-roots democratic spaces in which to work together, rather than directly the whole nation state. In this regard, twenty-first-century models of movements for social democracy and socialism have to pay sufficient attention to peoples' desire for more decentralized political and economic democracy.

Attempts at reciprocal aid in the forms of organizing local currencies and various cooperatives including workers' coops are potentially very important and should be promoted from the view of alternative strategies for new types of social democracy and socialism against neoliberalism.

Obviously such attempts to reactivate local economies must move in a direction of more local production and local consumption, and such a direction also contributes to the energy economy for green recovery. Conversely, green recovery strategies that promote soft energy paths must then help smaller-sized production of energy and economic activities in local communities. If realized, BI would be useful not just as a more egalitarian income (re-)distribution strategy, but also in spontaneous grass-root cooperative community movements.

As the actual experience of the capitalist economy in Japan after the sub-prime crisis is not steady and desirable, especially from the view of the majority of workers and socially weaker persons, alternative strategies are strongly required and need to be discussed. Further, international intellectual cooperation to discuss and work out desirable and promising strategies is highly desirable.

References

(Titles in square brackets are author's translation from Japanese.)

Boyer, R. (2013) *Overcoming the Institutional Mismatch of the Euro-Zone* (in Japanese, Tokyo: Fujiwara-shoten).
Harvey, D. (2011) *The Enigma of Capital and the Crises of Capitalism* (paperback edition, London: Profile Books.).
Itoh, M. (2000) *The Japanese Economy Reconsidered* (Houndmills: Palgrave).
——(2013) [*Why Japanese Economy Declined*] (Tokyo: Heibonsha).
——(2014) "Political Economy for 21st Century Models of Social Democracy and Socialism – Following up the Issues Raised by David Harvey," *World Review of Political Economy*, 4–4.
Iwata, K.(2013) [*Reflation is Correct*] (Tokyo: PHP Kenkyusho).
Keynes, J. M.(1936) *The General Theory of Employment, Interest and Money* (London: Macmillan).
Hamada, K. (2013) [*The USA Knows Japanese Economic Recovery*] (Tokyo: Koudannsha).
Lange, O. (1936, 1937) "On the Economic Theory of Socialism," *Review of Economic Studies*, October, February.
Marx, K. (1867) *Capital,* vol. 1. (London: Penguin, NLR, 1976).
Parijs, P. van (1995) *Real Freedom for All* (Oxford: Clarendon Press).
Tachibanaki, T. (1998) [*Japanese Economic Inequality*] (Tokyo: Iwanami-shoten).

Part 3

Crisis, austerity, and the extinction of capitalism?

9 A phase of transition away from capitalism

Robert Albritton

Introduction

Marx uses the concept "pure" as in "pure capitalism" at least fifty times in his later economic writings (*The Grundrisse, Capital, Theories of Surplus Value*), and there are many passages in which he refers to levels of analysis (though not using this term) that are more concrete than the abstract theory of pure capitalism. Following the work of Japanese political economists Kozo Uno (1980) and Thomas Sekine (1997), I believe it is possible to find material in Marx's later economic writings that can be utilized to build three levels of analysis: a theory of pure capitalism (i.e. a commodity-economic logic), a theory of phases of capitalism (mid-range theory), and the analysis of history. The theory of pure capitalism assumes that capital as a commodity logic is totally in charge of economic life, and with this assumption, the theory of pure capitalism's aim is to expose capital's deep structures that outline abstractly the main tendencies of capitalism that are always present, though their institutional manifestations in history may vary. Some of the central tendencies theorized at the level of pure capitalism include the following: the maximization of profit, the expansion of capital, the centrality of industrial capital, the exploitation of labor, the expansion of commodification, the speed up of the turnover of capital, and periodic crises (this list is not exhaustive).

These structural tendencies that are grounded in the theory of pure capitalism are quite abstract, and though they may form the basis of Marxian political economy, a mid-range theory of phases of capitalist development can help us understand the sequence of dominant or hegemonic forms of profit-maximization in different phases of capitalist development. While this is certainly open for debate, I believe that the historical sequence of phases that makes the most sense is first, a putting-out system (golden age between 1700–1750) combined with quasi-capitalist agriculture (Uno refers to this phase as "mercantilism," but this term can be misleading, since Uno means by it primarily the role played by merchants in capitalist putting-out production and not a perspective that focuses primarily on circulation as opposed to production), second, a competitive factory system (liberalism: golden age between 1840–1865), third, monopolistic corporations (imperialism: golden age between 1870–1914), and fourth, the mass production of consumer durables (golden age between 1947–70). There is debate amongst Unoists particularly over this last phase, which I have labelled "consumerism" (not to displace the primacy of production, but to emphasize the importance of mass consumption compared to earlier phases). I believe that the phase of consumerism had its golden age between 1947 and 1970 in the US, when unemployment was low and growth along with the rate of profit was high. I don't mean to suggest that this phase suddenly collapsed after 1970, but rather that it began to run into more and more problems that with the rise of global warming now seem increasingly to be insuperable, at least for capitalism.

Many refer to the current phase of capitalism as "neo-liberalism" because of its tendencies towards deregulation and privatization, and while there is some truth to this, it can be taken to mean that capitalism is becoming more capitalist or more successful as a phase of capitalist development. Contrary to such perspectives, I view neo-liberalism less as a new phase of capitalist development than as a desperate attempt to legitimize a dying capitalism by trying to enact ideals of its confident youth, ideals that were always filled with serious contradictions even at the height of nineteenth-century liberalism, and that are totally inappropriate to the current state of the global economy. Therefore, in this paper I will argue that the current phase of capitalism is most accurately seen as a phase of transition away from capitalism.[1]

The phase of transition from feudalism to capitalism lasted several centuries. But currently there are almost continual uprisings around the world, and future generations are likely to become yet more angry as they learn of the extent to which the present powers have lied about the seriousness of global warming, the exhaustion of the earth's resources, the growth of inequality, and about the lack of alternatives to capitalism. My argument in this essay is that we are now fairly early in a phase of transition away from capitalism, a transition that may end up being the most radical in all of human history.

If we are still early in the phase of transition away from capitalism, it is still worthwhile to theorize at a mid-range level to focus on the more enduring and causally powerful structures of capitalism, even though these structures lack the relative stability and success of the dominant structures in a proper phase of capitalism. In the near future changes in existing structures may start to occur at a more rapid pace, since there is no core mode of accumulation (i.e. a phase proper) that can expansively reproduce itself and provide a model for the rest of the world.

The United States is clearly the country that is most capitalist and most hegemonic in the post-World War II phase of capitalism. Therefore I focus on the United States to draw out aspects of its current economic and social practices, practices that indicate more the crumbling of capitalism's final phase (i.e. consumerism) than any relatively stable and expanded reproduction. While many consumer durables were important in the golden age of consumerism, the automobile stands out. It is likely the most popular commodity ever produced, and it is widely owned in advanced and advancing capitalist countries. Unfortunately, it uses up more of the earth's resources than any other commodity, and it contributes enormously to global warming. It turns out to be one of those deadly addictions that humanity must find ways to largely leave behind. The auto industry is an industry that desperately needs to be cut back, and yet given its centrality to capitalism and its power in the halls of government, this will be difficult to achieve. Indeed, recent experience suggests that the US government will bail out bankrupt auto companies precisely at a time when the global industry needs to be shrunk and consolidated.

In the current phase of crumbling consumerism/capitalism, much industrial production has either become highly automated, or, where labor is still an important input (as in clothing), it has shifted to low-wage countries.[2] As a result, high-income countries and their corporations depend more and more on monopoly rents, financial casinos, retailing cheap consumer goods manufactured elsewhere, and government handouts in order to survive. In recent studies the concept "financialization" has been utilized to understand the incredible expansion of debt and the betting on future prices known as "casino capitalism." And while capitalism has always had a global thrust, modern technologies have multiplied this thrust, both to exploit the cheapest possible labor and to find the cheapest land and resources. State intervention has always occurred to varying degrees in the history of capitalism, but an important characteristic of this phase of transition is a huge expansion of state intervention in order to deal with issues of corporate welfare, economic crises, and "perceived" security issues at home and abroad.

The line between mid-range theory and historical analysis is not sharp. Mid-range theory is more structural because it attempts to understand the basic tendencies of capital in terms of phase-specific dominant types that reproduce and expand. In an earlier book (Albritton 1991) I mainly focused on the dominant social forms that organize production, on degrees and types of commodification, and on struggles over major ideological, political, and legal forms. So, for example, following Uno and Sekine, I would ask questions such as the following: What are the dominant use-values and how is their production organized? Or to what extent is labor-power commodified and what sorts of ideological, political, and legal forms are used to try to contain labor's struggles against capital and maintain the dominant mode of accumulation?

Historical analysis may be broad in time and place or quite specific, and our understanding of history can be significantly advanced by the use of the two higher levels of analysis to clarify the relative causal power of interacting historical processes. Its main difference with mid-range theory is that it is less structural and focuses more on agency and change, or can focus on concrete or local detail. It is particularly important to strategic thinking, which requires a good understanding of the specificities of particular conjunctures, specificities that can bolster the most effective demands in mobilizing people.

This paper will not deal with strategic questions, but it will to some extent mix the three levels of analysis.

Should it turn out that years from now, when humanity looks back, and sees that at the beginning of the twenty-first century we were near the beginning of a transitional phase away from capitalism, then the perspective being offered here might be largely confirmed. Until then, it must remain at least to some extent speculative though possibly more accurate than some other perspectives. For instance, if we have an accurate grasp of capitalism's tendencies, we can predict with some confidence that it has not been able and will not be able to solve the human or ecological problems it faces. A phase of transition will be a phase of multiple crises and multiple forms of struggle linked to capitalism's core features such that in trying to deal with one crisis, capitalism will have a tendency to worsen others in ways that will further undermine the efforts to deal with the original crises. In short, the crises will tend to be increasingly mutually exacerbating in the long run, and as they converge, so will the people who are victimized by them, people who will become clearer and clearer about alternatives that will advance toward a more egalitarian, caring, just, democratic, free, non-violent, and sustainable world.

In this essay I want to focus on a small selection of very significant problems that are reaching crisis proportions. In particular, I want to address the decline of the welfare state and the burgeoning of health problems in the US. In relation to the decline of the welfare state I will address issues attendant to the rise of the prison industrial complex, military industrial complex, and corporate welfare. In relation to health problems in the US I want to address issues attendant to relations between prisons, the military, welfare state, and health, diet, and toxins in the environment. In the conclusion I will include a brief consideration of the growing global ecological crises.

The US welfare state in decline

The prison industrial complex

The development of the welfare state has been a major support for the legitimacy of the capitalist state going back as far as Bismarck in late nineteenth-century Germany, but it has particularly expanded since World War II. The legitimacy of capitalist states has been enhanced by offering public funding for education, research and development, health care, and welfare. These policies seemed to advance equality by supporting those who needed care or needed jobs. In Scandinavia the welfare state advanced to a level that many saw as a significant first step towards democratic socialism. In the US, the richest capitalist country in the world, the welfare state has run into serious problems, and it is not surprising to witness similar problems arising in many other states. Increasingly austerity policies are being put in place to deal with the debt crisis, policies that tend to cut spending on welfare. In the long-term the decline of the welfare state will likely trigger a crisis of legitimacy accompanied by mass uprisings. It is not surprising, then, to find the American state reluctant to cut back on prisons, defense, and homeland security. For, as a rule, the less legitimacy a government has, the more it has to rely on force and repression to continue governing. Arguably the expansion of a primarily beneficial welfare state in the US peaked in the late 1960s. President Johnson's "war on poverty" hardly got off the ground, and starting in the Reagan years in the 1980s, federal funding for "welfare" began to shift to the "war on drugs," prisons, and defence.

A major policy push by the Reagan presidency was the "war on drugs," which over the years has increased the prison population approximately four-fold, and has led to a militarization of domestic police forces (*The Economist* 2010b). As an indication of the militarization of US police forces in 1980 SWAT (Special Weapons and Tactics) teams were deployed in the US approximately 3,000 times and now this number has expanded to 50,000 times per year (*Toronto Star*, 2014). Further, the Department of Homeland Security has dispersed $35 million to police forces across the country to buy heavy weaponry such as armored personnel carriers. With only 5 percent of the world's population, the US has 25 percent of the world's prisoners (NAACP 2014). No state in the world comes close to incarcerating the same percentage of citizens than the US does.[3] In 2012 one in thirty-five or seven million Americans were in prison or under some form of correctional supervision (Schoenfeld 2013). An estimated 80,000 prisoners were in extremely debilitating solitary confinement (Allen 2014, p. 13). And even Homeland Security incarcerated over 22,000 immigrants, waiting for likely deportation (Hallett 2006, p. 21). It is perhaps no exaggeration, then, to refer to the US as "the world's largest penal colony" (Bichler and Nitzan 2014).

If young people cannot find their way to meaningful education leading to meaningful jobs, instead of becoming productive citizens, they may turn to gangs, drugs, and crime. Consider the fact that 35 percent of African-American youth between grades 7 and 12 have been suspended or expelled from school (NAACP 2014). Now also consider why African Americans are 6 times more likely to wind up in prison and Latinos 3 times more likely than White Americans, despite a more or less equal drug use across races and ethnicities (NAACP 2014). If trends continue, one in three black males will spend some time in prison during their lifetime. And finally, in many states this also means that the offender loses the right to vote for life.

Prisons were until recently a major growth industry with the state of California spending 9.5 percent of its budget on prisons as opposed to only 5.7 percent on universities, whereas 25 years ago it spent 4 percent on prisons and 11 percent on universities (*The Economist* 2010a, p. 37). Is it a surprise that California is now facing a severe budget crisis in part because it spends on average $50,000 per year on each of its 167,000 inmates, and even with 30,000 correctional officers, its prisons have become overcrowded and violent (Parenti 2008, p. 246). California's prisons have become so overcrowded and so expensive to run that it has now sent 8,302 prisoners out of state, mostly to less expensive and more repressive private prisons in other states (Buczynski 2014; Law 2013). This move by California is one way of responding to the US Supreme Court's demand that it do something to reduce the overcrowding of its prisons.

Given that once a person has a criminal record, it is hard to find employment, and that the unemployment rate for African-American men is typically over 25 percent, it is also not surprising to find an especially high recidivism rate for African-American prisoners. The recidivism rate for all prisoners in California no matter what race is above 70 percent. This suggests that incarceration is not a successful way of dealing with "crime" and that its main effect may be to raise the crime rate. Given recent austerity policies, the $70 billion per year spent on the prison industrial complex in the US is being rethought, but we may have to wait a long time before the high rates of incarceration are significantly reduced, given the need of private prisons to house enough prisoners to be profitable.

Is it really necessary to hand out life sentences to small-time drug pushers who happen to have been caught three times (as in California until recently), for currently one out of every eleven prisoners in the US has a life sentence and many more have long sentences for less than life (Mauer 2006). Does this terribly expensive and repressive way of dealing with crime have much to do with capitalism? The war on drugs had the effect of criminalizing black ghettos across the US, ghettos within which massive uprisings were occurring. The American state turned to force where its legitimacy was being challenged. The war on drugs was a total failure, but a lot of people made a lot of money off of drugs, prison building programs gave a strong stimulus to the economy, and uprisings were quelled.

From the mid-1960s to the mid-1970s there were black uprisings in most large cities in the US, and groups like the Black Panthers preached revolution. Black youth that did not end up fighting a tragic and fruitless war in Vietnam, filled the ranks of the unemployed. The war on drugs dealt with this problem by helping black youth to get hooked on highly addictive drugs such as "crack." This was not a very progressive way of dealing with black unemployment and black uprisings, and it was very expensive. Basically black youth caught in the cycles of poverty had a choice between selling drugs, unemployment, the military, a few sports, or prison. African Americans make up 58 percent of all youth admitted to state prisons, and since prisoners are not counted in unemployment statistics, the large number of incarcerated citizens greatly improves the unemployment statistics by underrepresenting the actual number of unemployed persons (Schoenfeld 2013; Western 2006, p. xii).[4] The prison system has become a terrible blight on the landscape of American capitalism. Building prisons and filling them created jobs and got Blacks off the street, while acting as a stimulus to a stagnant economy. The result has been called a "prison industrial complex." Instead of dealing with poverty in creative ways, one trend in the US is to put the poor behind bars.

But as we shall see, the "military industrial complex" has become the primary source for stimulus in the US Federal budget, so that the concept "military Keynesianism" (Keynesianism = demand management) becomes highly appropriate. This huge expansion of investment in state repressive apparatuses is a sure sign of capitalism in decay – a capitalist state that is losing its legitimacy both at home and abroad. But a state that is losing legitimacy must increasingly rely on force, manipulation, and divide and rule ideologies. Young Black males have become the most incarcerated group in all of history (Hallet 2006, p. 8). And as austerity measures come to the fore in US policy, the welfare state is shrinking and poverty rates are increasing. What an irony! Nothing did more to increase drug use in the US than the "War on Drugs", just as nothing has done more to spread terror in the world than the "War on Terror."

The military industrial complex

Because of the debt crisis and the turn to austerity, cutbacks in military spending are slated for the future, but the military is so well connected with every congressional committee that has anything to do with its budget, that it will be difficult to carry out any cutbacks even though those proposed are not very large. As Goodman (2013, p. 9) put it in his recent book "the defence budget is sacrosanct," and while it varies from year to year (in 2012 it was $682.5 billion), it generally hovers between 40 and 50 percent of total global spending on defense (Renner 2013). Further, at 60 percent of the total, the US dominates the world market in sales of military equipment. The pentagon deploys 1.5 million persons in 702 bases located in 130 countries and 6,000 bases located in The US (Hossein-Zadeh 2006, pp. 12–13). An estimated 85,000 private sector corporations benefit from defence contracts, as did 350 colleges and universities in 2002 when this was last studied. In 2003 MIT and Johns Hopkins received $842,437,294 from the Pentagon (ibid., p. 25). In fact 60 percent of all funding for basic research in the US comes from the Pentagon. And the Pentagon is not always very careful in accounting for its spending. According to a Defense Department report: "300 defense contractors in Iraq providing products or services to the Pentagon had been involved in fraud … During the decade of war, the Pentagon had forked over to the top 37 fraudulent corporations alone $1.1 trillion" (Jones 2013, p. 166). Halliburton, for example, did well at $39.5 billion. In fact the private contractors did so well that by 2011 there were more private workers than soldiers in Iraq and Afghanistan: 155,000 of the former and 145,000 of the latter (ibid., p. 164).

If we calculate the federal budget according to the true share that goes to defence and security spending, it amounts to 41.6 percent of the total (Hossein-Zadeh 2006, p. 14). The horribly destructive and senseless wars in Iraq and Afghanistan cost the lives of tens of thousands of Afghan civilians and over 500,000 Iraqi civilians. The final bill for these two wars is estimated to be as much as $4.4 trillion.

Since most military contracts are on a cost plus basis, cost overruns for weapons systems have become the norm. Furthermore, many systems are retired before they are ever deployed. Take the F-22 fighter jet, which was supposed to cost $35 million per plane and ended up costing $153 million. In the end 187 of these aircraft were produced at a total cost of $80 billion. The F-22 was parcelled out to forty-seven states for construction and parts, creating 28,000 jobs at its peak with 112,000 indirect jobs (Hartung 2011; Goodman 2013, pp. 331–32). All of this assured that Congress would support this project. To this day these planes have never been deployed and are not likely to be deployed in the future. They are to be replaced by the F-35 jet fighter that were supposed to cost $70 million per plane and recently this amount was raised to $133 million per plane. The first delivery was supposed to be in 2010, but has now been postponed to 2017. As might be expected the spending on this plane has been parcelled out to forty-eight states, and the total cost of building the proposed 2,440 F-35s and operating them over the next fifty years is estimated to be over $1 trillion (Goodman 2013, pp. 333–34). But most expensive of all has been the nuclear weapons systems developed by the US. They not only have the power to destroy the world many times over, but also from World War II to the present have cost an estimated $5 to $7 trillion, making this weapon system by far the most expensive (Goodman 2013, p. 344).

An estimated 40 percent of all corruption in international trade is related to the arms trade, and this occurs because such deals tend to be secrets among small numbers of people (Feinstein 2011, pp. 20–21). Unfortunately, in many parts of the world "power grows out of the barrel of a gun" (Mao Tse-Tung). Thus in South Africa, for example, while 345,000 people were dying of AIDS for lack of retroviral drugs, the government spent $10 billion on weapons in part because of bribes paid to an array of politicians (Feinstein 2011). Of the ten largest arms corporations in the world, seven are American, and the ten largest corporations controlled 62 percent of total international arms sales in 2005. The trends are toward greater and greater concentration, greater size, and greater profits for these producers of the means of killing. Between 2001 and 2011 the world's 100 leading arms producers (excluding China) more than doubled sales arriving at an astronomical $410 billion by 2011 (Godrej 2011, pp. 14–17).

It is not simply a question of corruption in the military, but also one of priorities. The lion's share of the money goes to corporations and not to soldiers who put their lives on the line. Let's consider for a moment the homeless in America, a large percentage of whom are veterans of wars. Counting homelessness is difficult precisely because many have no fixed address, many fluctuate in and out of homelessness, and because the definition of "homeless" varies. According to the Congressional Research Service, which is likely to have the most cautious and conservative estimates, in a 2012 point-in-time count, there were 62,619 homeless veterans in the US (Perl 2013). Further, 11 percent of all veterans are homeless compared to 35.5 percent of African-American veterans. Many homeless veterans suffer from a disability and deal with their suffering through substance abuse (Wood 2013). With the influx of veterans from the Iraq and Afghanistan wars, more attention has been given to this problem, and various government programs have attempted to reduce the number of homeless vets. Headway has been made, but not enough (Shane 2013). That such a situation would develop is an indicator of the extreme individualism characteristic of American capitalism. The slogan might as well be: "Let the hundreds of thousands of psychologically and physically damaged war vets find their own way to reintegrate into normal social life."

In 2012 it was estimated that 663,000 vets of the Iraq and Afghanistan wars out of at total of 2.3 million (one out of four) arrived home with service-related disabilities. While the 663,000 might be considered lucky not to be counted amongst the dead, it turns out that there were far more suicides amongst active duty soldiers than combat deaths (Jones 2013, p. 104). Of the 283,000 women deployed in the two wars an estimated one in three was raped and a surprisingly high percentage of men were also raped (Jones 2013, pp. 127–28, 153). This, no doubt, accounts for a proportion of those counted as having "service related disabilities" such as Post Traumatic Stress Disorders (PTSD).

Besides the disastrous foreign wars, there are on-going "private wars" amongst US citizens fanned by the sale of guns to private citizens. Twenty-five percent of all American adults own at least one firearm. In the first twenty-four days of 2014 there were seven school shootings in the US (Pitt 2014). Given that there are an estimated 283 million privately owned guns in the US, it is not surprising to find approximately 32,000 gun deaths a year and more than thirty per day with one-third of these being teenagers under 20 (Porter 2013). Tragically, homicide is the second leading cause of death for the 15–24 year old age group. Yes, the American gun industry is hugely profitable and the National Rifle Association is hugely powerful, but the degree to which the American economy's semi-well-being is tied to weapons and prisons is a strong indicator of a failing economy and society.

Corporate welfare

One of the myths of capitalist ideology is "consumer sovereignty," where presumably consumers spend their dollar "ballots" to maximize their utility and hence shape an economy to fit their wants. But what happens when an economy is kept afloat not by consumer sovereignty but by bribe-like millions spent by rich corporations to buy off members of Congress to spend tax-payers' money on a truly gigantic expenditure to support their particular incarceration and violence industry? And on top of this particular directing of tax funds, huge subsidies and incentives are given to make sure that certain sectors of the economy are profitable or that certain corporations locate production in particular places, hardly what one could call "consumer sovereignty." It would be an interesting study to find out how many producers would go bankrupt without continual subsidies and "incentives" from government. In other words, how many producers are not making a profit in strictly capitalist terms? Indeed, I wonder if any US manufacturing at all is still profitable without government incentives and subsidies?

Volkswagen considered 398 sites for building a new production facility in the US. Tennessee eventually won out by offering Volkswagen incentives worth more than half a billion dollars in taxpayers' money (Wikipedia 2014b). Alabama had offered Volkswagen the measly sum of only $385 million in incentives thus losing out to Tennessee. Apparently this is what it costs these days to get 1500 of those relatively high paying manufacturing jobs that more often than not have migrated away from the US to low wage countries. It has been estimated, however, that labor costs of this production facility will be less than those of other car makers in the US (assuming that Volkswagen can keep the unions out of the plant). Is capitalism healthy when huge incentives (a type of bribe?) have to be paid to corporations in order to get them to locate some of their production in a particular jurisdiction, and when they can threaten to leave at any time unless they receive yet more incentives?

States, counties, and cities are desperate to have job-creating production facilities located in their jurisdiction, because good industrial jobs have become so scarce in this age of transition. It is difficult to measure incentives because they can take so many forms and can come from so many directions. Some of the more popular forms include tax credits, cash grants, long-term low interest loans, low cost land, and low cost services and utilities. Because of its job-creating potential, manufacturing gets the most local incentives. The total to all companies is $80 billion a year and leading the pack in local incentives is GM at $1.7 billion per year. Pennsylvania was so keen to get some production facilities of Shell Oil that it offered tax credits worth $1.6 billion over twenty-five years. In this case Royal Dutch Shell, which made $31 billion in profits in 2011, hardly needed the incentive to stay profitable.

Incentives don't always work. In 2009 the state of Michigan gave General Motors $779 million in tax credits while GM had just received at $50 billion bailout from the federal government to stave off bankruptcy (Story 2012). Despite the bailout and tax credits, GM decided to close seven plants in Michigan. Political jurisdictions are desperate to get job-creating economic activities, so they compete with one another, and usually the one with the sweetest incentive package gets the investment. But the winner does not necessarily win. For another jurisdiction may come along and entice the facility to relocate to their yet sweeter incentive package.

While corporations receive more and more welfare, the poor are getting less. From 2004 to 2013 the number of US households requiring food stamps to make ends meet doubled. In 2013 one in five households or a total of 23,052,388 households were dependent on food stamps. The food stamp program (Supplemental Nutrition Assistance Program = SNAP) cost $79.6 billion in 2013, a 164 percent increase over a ten year period. As a part of its austerity program, the US government has cut back its support for food stamps including for 22 million children by an average of 7 percent. The resulting malnutrition will likely produce a lifetime of health problems for many of these children, and for seniors, military veterans, the unemployed, and the disabled. At the same time Congress has passed a $100 billion a year farm bill which will provide enormous subsidies to the 10 percent largest corn growers, subsidies which will make the otherwise uneconomic ethanol industry profitable, will cheapen high fructose corn syrup, the sweetener of choice in a good deal of junk food, and will cheapen beef, which is fattened mainly on corn feed. There is nothing wrong in principle with subsidies, but the US government is subsidizing disease and repression while it is cutting back on health and freedom.

Conclusions

My aim in presenting the above three examples is to indicate the extent to which the economy of the dominant capitalist state in the world has become dependent upon life support infusions, infusions that are replacing the welfare state with a penal state, a warfare state, and a state that provides welfare less and less to citizens and more and more to corporations or to the private sector in general (Simon 2007, p. 6). While since 2008 the US has been dealing with an accumulation crisis, the above statistics indicate what could become an increasing legitimization crisis as well. No doubt the future will manifest economic ups and downs, but current economic, political, and ideological trends indicate that capitalism may be entering a phase of transition that will become marked by increasing uprisings that may eventually become anti-capitalist. The decline of the American welfare state is simply one important indicator of what likely lies ahead.

Health in the US

Introduction

The US spends 18 percent of its GDP on health care each year, leading the world by far in having the most expensive health care system, and the trend is rising. Most other high income countries spend around half as much, yet have much better outcomes (Chernomas and Hudson 2013, p. 2). Over one half of all prison inmates in the US suffer mental illness, and according to Mark Engler (2011), "prisons have covered for government failure to provide mental health treatment." Globally on many other health issues, the US ranks poorly. Consider infant mortality. In the rankings of thirty-four OECD countries, the US is thirty-first, its life expectancy rankings are twenty-seventh, and its obesity rankings are last (Farmer *et al.* 2013). Perhaps most shocking is that for children under 5, the US mortality rate is forty-sixth in the world (Chernomas and Hudson 2013, p. 2).

Obesity is a significant risk factor for diabetes, heart disease, arthritis, mental illness, and many other debilitating health conditions. Between 2007 and 2012, the cost for treating diabetes alone increased by 41 percent (American Diabetes Association 2012). Obesity statistics indicate a health care system in serious danger of future bankruptcy. Add to this the statistics on substance abuse, and we find that the annual cost of addiction to tobacco, alcohol, and illicit drugs amounts to $600 billion in crime, lost work, and healthcare (National Institute on Drug Abuse 2013). Of course, a bankrupt health care system would seriously compromise the welfare state and would add to both the accumulation crises and the legitimacy crises, crises that are already building.

In part three of this paper I shall first connect with part two by indicating the relation between prisons and health and between the military and health, and the welfare state and health. I shall then turn to that all-important basis for health, which is diet. And finally, I shall briefly consider environmental pollution as it affects health.

Prisons, the military, the welfare state and health

The National Institute of Mental Health (NIMH 2013) estimates that in a given year one in four adult Americans experience at least one mental illness. This increases to one in three in the 18 to 25 age group and an estimated one in two amongst the prison population (Engler 2011). Indeed, the terrible prison overcrowding resulting from over 2.3 million Americans behind bars has turned prisons into breeding grounds for communicable diseases such as AIDS, tuberculosis, syphilis, and hepatitis. In a 2007 survey, it turned out that prisoners had AIDS at 2.4 times the rate of the non-prison population.

Veterans returning from Iraq and Afghanistan often suffer from post-traumatic stress disorder (PTSD) and/or traumatic brain injury (TBI). Of the 2.4 million Americans who fought in Iraq and Afghanistan, it has been estimated that 600,000 suffer from PTSD, TBI, or depression, and well over 200,000 are behind bars with 50 percent of them having committed violent crimes. Given the high rate of depression, it is not surprising to find that the suicide rate for veterans is 300 percent the national average. The Veterans Administration suicide crisis hot-line averages approximately 17,000 calls a day, and even so US veterans from all wars including Vietnam committed suicide at an average rate of 500 a month (Wood 2013). Sadly, suicide is not only reducing the ranks of veterans, but also is the third leading cause of death for young people between 15 and 24 and the second highest cause of death for those between 25 and 34. The highest cause of death for the 15 to 24 age group is auto accidents and homicide is second. And for the 25 to 34 group the highest cause is poisoning (which could be suicide or accidental overdose) and number three is auto accidents with homicides at number 4 (National Institute for Mental Health 2007). In a recently released report by the CDC (Will 2014) at 38,329 deaths per year, drug overdose was the number one "accidental" killer of Americans between 25 and 64 years of age in 2010.

Diet

Diet is perhaps the strongest overall determinant of health, particularly in countries like the US where the widespread consumption of junk food has been the primary cause of an obesity epidemic (Wikipedia 2014a). The only country with a higher obesity rate is Mexico, where almost everyone drinks soft drinks or alcohol in one form or another. The purveyors of junk food are essentially the purveyors of sugar, fat, and salt in quantities that can be ruinous to the health of the many people who consume junk food. While all three can in excess negatively impact health, the effects of sugar undermine health the most. Recent research shows that people who get 25 percent or more of their daily calories from added sugar have three times the risk of dying from heart disease (Picard 2014). Further, high levels of sugar consumption are the major cause of obesity and diabetes. But despite these findings, sugar consumption remains high in the US. This occurs because food producers have known a little secret for a long time, namely that sugar is quasi-addictive or just plain addictive, depending upon how you define the word. As a result many people crave sugar, and this craving is often established at a young age when lifetime eating habits are created. It follows that in the food industry added sugar increases sales and profits enormously.

According to a 2010 CDC report 74.1 percent of American adults are overweight and 35.7 percent are obese, while as many as 25 percent of US children and adolescents are obese. This study also claimed that obesity is a contributing factor in between 100,000 and 400,000 deaths a year. The direct and indirect costs of obesity have been estimated to amount to $117 billion per year, and by 2030 obesity will account for 21 percent of all medical costs in the US. Finally it is estimated that by 2050 one in three Americans will have diabetes (American Diabetes Association 2012).

The junk food industry, based largely on unsustainable industrial farming, is powerful enough to buy off politicians at every level of government. As a result the industry receives all sorts of direct and indirect subsidies including incentives. The largest subsidies go to the largest farms that grow corn. Between 1995 and 2012 corn farmers received $84.4 billion, and the largest 10 percent of the farms received 72 percent of the total. Corn eaten directly by humans as corn on the cob, cornmeal, popcorn, etc. is a healthy food, but much of the corn becomes feed for cattle, becomes converted into high fructose corn syrup (HFCS), or into ethanol, an industry that would not exist at all were it not for government subsidies and incentives. The cheaper feed for cattle cheapens the hamburger that goes to burger chains, and because of import duties on cane sugar, and subsidies for HFCS, the latter is the cheapest sweetener; hence, it winds up in most soft drinks and many processed foods. HFCS is a major cause of obesity, for 37 percent of added sugar in the American diet comes from sugar-sweetened (mainly HFCS) beverages (Beck 2014; Laskawy 2013). The US government, then, is not subsidizing healthy foods anywhere near the extent that it is subsidizing the unhealthy foods that undermine the health of Americans. The recent farm bill passed by Congress reduced the funding to the 47,636,082 million Americans who depend on food stamps, while large subsidies to industrial farms continued (Jalonick 2014; *CNSNEWS* 2014).

Furthermore, the corn subsidies have led to acreages far in excess of any other crop, and corn is one of the least environmentally friendly crops. Corn growing is heavily chemicalized and mechanized making it a heavy contributor to toxins in the environment and greenhouse gases. Where rainfall is insufficient corn needs lots of water, thus draining crucial aquifers (Kumar 2013). In many areas of the American mid-west the run-off from confined animal feeding operations (CAFOs) combined with that from crop fertilizers flows down the Mississippi and other rivers contributing to the creation of a giant dead zone in the Caribbean, where nothing much can live except algae. This dead zone that is expanding into the Caribbean is already larger than the state of New Jersey.

If "diet" is expanded to refer to anything that we ingest in our bodies, it would include all of the drugs or mood altering substances that we ingest. In 2008 it was found that 8.9 percent of Americans over 12 take illegal drugs, and this number is up from 5.8 percent in 1992. According to The Center for Disease Control (CDC), there were 14,218 deaths from taking illegal drugs in 1995 compared to 37,792 deaths in 2008 (*The Economist* 2012, pp. 31–32). Also it is worth noting that in 2008 25 percent of the prison population consisted of non-violent drug offenders, who were in prison largely because of the war on drugs.

On average every adult American takes ten prescribed drugs. A recent trend has seen an explosive expansion of abusing "prescription" opioids (any drug resembling morphine or cocaine as pain killers). In 2000 pharmacies gave out 174 million prescriptions for opioids, and this has increased to 257 million prescriptions by 2009. And, as one journalist put it, "presumably America did not become a 48 percent more painful place during those nine years" (*The Economist* 2012, pp. 31–32). Indeed, there is an alarming increase of addiction to prescription drugs, particularly painkillers with the result that on average forty people die of an overdose every day (Jones 2013, p. 114).

A toxic environment

According to leading epidemiologist Devra Davis (2007, p. 9) about 1,000 of the over 80,000 chemicals used widely have had adequate toxicity tests, primarily because the time and cost of such tests cuts into profits or into state revenues. As a result, American citizens are blind to the fact that they are guinea pigs in a huge and largely unmonitored test of possible toxins in their environment. Toxins, whose effects are long-term or whose effects depend on interaction with other toxins, are the least likely to be discovered even though they can be extremely damaging. One would think that testing chemicals for their carcinogenic effects would be a very high priority, given that on average

1500 Americans die each day of cancer and there are hundreds of known carcinogens in the environment (Physicians for Social Responsibility 2014).

Chemical companies are interested in short-term profits and not long-term costs, and mainly for this reason governments are loathe to require stringent testing regimes for new chemicals. After all, not only can the long-term be ignored in the short-term, but also long-term testing of chemicals and their interactions would be costly. Since profits of the chemical industry are at stake, researchers are very cautious in declaring connections between chemical exposures and particular health issues, and since it is very difficult to totally prove a direct one-to-one causal connection, many drugs that should be pulled from the market are not. Furthermore, the chemical companies that would lose profits generally pay off scientists to provide "studies" that counter those that do find a chemical to be toxic. Even the strong connection between tobacco smoke and lung cancer was ferociously attacked by the cigarette companies, such that it took over twenty years to firmly establish a causal connection. Now it is known that the primary cause of lung cancer, the most common and deadly cancer in the world, is smoking tobacco. Based on the 1.59 million lung cancer deaths globally in 2012 (Grant 2014) and general smoking trends globally, it has been estimated conservatively that at least one billion people will die from smoking tobacco or from second hand smoke in the twenty-first century (Brandt 2007, p. 14).

It is very hard to explain the sudden growth of certain new diseases without reference to the spread of toxins in the environment (MacDonald 2014). We have known for some time that there are many carcinogens in the environment, and it has been estimated that they account for 34,000 deaths a year in the US (Physicians for Social Responsibility 2014). According to leading cancer epidemiologist Devra Davis (2007, p. 4), one out of two American men, and one out of three women, will have cancer in their lifetime.

As shocking as the cancer statistics may seem, the CDC (2013) has found that one in six children between 3 and 17 have one or more disability likely caused by toxins in the environment. Autism has an annual growth rate of between 10 and 17 percent, and it is estimated that its treatment over a normal lifespan would amount to $3.2 million per person (Autism Society 2014). Now the annual cost for treating autism in the US is $60 billion and in ten years it is estimated that it will increase to between $200 and $400 billion. What can explain the 600 percent growth of autism in 20 years, such that one in every eighty-eight children born in the US in 2008 suffered from Autism Spectrum Disease (CDC 2013)? Or what can explain the 50 percent increase in ADHD in the past ten years (Gordon 2014)? There also appears to be an increase in allergies, hay fever, asthma, and cancer amongst children (American Academy of Allergy Asthma & Immunology 2013). Most doctors and researchers think that these changes are caused by toxins in the environment, but they mostly end their studies with a plea for more studies even when the toxic properties of certain chemicals are strongly indicated. An exception is a recent study published in the *Lancet Neurology Journal* (Pearson 2013). The authors claim that the world is facing a pandemic of neurodevelopmental toxicity. Commenting on the study Dr. Blakely, a toxicology professor at the University of Saskatchewan, claims "The fetus is uniquely susceptible to developmental disorders ... that can lead to immune and behavioral, as well as reproductive dysfunction later in life" (Pearson 2013).

Besides the alarming growth of childhood diseases, there are also alarming changes in reproductive health and fertility. At least 12 percent of US women expressed difficulty getting pregnant and carrying the pregnancy to term in 2002. This was an increase from 1982 of 40 percent. Testosterone levels and sperm counts have declined in adult US males, and testicular cancer has increased 60 percent from 1973 to 2003. In the US girls are experiencing puberty at an earlier and earlier age. All of these changes are likely due to toxins in the environment (Safer Chemicals 2010).

For an aging population, the growth of Alzheimer's disease is particularly important. Currently one in nine over 65 has this illness, and its incidence is expected to double by 2050, raising its annual cost to $1.2 trillion from the 2013 cost of $203 billion (Alzheimer's Association 2013). In short, the above examples indicate that the US has a rapidly expanding disease burden, one that will certainly bankrupt its health care system. Because of the primacy of capitalism's profit orientation, its preoccupation with the short-term profits, and its rush to get chemicals onto the market, capitalism has led us into a life in which toxins are too omnipresent to be avoided. An economic system that so undermines the health of humans and of the environment is undermining life itself.

Conclusions: the need for global change

Human beings have never had to face something so daunting as global warming and the looming shortages of non-renewable natural resources (Albritton 2013). Capitalism is the main deep cause blocking the way to necessary changes. The "path dependency" of capitalism is very resistant to change, but change it must. Its roots are deep and require radical change guided by radical thought. We need to think about things so basic as time and space in new ways. Temporally we will need to think about the long-term much more as if it were the short-term, or else there may be no long-term. Spatially our primary loyalty must shift from being citizens of states to citizens of the world. These changes are necessary because global warming and shortages of non-renewables are world-wide issues, and because our lack of action now may severely reduce the options of future generations.

As the most powerful and wealthy capitalist country in the world, the US could in principle take a lead in advancing sustainability, but for the very reason that it is also the most capitalist country in the world, it is least likely to deal effectively with problems of sustainability. Put simply, the dilemma is that the most powerful country is with regard to sustainability the least effective. It is only when a large majority of Americans understand this and rise up *en mass* to demand and implement change, that significant steps towards sustainability can be achieved. By saying this I don't mean to imply that all other people of the world need to wait upon the awakening of Americans. Indeed, sustainability is a global issue that in the first instance needs to be dealt with globally. But to be fully democratic and effective global decision making needs to be rooted as much as possible at a local level. In principle modern information technology should make this more possible.

It is climate change that is perhaps hitting people around the world the hardest at this point in time, and no doubt extreme weather is just a start compared to what is coming. Life anywhere near the equator will become unbearably hot to a point where crops will not grow and forests including the Amazon forest will burn to the ground. Extreme weather will produce drought and flooding in different parts of the world. Water shortages will make life in many areas extremely difficult. Acidification of the oceans will undermine ocean life. And ultimately the melting of the world's ice will raise ocean levels over 200 feet. As food and water shortages grow, it will become more and more necessary to reach international accords on their equitable and sustainable distribution and hence on the global distribution of wealth in general.

I have only dealt with a few of the many problems and crises the future generations will need to resolve, and I have dealt with them mainly within the context of the world's leading capitalist power, the US. I believe that even my small sampling supports the perspective that we are in a phase of transition away from capitalism. Even these few problems might seem overwhelming, but the dominant capitalist ideology is one of denial, divisiveness, and escape. Given the lack of problem orientation in the dominant media, it is important to face up to our situation in realistic ways. It is then that we can think and act towards effective transformations, for we cannot afford a transition that takes hundreds of years, as the one from feudalism to capitalism. Time is not money, it is the future – the future of life on earth.

Notes

1 Bichler and Nitzan's (2014) notion of "systemic crisis" suggests that capitalism as a whole is on the way out, a position that is similar to my "phase of transition."
2 According to Bichler and Nitzan (2014, p. 12) manufacturing "currently accounts for a mere 10–20 percent of all business activity." For Marx industry is at the center of capitalism, so its decline is a strong indicator of capitalism's decline.
3 In the US 743 citizens out of every 10,000 are in the prison system, for Canada 117 citizens out of 10,000, and for Japan 58 out of 10,000.
4 According to Western (2006, p. xii) "The U.S. Census Bureau's labor force survey … estimated that 46 percent of young black male dropouts were employed, but this number dropped to 29 percent once prison and jail inmates were counted."

References

Albritton, R. (1991) *A Japanese Approach to Stages of Capitalist Development* (New York: St. Martins Press).

——(2013) "Marxist Political Economy and Global Warming," *International Journal of Pluralism in Economics Education*, 4(3).

Allen, K. (2014) *The Toronto Star*, February 15, p. 13.

Alzheimer's Association (2013) "Alzheimer's Disease: Facts and Figures," available at: www.alz.org?downloads/facts_figures_2013.pdf [accessed January 22, 2014].

American Academy of Allergy Asthma & Immunology (2013) "Allergy Statistics," available at: www.aaaai.org [accessed February 2, 2014].

American Diabetes Association (2012) "Economic Costs of Diabetes in the US," available at: www.ncbi.nlm.nih.gov./pubmed/23468086 [accessed February 6, 2014].

Autism Society (2014) "Facts and Statistics," available at: www.tutism-society.org/about-autism/facts-and-statistics.html [accessed February 8, 2014].

Beck, L. (2014) "Where Sugar is Hiding in Your Diet," *The Globe and Mail*, February 11, p. L7.

Bichler, S. and J. Nitzan (2014) "No Way Out: Crime, Punishment and the Capitalization of Power," available at: http://dx.doi.org/10.1007/s10611-013-9505-3 [accessed January 26, 2014].

Brandt, A.M. (2007) *The Cigarette Century* (New York: Basic Books).

Buczynski, B (2014) "Shocking Facts About America's For-Profit Prison Industry," available at: http://truth-out.org/news/item/21694-shocking-facts-about-americas-for-profit [accessed February 11].

Center for Disease Control and Prevention (CDC) (2013) "Facts About Developmental Disabilities," available at: www.cdc.gov/ncbddd/developmentaldisabilities/facts.html [accessed February 19, 2014].

Chernomas, R. and I. Hudson (2013) *To Live and Die in America: Class, Power, Health, and Healthcare* (London: Pluto Press).

CNSNEWS (2014) "Record 20 % of Households on Food Stamps in 2013," available at: http://cnsnews.com/news/article/ali-meyer/record-20-households-food-stamps [accessed February 15, 2014].

Davis, D. (2007) *The Secret History of the War on Cancer* (New York: Basic Books).

Engler, M. (2011) "America: Life in Prison Nation," *New Internationalist*, 446, October.

Farmer, P., J. Y. Kim, A. Kleinman and M. Basilico (eds) (2013) *Reimagining Global Health: An Introduction* (Berkeley: University of California Press).

Feinstein, A. (2011) "The Shadow World," *New Internationalist*, 448, December, pp. 20–21.

Godrej, D. (2011) "Anxieties of Influence," *New Internationalist*, December, 448, pp. 14–17.

Goodman, M. (2013) *National Insecurity: The Cost of American Militarism* (San Francisco, CA: City Lights Press).

Gordon, A. (2014) "'Neurotoxicants' hindering brain development of children," *Toronto Star*, February 15, p. 8.

Grant, K. (2014) "Mapping Cancer," *The Globe and Mail*, February 4, A8–9.

Hallett, M. A. (2006) *Private Prisons in America: A Critical Race Perspective* (Charlotte: University of North Carolina Press).

Hartung, W. (2011) "Washington's White Elephant," *New Internationalist*, December, 448, pp. 18–19.

Hossein-Zadeh, I. (2006) *The Political Economy of U.S. Militarism* (New York: Palgrave Macmillan).

Jalonick, M.C. (2014) "US Senate Passes $100 billion per year farm bill." *The Globe and Mail*, February 5, p. B10.

Jones, A. (2013) *They Were Soldiers: How the Wounded Return from America's Wars—The Untold Story* (Chicago, IL: Haymarket Books).

Kumar, S. (2013) "Looming threat of water scarcity", March 19, available at: http://vitalsigns.worldwatch.org/vs-trend/looming-threat-water-scarcity [accessed January 23, 2014].

Laskawy, T. (2013) "Corn free: cutting back on our dominant crop is easier said than done" [online], available at: http://grist.org/food/corn-free-cutting-back-on-our-dominant-crop-is-easier-said-than-done/?utm_campai [accessed July 12].

Law, V. (2013) "California Ships Prisoners Out of State to 'Reduce' Its Prison Population," *Truthout*, Dec. 6. Available at: www.truth-out.org/news/item/20405-california-ships-prisoners [accessed January 26, 2014].

MacDonald, G. (2014) "The 'Silent Epidemic' Hurting Our Children," *The Globe and Mail*, February 17.

Mauer, M. (2006) *The Race to Incarcerate* (New York: The New Press).

Mitchell, A. (2009) *Sea Sick: The Global Ocean in Crisis* (Toronto: McClelland & Stewart).

NAACP (2014) "Criminal Justice Fact Sheet," available at: www.naacp.org/pages/criminal-justice-fact-sheet [accessed February 28, 2014].

National Alliance on Mental Illness (NAMI) (2013) "Mental Illness: Facts and Figures," available at: www.nami.org [accessed February 2, 2014].

National Institute on Drug Abuse (NIDA) (2013) www.drugabuse.gov [accessed February 2, 2014].

National Institute of Health (NIH) (2007) "Suicide in the US," publication # 06–4594. Available at: www.nimh.nih.gov/health/ … /suicide-in-the-us-statistics-and-prevention [accessed February 4, 2014].

——(2013) "The Numbers Count: Mental Disorders in America," available at: www.nimh.nih.gov/health/publications/the-numbers-count-mental-disorders-in-america/index.shtml [accessed February 7, 2014].

Parenti, C. (2008) *Lockdown America: Police and Prisons in the Age of Crisis* (London: Verso).

Pearson, C. (2013) 'Doctors Link Toxic Chemicals And Reproductive Health Problems,' available at: www.huffingtonpost.com/2013/09/23/toxic-chemicals-health_n_397 [accessed February 17, 2014].

Perl, L. (2013) "Veterans and Homelessness," *Congressional Research Service* available at: www.fas.org/sgp/crs/misc/RL34024.pdf [accessed January 29, 2014].

Physicians for Social Responsibility (2014) "Cancer and Toxic Chemicals," available at: www.psr.org [accessed February 2, 2014].

Picard, A. (2014) "High Sugar Diet Shown to Triple Risk of Dying from Heart Disease," *The Globe and Mail*, February 4, pp. 1, 14.

Pitt, W.R. (2014) "An Open Letter to Lovers of the Gun," *Truthout*, January 24. Available at: www.truth-out.org/ … /21422-william-rivers-pitt-an-open-letter-to-lovers-of-the-gun [accessed February 5, 2014].

Porter, H. (2013) "American gun use is out of control. Shouldn't the world intervene?" available at: www.theguardian.com/commentisfree/2013/sep/21/american-gun-ou [accessed February 4, 2014].

Renner, M. (2013) "Military Expenditures Remain Near Peak," *Vital Signs*, Worldwatch. Available at: www.vitalsigns.worldwatch.org [accessed February 20, 2014].

SAMHSA (2012) "National report finds one-in-five Americans experienced mental illness in the past year." Available at: www.samhsa.gov/newsroom/advisories/1201185326.aspx [accessed February 18, 2014].

Safer Chemicals (2010) "Reproductive Health and Fertility Problems," available at: http://health report.saferchemicals.org/reproductive.html [accessed February 14, 2014].

Schoenfeld, H. (2013) "Five Things Everyone Should Know About US Incarceration," *Aljazeera*, March 26.

Sekine, T. (1997) *An Outline of the Dialectic of Capital*, vols. I & II (London: Macmillan Press).

Shane III, L. (2013) "Number of Homeless Vets Drops," *Stars and Stripes*, November 21.

Simon, J. (2007) *Governing Through Crime* (Oxford: Oxford University Press).

Story, L. (2012) "As Companies Seek Tax Deals, Governments Pay High Price," available at: www.Nytimes.com/ … /how-local-taxpayers-bankroll-corporations.html [accessed February 2, 2014].

The Economist (2010a) "Jailhouse Blues," February 13, p. 37.

——(2010b) 'Rough Justice,' July 24, p. 13.

——(2012) "Pills and Progress," February 11, pp. 31–32.

The Toronto Star (2014) "America's Thick Blue Line," March 29, p. WD8.

Uno, K. (1980) *Principles of Political Economy* (Sussex: Harvester Press).

Western, B. (2006) *Punishment and Inequality in America* (New York: Russell Sage Foundation).

Wikipedia. (2014a) "Obesity in the US," available at: en.wikipedia.org/wiki/Obesity_ in_the_United_ States [accessed February 1, 2014].

——(2014b) "Volkswagen Chattanooga Assembly Plant" [accessed February 2, 2014].

Will, V. (2014) "America's Overdose on Overdoses," *Toronto Star*, March 1, WD 8.

Wood, D. (2013) "Iraq, Afghanistan War Veterans Struggle With Combat Traumas," available at: www.huffingtonpost.com/ … /iraq-afghanistan-war-veterans-combat-trauma [accessed January 28, 2014].

10 Not just another crisis

How and why the Great Recession was different

Maria N. Ivanova

The Great Recession of 2007–9 has often been referred to as the most severe economic downturn since the Great Depression. According to the official verdict of the National Bureau for Economic Research announced in September 2010, the trough of the recession was reached in June 2009 and a recovery followed. But said recovery has been different from any other in postwar US history. By 2010 corporate profits surpassed the previous 2006 peak and have risen strongly ever since. Investment, however, has remained sluggish. In 2012, more than three years after the official end of the Great Recession, real net private domestic investment was about 46 percent of its 2006 level. This peculiar co-existence of growing profit margins and weak investment has puzzled numerous analysts. But nowhere is the dubious character of the recovery more obvious than in the US labor market where employment has not yet recovered to its pre-recession level. Moreover, the complexity of the labor market situation extends beyond the slow pace of job creation and is compounded by the interplay of pre-existing tendencies, such as the continuous transformation of the occupational structure of the US economy which has been skewed towards the proliferation of low-skill, low-wage jobs, and novel ones, such as the rise of long-term unemployment. These realities suggest that the once celebrated "great American job machine" may have become a thing of the past and, arguably, is increasingly unlikely to return.

This chapter draws some parallels between the Great Recession and the Great Depression in the United States (US) in order to highlight the unique character of the recent downturn. It further outlines significant tendencies in the US labor market which are considered emblematic of the profound transformations that the American economy and society have been undergoing. A closer look at the 1920s and the 2000s reveals a number of similar characteristics underpinning the structural fragility of the American economy then and now. Those characteristics include the following: sluggish wages growth and falling labor share of national income, rising inequality with heavy concentration of wealth gains at the top levels of income distribution, mounting indebtedness among lower- and middle-income households, surging corporate profits and a corporate saving glut seeking financial ventures.

However, my key argument is that despite various structural similarities between the Great Depression and the Great Recession, the latter is a crisis of a different kind whose impact and far-reaching consequences have rendered useless traditional policy tools, such as demand stimuli and institutional adjustments.

The asset bubbles then and now

Both the Great Recession and the Great Depression were preceded by a stock market and a housing bubble, although in a reversed order. The economic expansion of the 1920s was accompanied by a real estate bubble which peaked around 1925 and deflated rapidly thereafter. The bubble was of remarkable proportions: in four consecutive years between 1924 and 1927, the share of housing construction in GDP exceeded 8 percent. Ever since this figure has only been approximated but never repeated, let alone exceeded. For comparison, during the most recent housing bubble the share of residential construction in GDP peaked at 6.2 percent in 2005 (Field 2011, pp. 232–33). The fallout of the 1920s bubble did not bring about an economy-wide collapse; the rest of the economy continued to expand in the second half of the decade. A stock market bubble started developing around March 1928. Its peak was reached in the late summer of 1929, followed by the dramatic crash of October 29 which has been symbolically associated with the beginning of the Great Depression.

In the recent period, the US economy went through the so-called dot-come bubble in the late 1990s, whose burst in 2000 was followed by one of the mildest recessions in postwar history while the financial sector remained largely unaffected. The Great Recession was triggered by the collapse of the biggest housing bubble since the Great Depression which was the culmination of the longest sustained boom of US residential investment and housing construction in postwar history that took place between 1992 and 2006. Housing starts in the early 2000s reached levels unseen since the early 1970s. New residential construction exceeded 2 million units in 2005 and peaked at an annual rate of 2.1 million units in the first quarter of 2006. New home sales exceeded 1 million in 2003–04 and peaked at 1.28 million in 2005. For comparison, new home sales averaged 608,000 in the 1980s and 698,000 in the 1990s. Housing prices also reached unprecedented heights in the 2000s. According to the S&P/Case-Shiller National Index, house prices increased by 11 percent in 2002, 11 percent in 2003, 15 percent in 2004, and 15 percent in 2005.

The housing bubble of the 1920s appears to have been neither the trigger of the Depression nor its most important cause while in 2007–08 there was a direct link between the burst of the real estate bubble and the run on the (shadow) banking system which triggered the Great Recession. Still, the analysis of the recent real estate financial collapse can benefit from a comparison with the 1920s not only because of some striking similarities in the booms of residential construction that preceded both crises but also because of important differences.

Many factors that accompanied the recent housing boom and bust were also present in the 1920s. For example, in both cases there was an initial easing of the monetary policy of the Federal Reserve that, according to many accounts, played a role in the credit boom that nurtured the bubbles. There was an expansion of mortgage lending which eventually led to the lowering of lending standards, although to different degrees. Mortgage securitization was also present in the 1920s but in a still undeveloped form. Most mortgage-backed securities (MBSs) were limited to pools of mortgages on apartments or other commercial properties, as opposed to mortgages on owner-occupied housing (Field 2013).

One of the most significant differences between then and now concerns the complete absence of government housing policies in the 1920s and, in particular, of any commitment to expand homeownership. While there was some loosening of lending standards in the 1920s, its degree appears quite modest by comparison. The typical mortgages required 40 to 50 percent down payment and were of relatively short duration, five to seven years at most, which limited bank exposure. There was no practice of lending to individuals and households with a significant risk of default. The absence of deposit insurance was another factor that encouraged more prudent lending behavior by financial institutions (White 2009).

There are barely any scholarly accounts of the Great Depression that point to housing as being among its primary causes (Gjerstad and Smith [2009] represents a notable exception). Such a case seems difficult to make partly because of the time gap between the housing peak in 1925–26 and the beginning of the economic downturn in the summer through fall of 1929. In fact, employment and output continued to grow even when housing prices and construction spending declined in the second half of the 1920s. The housing market itself had shown some signs of recovery by 1929. However, despite the gap between the housing peak and the general economic downturn that started in the 1929, the two events are by no means unconnected. Evidence shows, for example, that cities where the housing boom was most pronounced in terms of construction investment, rising housing prices, and homeownership rates also experienced the greatest decline in housing values and homeownership rates along with the highest rates of foreclosures in the early 1930s (Brocker and Hanes 2013). Furthermore, the overbuilding that took place over the 1920s is certainly a part of the explanation for why new construction and housing in general remained depressed longer than the rest of the economy with signs of recovery starting to appear in the late 1930s and only with significant government support.

As Galbraith (2009 [1954]) remarks, it is easier to explain the 1929 stock market crash than the Depression that followed. Indeed, establishing a direct connection between the stock market crash and the ensuing general economic downturn is actually not much easier than establishing a connection between the housing bubble and the Depression. Financial bubbles have occurred with relative frequency throughout history but they have not always induced deep recessions or depressions. Why does the burst of one bubble trigger economy-wide and global collapse while the effects of another remain limited? The view taken here is that neither the outbreak nor the severity of the Great Depression and the Great Recession can be fully understood by focusing on the particular features of the stock market or the housing bubble. Rather, the structural fragility of the economy that manifested itself in these bubbles was the underlying reason for the economy-wide collapse that followed.

The fundamental fragility of the economy then and now

The Great Depression and the Great Recession were triggered, respectively, by a stock market and a housing bubble. But to trigger something does not mean to cause it. Pre-existing structural imbalances in the economy were the reason why the burst of a speculative bubble induced a general economic collapse. A closer look at the boom and the bubble of the 1920s and the 2000s reveals a number of similar dynamics. In both cases, economic expansion was preceded and paralleled by years and even decades of sluggish wage growth relative to productivity growth, although the stagnation of labor income has been much more pronounced in the recent period. Over the last four decades, real incomes in the US have followed a general downward trend, while the peak level reached in the early 1970s was never regained. The boom of the 2000s represented no deviation from this trend. Real average weekly earnings in the private nonfarm sector remained almost flat in 2002–08. At the height of the boom in 2007, the median household income was $55,627, which was 9 percent lower than the 1999 peak of $56,080. In 2012, the median household income ($51,017) was still 8.3 percent below the 2007 level (US Census Bureau 2013).

Accounts of labor income growth in the 1920s have often been exaggerated. Manufacturing was the leading sector of the economy and even there wage growth was far from spectacular, and most importantly, it was lagging behind the growth of property income. There was a substantial increase in the real annual earnings of manufacturing workers in 1922–23 after a significant decline during the recession of 1921. Real wages of manufacturing workers remained flat in 1923–27 followed by a 6 percent increase during 1928 (Brissenden 1929; Douglas 1929). As will be discussed below, the growth of property income during the same decade was much stronger. Sluggish wage growth relative to profit growth then and now translated into a decline in the labor share of national income (Ivanova 2014; Jacobson and Occhino 2012; Kristal 2013; Steindl 1952).

The fall in the labor share of national income over the last four decades has been accompanied by rising income inequality. The GINI index for households which reached a postwar low of 0.386 in 1968 has been continuously on the rise since the mid-1970s and reached 0.477 in 2011–12. A similarly dramatic increase in income inequality also characterized the 1920s. The share of disposable income for the lower 93 percent of the nonfarm population fell from 71 percent in 1919 to 61.29 percent in 1929; correspondingly, the GINI index increased from 0.359 to 0.4828 in the same period (Smiley 2000). Then and now, income gains have been heavily concentrated at the very top of the income distribution. As shown by Piketty and Saez (2013), the evolution of the top incomes over the last century has been U-shaped. The share of total income accruing to the top 10 percent exceeded 45 percent in 1928 (and reached almost 50 percent if capital gains were included), declined sharply during the Depression, remained below 35 percent in the postwar decades and started to increase again in the early 1980s. It crossed the 45 percent mark in 2005 and reached 50 percent including capital gains in 2007. In 2012, the top-decile income share including capital gains stood at 50.4 percent – the highest level since the beginning of the series in 1917.

Under the combination of strong income gains at the top and relative wage stagnation at the bottom, the housing and consumption booms of the 1920s and the 2000s were fueled and sustained by growing household indebtedness, particularly among low- and middle-income households, along with the luxury spending of upper-income households (Barba and Pivetti 2009; Brennan 2014). Between 2000 and the peak year 2007, residential mortgage debt out-standing almost doubled from $6.1 trillion to $11.96 trillion. The growth of mortgage debt in the 1920s was even more spectacular (although from much lower levels in absolute terms). According to Persons' (1930, p. 104) estimate, from 1920 to 1929 total residential mortgages outstanding increased from $11.1 billion to $27.1 billion or 140 percent. Consumer credit was also on the rise. Largely due to the widespread use of installment credit for the purchase of consumer durables, consumer debt as a percentage of household income doubled from 4.68 percent in 1920 to 9.34 percent in 1929 (Olney 1991, pp. 87–90, Table 4.1). Between 2000 and the peak year 2008, outstanding consumer credit (revolving and non-revolving) rose from $1.74 trillion to $2.55 trillion or about 46 percent. Total household debt (residential mortgage debt and consumer debt) peaked at 138 percent of disposable personal income in 2007.

Another similarity between the 1920s and the 2000s concerns the emer-gence of a saving imbalance as a result of rising income inequality epitomized in the larger share of national income accruing to the propertied classes and the so-called working rich. In the 1960s and the 1970s personal saving was generally about 9 and occasionally above 10 percent of disposable income. This share has continuously declined since the mid-1980s to reach 1.5 percent in 2005. The decline has not been uniform as high-income households tend to save more than low- and middle-income households both in absolute and relative terms. Since 1989, saving rates for the upper two income quintiles have trended upward, but the difference has been most pronounced in the top quintile whose saving as a share of income has risen from 22 percent in 1989 to 37.1 percent in 2012. Unlike the 2000s, the 1920s were characterized by a general rise in aggregate saving even though, then as well as now, saving rates differed strongly across the various income classes. However, in 1929 as in the present day, the savings of the majority of the population constituted a negligible portion of total saving. Thus, rising incomes of individuals and households in the upper-income brackets ($5,000 and above) were primarily responsible for the growth in total saving (Moulton *et al.* 1934).

A further similarity between the 1920s and the 2000s concerns the impressive growth of property income relative to labor income. According to Kreps' (1935, p. 565) estimate, while total labor income increased 29 percent between 1922 and 1929, interest and dividend payments more than doubled from $6.5 billion to $13.28 billion. The net profits of the 135 leading industrial corporations increased 150 percent from $840.2 million in 1922 to over $2 billion in 1929 while their retained earnings in 1929 were $732.2 million compared to 297.2 million in 1922 (Sloan 1936, p. 41). Total cash holdings of all corporations increased $5.6 billion between 1925 and 1929 (Moulton *et al.* 1934, p. 153). After the beginning of the Depression, the fall of labor income was much greater than the fall of property income (Kreps 1935). Corporate profits declined but did not collapse. As reported by Sloan (1936, p. 40), in 1933, the 135 leading industrial corporations still had $710 million more cash in their coffers than in 1922 and that amount was down from the peak figure in the same period by less than $400 million.

Similarly, in the recent period, property income has risen out of proportion to labor income even if the strong contribution of the salaried working rich is considered. The upward trend of corporate profits since the second half of the 1990s was briefly interrupted by the Great Recession, only to further accelerate in its aftermath. While corporate profits almost tripled in 2000–2012, wages and salaries increased by only 30 percent. The wage share of national income declined 4 percent over that period. Rising profits translated into strong growth of retained earnings which averaged $407 billion in 2002–06 and over $800 billion in 2010–12. The transformation of the US non-financial corporate sector from a net debtor in the 1970s and 1980s to a net lender in the 2000s along with the accumulation of huge corporate cash holdings reaching $1.62 trillion in 2011 have sparked a considerable amount of research, discussion, and controversy with regard to its causes (e.g. Armenter and Hnatkovska 2011; Bates *et al.* 2006; Sánchez and Yurdagul 2013).

In sum, two causal mechanisms underlay the structural fragility of the economy then and now. First, the relative stagnation of labor income represents the key factor behind rising income inequality and a potential drag on consumption which was temporarily alleviated by credit expansion; hence, the rising household debt levels which eventually became unsustainable. Second, rising corporate profits created an overhang of idle money, eager to lend itself to speculative ventures, which played a key role in fueling the stock-market bubble of the 1920s and the housing bubble of the 2000s (Ivanova 2014).

What happened to the Great American Job Machine?

Despite the similarities discussed above, this chapter argues that the Great Recession was a crisis of a different kind whose repercussions are quite unlikely to be resolved with demand stimuli, policy or institutional adjustments, that is, the type of solutions that once worked well to support the relative stability of capital accumulation in the postwar period. For the American economy then and now is fundamentally different.

The US labor market is the area where an actual recovery from the Great Recession is still outstanding. The fall in the official unemployment rate from 10 percent in October 2010 to 6.7 percent as of December 2013 is to a large extent attributable to a fall in the labor force participation rate. The latter has declined from its peak of over 67 percent in the late 1990s to 62.8 percent in December 2013 which is a level unseen since the late 1970s. Seasonally adjusted total nonfarm employment peaked at about 138.4 million in December 2007–January 2008, sank rapidly afterwards to remain below 130 million between September 2009 and October 2010. At the end of 2013, total job count for nonfarm employment was still 1 million less than in January 2008. The total number of full-time employed persons, defined as those working 35 hours or more per week, declined from its peak of 121.9 million in November 2007 to 117.3 million in December 2013.

A novel feature of the Great Recession and the following troubled recovery has been the rise and persistence of long-term unemployment. Between the late 1980s and 2007, the US enjoyed somewhat lower rates of unemployment and significantly shorter unemployment spells than other advanced countries. Between 1948, when official records began, and 2008, the average number of weeks spent in unemployment never exceeded 20. This number increased significantly during the Great Recession and doubled in its aftermath. In 2011 and 2012, the average number of weeks spent in unemployment was 39.4. Between January 2008 and January 2009, the number of long-term unemployed (those out of work for 27 weeks or more) doubled to reach 2.6 million. In January 2008, 17 percent of the unemployed were long-term unemployed. In January 2009, the percentage was 22.4. By January 2010, the number of long-term unemployed reached 6.3 million, that is, 42.6 percent of all unemployed. Fast forward to January 2014; after almost 5 years into the "recovery," there were still 3.6 million long-term unemployed accounting for 35.8 percent of all unemployed.

The present conditions in the US labor market have been strongly influenced by the cumulative and mutually reinforcing effects of two related tendencies: the deepening job polarization along with the growth of low-paid, often part-time work, and the weakening of the connection between output and employment growth. These tendencies are a result of the transformation of the industrial and occupational structures of the US economy which has been part and parcel of the global restructuring of production since the 1970s.

In the two decades preceding the Great Recession, the US labor market served as the poster child and vindication of the paradigm of labor flexibility which represented at its core a philosophy and practice of insecure employment. Job destruction was said to encourage job creation and thus a virtuous cycle of labor market dynamism. Overall, there was a significant increase in the employment–population ratio with low unemployment rates and exceptionally short unemployment spells. This labor market dynamism, however, had more than one dark side. On the one hand, the dismantling of employment protection enabled the proliferation of part-time, low-paid, no-benefit jobs thereby turning job insecurity into a structural feature of the American way of life. The erosion of stable employment relations took its toll on the individual workers, and on society as a whole, in terms of growing human insecurity and psychological distress. On the other hand, the occupational structure of the US economy has undergone a deep transformation epitomized in the so-called job polarization, which refers to the disproportionate expansion of job opportunities in high-skill high-wage occupations along with low-skill, low-wage occupations, coupled with shrinking opportunities in middle-wage, middle-skill white-collar and blue-collar occupations. During the 1980s, there was an almost uniform rise in different employment categories and skill levels with occupations below the median skill level actually declining and occupations above the median increasing as a share of employment. This situation started to change in the 1990s and by the early 2000s the change had reached dramatic proportions. Employment growth in 1999–2007 was heavily concentrated among the lowest three deciles of occupations. In deciles four through nine, employment shares actually declined while in the highest decile of occupations, employment shares remained flat (Autor 2010). The deepening income inequality in American society is to a large extent a consequence of this transformation of the occupational structure of the US economy which, according to Mouw and Kalleberg (2010), explains about 66 percent of the increase in wage inequality between 1992 and 2008. The overwhelming majority of jobs created in the aftermath of the Great Recession have been concentrated in low-wage sectors, such as retail, professional and business services, leisure and hospitality, and healthcare.

Considering the present sluggish employment recovery, one may be tempted to draw a parallel to the 1930s as employment then similarly did not recover back to its 1929 pre-depression peak until 1940. But the similarity between the two situations is largely superficial while the differences, determined, among other things, by the particular dynamic between output and employment then and now, are fundamental. In the early years of the Depression, output declined more than employment: between 1929 and 1933, real GDP dropped by 31 percent while employment fell by 18 percent which was to a significant extent due to the employers' conscious attempt to retain workers by reducing labor hours (Neumann *et al.* 2013). By contrast, between 2007 and 2009, output declined by 4.7 percent while employment fell by 6.3 percent (Freeman 2013). Furthermore, employment growth has lagged significantly behind output growth during the recovery. The progressive weakening of the relation between output and employment growth is another manifestation of changing labor market conditions in the US. Signs of this weakening have been observed for decades and, particularly, during the "jobless recovery" in the early 2000s when employment took longer than ever before in the postwar period to recover back to the pre-recession level. During the recovery following the Great Recession, the weak relation between output growth and employment growth has turned into a virtual disconnect. From the end of the recession through 2012, GDP increased by 7.5 percent while employment increased by only 1.2 percent (Freeman 2013).

The persistent weakness in the US labor market is to a significant extent due to the weakness of domestic investment which has remained unusually low in recent years. At the same time, it is important to emphasize that a general slowdown of investment in fixed capital formation has characterized the development of the US economy since the late 1960s. The final section of this chapter is an inquiry into key development trends in the US economy over the last several decades that may shed light on the factors and tensions underlying the unique character of the Great Recession.

How and why the Great Recession was different

Both the Great Depression and the Great Recession were crises of over-accumulation. But in the first case, the underlying problem appears to have been overinvestment relative to consumer demand against the backdrop of labor abundance and low wages that ultimately drove the economy into an underconsumption trap; hence the depth, length, and severity of the slump (Devine 1983, 1994). Consumption in highly unequal societies depends critically on the combination of continuous borrowing by low- and middle-income households and the luxury spending of the rich. In time, the relative importance of the latter is bound to increase as rising debt-to-income ratios impede further borrowing. By 1929, credit was stretched to its limits and creditworthy borrowers were increasingly hard to come by. The loss of fortunes by rich individuals and households as a result of the stock market crash led to falling demand for luxury goods. Producers responded by curtailing investment. These factors clearly point to weak demand as being the primary cause for the depth and severity of the crisis. But the productive structure of the US economy was substantially sound and bore a significant growth potential. As argued by Field (2011), the US economic and military success in the postwar decades rested upon the dramatic expansion of potential output during the Depression years due to the combination of continued growth of multifactor productivity in manufacturing and the spillover effects in transportation and distribution resulting from the extension of public infrastructure. The extra-ordinary level of profitability reached during World War II significantly overshot both the historical pre-depression and the postwar trend. This "leap forward" was the result of technological change manifest in a 40 percent increase in multifactor productivity and associated with an 'autonomous' substitution of equipment for structures in the capital stock (Duménil *et al.* 1993).

The present situation is different and significantly more complex. The problem of overaccumulation of capital is now more severe than ever before.

Crises and depressions prior to the Great Depression were relatively frequent events that were allowed to run their course. There was no economic policy, no government intervention, no functioning lender of last resort. Market adjustment occurred through the fall in asset values resulting in the destruction of fictitious and real capital. This cleared the way for a new cycle of economic growth in the process of accumulation. In other words, overaccumulation in the pre-depression period was a temporary phenomenon which was regulated by "the market." This dynamic changed after World War II. "Big Government" and "Big Bank," in Hyman Minsky's now famous terms, took charge of economic management and worked hard to avert deep recessions and depressions by preventing, in time of crisis, the massive collapse of profits and asset values, and, correspondingly, the destruction of (over)accumulated capital. As a result of decades-long government efforts at "stabilizing" capitalism, overaccumulation has become a permanent feature of the latter. The American and global economy is dominated by "too-big-to-fail" firms that enjoy an implicit government guarantee that they would never be allowed to fail because of feared contagion risks and snowball effects. Moreover, there is over $100 trillion of investable wealth in the global economy including the assets of high-net-worth individuals, pension, insurance, and mutual funds, sovereign-wealth funds, corporate cash holdings, etc. – an ocean of idle money looking for profitable ventures. The problems resulting from the global overaccumulation of investable capital are further magnified by the workings of the hyperactive financial system eager to invent, reap, and harness new profit opportunities.

Overaccumulation lies at the very root of the recent downturn. And this is why it has been so difficult to categorize the Great Recession as either a demand-side or a supply-side crisis. Curiously, it bears some elements of both. Structural inadequacy of aggregate demand was one of the factors underlying the recent downturn. The overextension of credit was among the key reasons why effective demand appeared healthy before the crisis. The curtailment of credit through tightening of lending standards, prompted by rising debt burdens and insolvency of borrowers, accounted to a significant extent for the drop of consumer demand after the crisis started. The full effects of rising debt levels on the American economy have not yet been felt but are bound to be. The demography of debt distribution characterized by a considerable increase of the debt burden on younger generations is likely to alter the whole dynamics of consumer spending in the future. Furthermore, the structure of US consumer spending is characterized by a heavy orientation towards imported goods as manifested in the huge trade imbalance resulting from the deficit on the balance on goods which reached $847.8 billion in 2006. Fifty-five percent of the latter amount came from the combined deficits in consumer goods and automotive vehicles, parts, and engines. Despite an overall decline in the current account deficit, the deficit on the goods balance was still $741.5 billion in 2012 and most unlikely to significantly decline in the near future. This structure of US consumer spending explains why buoyant demand during the bubble years and beyond has done relatively little to stimulate domestic investment.

On the supply side, there are also considerable challenges, although of a somewhat unusual kind. The most serious indicator of supply-side trouble – falling profit rates or return on investment – seems to be absent (Basu and Vasudevan 2013; Smithers 2013). With minimal interruptions, the US corporate sector has enjoyed high and rising total profits since the mid-1990s. The present puzzling coexistence of high profit margins and sluggish investment has spurred a considerable amount of discussion identifying a number of probable causes. The problem of weak demand as a result of the combination of, on the one hand, a large share of imported goods in the consumer basket, and sluggish income growth, rising inequality, and debt burdens, on the other, was already noted above. Other accounts point to a general slowdown in capitalism's capacity to innovate in a way that could spur new investment and raise productivity growth to levels comparable with the postwar Golden Age. Following Gordon (2012), economic growth over the last 250 years has been directly correlated with the major technological innovations resulting from the so-called Industrial Revolutions. Many of these innovations and their spin-offs were unique, one-time events that cannot be repeated. Consequently, a slowdown in the rate of investment and growth is unavoidable. A different but not contradictory explanation put forward by the Monthly Review School points to the tendency to monopolization, characteristic of American capitalism, which erodes competition and reduces the incentive to innovate (Foster and McChesney 2012). Some explanations attribute the present weakness of investment to changes in corporate behavior as a result of linking management compensation to company performance. The latter is typically measured either by changes to earnings per share, or the ratio of after-tax profits to net worth (return on equity), or by an increase in share prices. The growing share of performance-based bonuses in management compensation has reoriented the focus of company management towards raising short-term profits at the expense of long-term investment (Smithers 2013).

The alternative explanations of the peculiar coexistence of high profit margins and weak investment are not mutually exclusive and may be viewed as pointing to different aspects of a complex problem. As noted above, the general slowdown of capital accumulation in the US is not a recent phenomenon but a tendency that goes back to the late 1960s. The initial causes of this tendency can be located in the profitability crisis of the Fordist model. Remarkably, the transnationalization of production, which was the central solution to this crisis, has further aggravated the general slowdown of domestic investment. Since the early 1980s, a growing share of US corporate profits has come from the overseas operations of US multinational companies. This rest-of-the-world share of corporate profits averaged about 27 percent in the first decade of the 2000s. The global restructuring of production through the offshore outsourcing of labor-intensive production stages has played an important role in raising the overall profitability of the US corporate sector. However, the global restructuring of production has also transformed the domestic economic structure, lowered investment demand, and permanently altered the employment prospects of the US economy. The Great Recession may have opened the door to a different world but did not create it. The forces underlying the tendencies discussed above have been at work for decades. The recent upheaval merely exposed and accelerated their effects.

References

Armenter, R. and V. Hnatkovska (2011) "The Macroeconomics of Firms' Savings," *Federal Reserve Bank of Philadelphia Working Paper* No. 12–1.

Autor, D. (2010) "The Polarization of Job Opportunities in the US Labor Market: Implications for Employment and Earnings," Center for American Progress and The Hamilton Project. Available at: http://cdn.americanprogress.org/wp-content/uploads/issues/2010/04/job_polarization_report.html [accessed March 1, 2014].

Barba, A. and M. Pivetti (2009) "Rising Household Debt: Its Causes and Macro-economic Implications – A Long-Period Analysis," *Cambridge Journal of Economics*, 33: 113–37.

Basu, D. and R. Vasudevan (2013) "Technology, Distribution and the Rate of Profit in the US Economy: Understanding the Current Crisis," *Cambridge Journal of Economics*, 37: 57–89.

Bates, T. W., K. M. Kahle and R. M. Stulz (2006) "Why Do U.S. Firms Hold So Much More Cash Than They Used To?" *NBER Working Paper No. 12534* (Cambridge, MA: National Bureau of Economic Research).

Brennan, D. M. (2014) "'Too Bright for Comfort': A Kaleckian View of Profit Realisation in the USA, 1964–2009," *Cambridge Journal of Economics*, 38: 239–55.

Brissenden, P. F. (1929) *Earnings of Factory Workers, 1899–1927* (Washington, DC: US Government Printing Office).

Brocker, M. and C. Hanes (2013) "The 1920s American Real Estate Boom and the Downturn of the Great Depression: Evidence from City Cross Sections," *NBER Working Paper No. 18852*, (Cambridge, MA: National Bureau of Economic Research).

Devine, J. D. (1983) "Underconsumption, Over-Investment and the Origins of the Great Depression," *Review of Radical Political Economics*, 15(1): 1–27.

——(1994) "The Causes of the 1929–33 Great Collapse: A Marxian Interpretation," *Research in Political Economy*, 14: 119–94.

Douglas, P. H. (1929) "Wages," *American Journal of Sociology*, 34(6): 1021–29.

Duménil, G., M. Glick and D. Lévy (1993) "The Rise of the Rate of Profit during World War II," *Review of Economics and Statistics*, 75(2): 315–20.

Foster, J. B. and R. W. McChesney (2012) *The Endless Crisis* (New York: Monthly Review Press).

Field, A. J. (2011) *A Great Leap Forward: The 1930s Depression and U.S. Economic Growth* (New Haven, CT: Yale University Press).

——(2013) "The Interwar Housing Cycle in the Light of 2001–11: A Comparative Historical Approach," *NBER Working Paper No. 18796* (Cambridge, MA: National Bureau of Economic Research).

Freeman, R. B. (2013) "Failing the Test? The Flexible U.S. Job Market in the Great Recession," *The ANNALS of the American Academy of Political and Social Science*: 650–78.

Galbraith, J. K. (2009 [1954]) *The Great Crash 1929* (Boston, MA: Houghton-Mifflin).

S. Gjerstad and V. L. Smith (2009) "Monetary Policy, Credit Extension, and Housing Bubbles: 2008 and 1929," *Critical Review*, 21(2): 269–300.

Gordon, R. J. (2012) "Is US Economic Growth Over? Faltering Innovation Confronts the Six Headwinds," *NBER Working Paper No. 18315* (Cambridge, MA: National Bureau of Economic Research).

Ivanova, M. N. (2014) "The Great Recession and the Great Depression in Comparative Perspective," unpublished manuscript.

Jacobson, M. and F. Occhino (2012) "Labor's Declining Share of Income and Rising Inequality," Federal Reserve Bank of Cleveland, Economic Commentary, September 25.

Kreps, T.J. (1935) "Dividends, Interests, Profits, Wages, 1923–35," *Quarterly Journal of Economics*, 49(4): 561–99.

Kristal, T. (2013) "The Capitalist Machine: Computerization, Workers' Power, and the Decline in Labor's Share within U.S. Industries," *American Sociological Review*, 78 (3): 361–89.

Moulton, H. G., M. Leven and C. Warburton (1934) *America's Capacity to Consume* (Washington, DC: The Brookings Institution).

Mouw, T. and A. L. Kalleberg (2010) "Occupations and the Structure of Wage Inequality in the United States, 1980s to 2000s," *American Sociological Review*, 75 (3): 402–31.

Neumann, T., J. Taylor and P. Fishback (2013) "Fluctuations in Weekly Hours and Total Hours Worked Over the Past 90 Years and the Importance of Changes in Federal Policy Toward Job Sharing," *NBER Working Paper No. 18816* (Cambridge, MA: National Bureau of Economic Research).

Olney, M. (1991) *Buy Now, Pay Later: Advertizing, Credit and Consumer Durables in the 1920s* (Chapel Hill: University of North Carolina Press).

Persons, C. E. (1930) "Credit Expansion, 1920 to 1929, and Its Lessons," *Quarterly Journal of Economics*, 45: 94–130.

Piketty, T. and E. Saez (2013) "Top Incomes and the Great Recession: Recent Evolutions and Policy Implications," *IMF Economic Review*, 61(3): 456–78.

Sánchez, J. M., and E. Yurdagul (2013) "Why Are Corporations Holding So Much Cash?" *The Regional Economist*, Federal Reserve Bank of St. Louis, January.

Simpson, H. D. (1933) "Real Estate Speculation and the Depression," *American Economic Review*, 23(1): 163–71.

Sloan, L. H. and Associates (1936) *Two Cycles of Corporation Profits: 1922–1933 and 1934–19XX* (New York: Harper).

Smiley, G. (2000) "A Note on New Estimates of the Distribution of Income in the 1920s," *Journal of Economic History*, 60(4): 1120–28.

Smithers, A. (2013) *The Road to Recovery: How and Why Economic Policy Must Change.* (Cornwall: Wiley).

Steindl, J. (1952) *Maturity and Stagnation in American Capitalism* (New York: Monthly Review Press).

US Census Bureau. (2013) "Income, Poverty, and Health Insurance Coverage in the United States: 2012," September (Washington, DC: US Government Printing Office).

White, E. N. (2009) "Lessons from the Great American Real Estate Boom and Bust of the 1920s," *NBER Working Paper Series*, No. 15573 (Cambridge, MA: National Bureau of Economic Research).

11 Competitiveness or emancipation?

Rethinking regulation and (counter-)hegemony in times of capitalist crisis[1]

Hans-Jürgen Bieling and Ulrich Brand

Introduction

International Political Economy (IPE) and Comparative Political Economy (CPE) analyses are in great demand. They struggle hard, however, with the challenge to understand the dynamics and the complexity of the multiple crises of capitalism and the dominant way to deal with it, i.e., the politics of austerity. The answers provided not only depend on empirical knowledge, but also on the general theoretical assumptions about the nature and modes of reproduction in the realm of international political economy.

Given the long-standing predominance of institutionalist perspectives, it is no surprise that such approaches, e.g. the Varieties of Capitalism approach (VoC, cf. Hall and Soskice 2001), still prevail within the recent political economy debates. Theoretically more sophisticated institutionalist points of view are sometimes pooled under the heading "post-VoC" (cf. Hancké *et al.* 2007; Hall and Thelen 2009; Höpner 2009; Streeck 2010, 2011a) and they still dispose of considerable interpretive power. This power is, however, overrated in some regards. First, irrespective of the important insights into the specific institutional organization of capitalist models of development, in terms of the presumed ontology, institutionalist IPE/CPE has no deeper understanding of capitalism grounded in a social theory. It therefore runs short in taking transnational social relations, including given power relations, structures of domination, and the concrete forms of socio-economic, cultural and socio-ecological reproduction into sufficient systematic account. Second, this neglect corresponds with a quite narrow, if not one-sided, cognitive interest. Most scholars in the institutionalist tradition are primarily concerned about the particular institutional settings and their complementary arrangement as a precondition for the promotion of economic growth and national competitiveness. Third and consequently, this precondition also has important normative implications. So, institutionalist concepts of capitalism neither systematically address structurally inscribed forms of domination and humiliation, the unjust distribution of life chances, or the destruction of bio-physical conditions, nor do they address forms of emancipatory engagement pointing beyond the existing capitalist order.

In view of such shortcomings this paper aims to criticize the presumed intellectual superiority of institutionalist Political Economy. We will go about this aim in four steps. The following section provides a short outline of the key assumptions and influential contributions of institutionalist IPE/CPE and their respective analytical strengths and shortcomings. In order to overcome these deficiencies, the third section conceptually develops a political sociology and political ecology of today's capitalism by drawing on insights from Marxist, regulationist, neo-Gramscian and neo-Poulantzian Political Economy debates. We intend to show that an adequate understanding of current, crisis-driven capitalist development should refer to aspects such as the contested forms of (inter)national steering and regulation, of struggles for hegemony within civil society, and of transnational (inter-)dependencies, uneven development and imperial control. In the fourth section, we use those concepts to analyze and interpret the recently established austerity agenda and its implications on social (re-)production, societal power relations, and social-ecological transformation. Finally, we reflect to what extent current developments may open new ways towards emancipatory alternatives.

Strengths and shortcomings of institutionalist versions of political economy

The recent prominence of institutionalist Political Economy, above all CPE, has to be understood against the background of its past history and its important analytical insights. The pedigree of institutionalist CPE finds its origins in the German historical school and Thornstein Veblen's institutional-sociological economics. It proceeds to Andrew Shonfield's (1965) analysis of particular national styles of state intervention, Michael Porter's (1990) study of the impact of different institutional settings on innovation and competitiveness, and to Michel Albert's (1993) "Capitalism against Capitalism" which distinguishes between the models of Rhineland and Anglo-Saxon capitalism. In a way, the prominent VoC approach which differentiates between Liberal Market Economies (LMEs) and Coordinated Market Economies (CMEs) represents an academically stylized version of Albert's attempt to highlight the specific territorial, and, above all national, features of capitalist institutional organization (cf. Hall and Soskice 2001). In this sense, a core assumption of the VoC approach is that capitalist models are formed by formal and informal institutional modes of coordination and that the complementary arrangement[2] of these institutional modes determines the economic performance and international competitiveness of individual models.

Contrary to neoclassical economics, therefore, institutionalist CPE takes the institutional conditions and contexts of economic development seriously. Most scholars of this line of thinking offer a historical understanding of capitalist development and its dynamics. Furthermore, they have a rather broad view on institutions, including informal rules, conventions, and practices of societal reproduction. This implies that the term capitalism is not restricted to the economic system or the market but also considers different arenas and modes of embeddedness. Moreover, institutional CPE is also critical of the modernization of theoretical conceptualizations which imagine a superior path of development, that is, a so-called best practice model, to which all others should orient. Hence, the focus is on the continued institutional, cultural, and political diversity of capitalist models and their specific trajectories while trendy but too polarizing globalization and convergence arguments are rejected.

Next to these and other merits of institutionalist CPE, there are, however, certain analytical limits. In terms of the VoC approach, critics have worked out and emphasized above all the following deficits (cf. Bieling 2011; Bruff 2011; Beck and Scherrer 2013): only a half-hearted break with neoclassical economics; a firm-centered perspective insensitive to macroeconomic conditions; a rationalist ontology concerning the actors; and a rather simplifying typology which only refers to two ideal-types and neglects all other models as institutionally incoherent and therefore less efficient. From our perspective, these criticisms are important. With respect to our argument, other conceptual flaws need to be emphasized:

- A first flaw concerns the dynamics and the nature of social change and transformation (cf. Kang 2006: 15f). These are often underrated, as institutionalist Political Economy tends to emphasize phenomena of formal institutional persistence without being sensitive to their simultaneous (but sometimes also uneven), often incremental, informal, and practical transformation.
- A second flaw is related to the first one and refers to the very understanding of capitalism. Most institutionalist political economists regard capitalism only as an institutionally embedded ensemble of market relations. Of course, the firm-centric perspective sometimes requires taking forms of production and the organization of labor into account, too. However, markets and companies are primarily seen as more or less efficiently guided spheres of shareholder and manager control, but not as terrains of power also shaped by other – sometimes opposing – social forces such as trade unions, social movements, non-governmental organizations (NGOs), or state actors which do not see their role in exclusively securing the economic benefit of the firms. This conceptual disinterest in the mutual conditionality of capitalism and social power relations is not confined to the area of work and production. It also covers the sphere of reproduction, that is, public and private households, the ways that organizational patterns correspond with particular social relations in terms of gender, ethnicity, and class as well as the institutionally and discursively embedded forms of the societal appropriation of nature, i.e. the bio-physical conditions of (re-)production.
- The thin social-theoretical background of institutionalist Political Economy is also reflected in a third flaw. Basically, the state is seen as a public authority and regulatory instance which sets economic rules. This is not

wrong but a rather simplifying instrumentalist view of the state whose social content and character remains underexplored. In other words, institutionalist CPE works with a flat ontology of state-market-interaction that tends to reify or fetishize both the market and the state. As an expression of the "productivist bias," a similar fetishization takes place with respect to two powerful dispositives of capitalist societies, i.e., growth and competitiveness. It is not seen that growth and competitiveness themselves are complex social relations which secure certain modes of production and living, class and gender relations, hegemonic orientations and understandings of a "good life," the dominance of a hierarchically structured capitalist world market, and destructive societal-nature relations.

- Finally, most institutionalist Political Economy conceptually suffers from a methodological nationalist perspective. Of course, there are good reasons to reject an immediate equation of the recent phase of globalization with overall convergence. Most institutionalist scholars know that national capitalist models are under the influence of world market developments and trans- or supranational institutional arrangements. Nevertheless, these spheres are regarded as exogenous and not constitutive to national capitalist models. Neither their mutual – mostly asymmetrical – interpenetration nor their rivaling nature, or in other words: the "uneven and combined development" (Trotsky 1977, p. 26f.; Smith 1984; of capitalism is taken up as a conceptual challenge).

A substantial and critical analysis of the current age of transnational austerity has to address the listed flaws. Quite a few institutionalist Political Economy scholars have moved in this direction. Partially adopting insights from historical materialist Political Economy, they have outlined a conceptually more comprehensive and dynamic framework of institutional embeddedness, capable of not only analyzing inter-national but also inter-temporal capitalist change (cf. Jackson and Deeg 2012; Nölke *et al.* 2013). Moreover, they delved more intensively into the specific external economic integration as an important component of particular trajectories of capitalist development, for instance, financialized or export-led accumulation (cf. Kalinowski 2013); and they have also applied the acquired insights to European integration and the crisis of Economic and Monetary Union (EMU) (cf. Hall 2012).

Perhaps Wolfgang Streeck (2010, 2011a, 2011b) has gone furthest with the move towards a more social-theoretically and critically grounded understanding of today's global capitalism. He has not only worked out a more complex institutional and socio-economic analytical heuristic but also a theoretically compelling and challenging interpretation of the capitalist prologue to the current crisis. According to Streeck, capitalist development – under conditions of democratic rule – is inherently conflictual due to class-based structural distributional struggles which are only temporarily balanced by, more or less, operational institutional arrangements (cf. Streeck 2011b). For instance, since the late 1960s the tension between rising wages and a shrinking rate of profits was softened by the acceptance of higher inflation; then, from the late 1970s onwards, given the impairment of money holders and national competitiveness, social peace was secured at the cost of rising public indebtedness; and as this strategy reached its limits in the early 1990s, the stimulation of financial markets and an increase of private household debt enabled the way out of the crisis. Meanwhile, after the bursting of the financial bubble and the subsequent political rescue of the financial system, much of private debt has been transformed into – even further increasing – public debt so that austerity measures seem to be an unavoidable "solution."

Obviously, this remarkable modification of institutionalist Political Economy is driven by the attempt to emphasize the conflictual, crisis-prone, and capitalist nature of so-called market economies, including the difficulties of generating political legitimacy. In that sense, therefore, we can agree with David Coates (2014, p. 22ff) that Streeck has produced a rupture within institutionalist political economy debates, but still remains trapped in the institutionalist paradigm. This shows up in certain formulations, for instance, when Streeck (2011b, p. 164) writes about capitalism as becoming "more like itself, revealing in the course of its development its 'true nature', or its 'essence'" or when he pits a "state people" (Staatsvolk) against a "market people" (Marktvolk) instead of looking at their overlapping social-structural commonalities (cf. Streeck 2013, p. 119ff). Obviously, Streeck is more interested in capitalism as an unfolding logic of development than as a particular social formation which is based on a particular organization of work, reproduction, and exploitation, complex civil society networks and contested public discourses, and specific forms of domination and control structuring the living conditions of social groups and classes (cf. the critiques by Brie 2013; Demirovic 2013). From our point of view, all these dimensions are crucial for understanding today's capitalism including its inherent contradictions, crisis processes, and emancipatory alternatives.

Capitalism as a complex formation of contested social relations

The critique of institutionalist Political Economy leads us to the conclusion that a more comprehensive and critical understanding of capitalism should be based less on theoretical off-springs of historical and actor-centered institutionalism and more on Karl Marx and the rich tradition of historical materialist research. In the following, we will show that not only classical historical materialist theorists, but also more recent theoretical currents such as the French regulation school, neo-Gramscian IPE and neo-Poulantzian state theory have contributed to an understanding of capitalism as a complex social formation whose inherent dynamics of "uneven and combined development" are not restricted to the economic realm. On the contrary, by emphasizing political sociology and political ecology dimensions of historical materialist Political Economy, we aim to highlight that the contradictory and uneven development of capitalism also includes specific bio-physical and social forms of life and production.

Social relations of production and reproduction and their capitalist regulation

According to Marx, capitalism represents a social formation whose development is driven by capital's insatiable desire to increase profits through more intensive or extensive strategies of investment. The accumulation imperative, therefore, has fundamental and far-reaching implications. One of these implications is that "[t]he bourgeoisie cannot exist without constantly revolutionizing the instruments of production, and thereby the relations of production, and with them the whole relations of society" (Marx and Engels 1998, p. 243).

Next to its inherently revolutionary nature, a second implication is capital's tendency to create the world market (cf. Marx 1973, p. 408). Extensive accumulation and the production of exchange value via commodities and competition represents the material background against which the bourgeoisie cultivates a cosmopolitan orientation. Capitalist development is, however, not a one-dimensional process. It should rather be seen as a dialectical process of the *unifying* forces of the societies under the dominance of the capitalist mode of production and, at the same time, continuous territorially *differentiating and fragmenting* dynamics. Hence, the analysis of societies with similar economic structures does not obviate the actuality of such societies: "due to innumerable different empirical circumstances, natural environment, racial relations, external historical influences, etc. from showing infinite variations and gradations in appearance, which can be ascertained only by analysis of the empirically given circumstances" (Marx 1968, pp. 331, 555; Röttger 2008). Apart from the concrete empirical circumstances, such features are, however, a systematic product of capitalist development as its spatially and temporarily uneven nature (Smith 1984). This is strongly determined by the role of a national economy within the international division of labor, that is, the specific mode of integration into the world market. The world market is not an external given which requires adequate accommodation (competitiveness). It is in itself a mode of the reproduction of capitalist societies and a terrain of various struggles.

As societies under the dominance of the capitalist mode of production are subject to an imperative that commodifies social relations, and especially the work force, this is also true for land and nature. Already Marx (1976, p. 638) noticed the destructive capacities of capitalism, as its mode of production "only develops the techniques and the degree of combination of the social process of production by simultaneously undermining the original sources of all wealth – the soil and the worker" (cf. also Altvater 1993). However, "nature" should not be conceived as something outside society, but as a societal or political relation (Brand and Wissen 2013), particularly in terms of the use of land, resources, and sinks. Therefore, societal nature relations are an integral part of any social relations of (re)production. They are linked to historically concrete power relations and structures of domination and domination over nature is closely linked to societal domination. This is the reason why we prefer the term "societal nature relations" in order to highlight the strong interrelatedness without denying that "nature" has at the same time its own material properties independent of its societal constitution. We will show below that both the current crisis and austerity politics are based on and shape particular societal nature relations. At the same time, we are going to argue that hegemonic societal nature relations are in a very ambiguous way a stabilizing moment within the crisis.

Mainly preoccupied with the "capitalist mode of production," Marx elaborated the general conditions and "laws" of capitalist development (which he always understood against the background of historically concrete dynamics, struggles, and contingencies). Later and in light of historical developments like the post-World War II phase of capitalism, historical materialist research has tried to complement Marx's abstract theoretical reflections by more midrange or meso-level theoretical conceptualizations. In that context, the French regulation school was an important advancement. Its major impulse was to differentiate – both in time and space – more specifically between different types of capitalist formation within capitalism itself in order to get a better understanding of how capitalist contradictions, conflicts, and crisis processes are mediated by specific – discursively and politically structured – institutional arrangements and forms of regulation (cf. Lipietz 1988). While some scholars were primarily interested in the comparative analysis of particular national types of capitalism (cf. Amable 2003; Bohle and Greskowits 2012; Becker and Jäger 2012), others tried to identify temporarily distinct phases of capitalist development (cf. Albritton *et al.* 2001; Brand and Raza 2003; Atzmüller *et al.* 2013).

The concrete analysis of capitalist formations is based on a range of mutually related analytical concepts such as "regime of accumulation." An accumulation regime denotes a package of social forms of organizing production, temporal periods of capital valorization, demand, but also the relationship with non-capitalist forms of production. The complementary concept is the mode of regulation which refers to the institutional embeddedness of macro-economic coherence, i.e. to the "totality of institutional forms, networks, explicit and implicit norms that all guarantee the compatibility of modes of conduct within the framework of a regime of accumulation, corresponding to social conditions as well as transcending their conflictive properties" (Lipietz 1988, p. 24). In this sense, the concept of the mode of regulation is very comprehensive. Among other aspects, it includes above all the wage and money relation, the state, competition between companies and integration into the world market (cf. Aglietta 2001; Becker 2002). Feminist scholars argue that asymmetric gender relations are inherent to capitalist development (albeit not reduced to it) and that macro-economic and societal stability has to do with more or less accepted gendered identities and divisions of labor

(Sauer 2013, Aulenbacher and Riegraf 2013). In addition to "regime of accumulation" and "mode of regulation," regulationist scholars sometimes refer to two complementary analytical concepts (cf. Lipietz 1994). The concept of a "hegemonic bloc" accentuates the Gramscian influence on the regulation school by highlighting the concrete social forces and alliances which organize the interaction of accumulation and regulation by struggling about public consensus and possible material compromises. In a way, the other concept of a "societal paradigm" might be the outcome of such struggles while also taking the technological and industrial conditions, i.e., the concrete material and energy dimensions of capitalist accumulation, including forms of production and labor organization, into account.

The briefly sketched turn towards the analyses of historically concrete capitalist formations implies some very important theoretical innovations. First, the regulationist approach assumes that capitalist formations are not only determined by capitalist forms of (re-)production but also by a range of non-capitalist social, institutional, ideological, and political dimensions. Moreover, the latter non-economic dimensions are seen as constitutive for capitalist accumulation as they may socially or institutionally embed and foster capitalist development or provide fields for potential capitalist penetration. Second, the societal embeddedness of capitalist accumulation is a much more complex and contested phenomenon than institutionalist Political Economy assumes. The regulationist school opens ways towards a political sociology and political ecology of capitalist development that take into account important and otherwise neglected analytical dimensions.

(Trans-)national relations of power, domination, and hegemony

Given the complex and comprehensive view of the social embeddedness of capitalist accumulation in labor, production and reproduction, norms and ideologies, subjectivities and bodies, and nature, the regulationist approach represents an important theoretical advancement for historical materialist thinking. Nevertheless, it is not without its own "blind spots" and therefore needs some further specification. From our point of view, these specifications concern above all the following two points (cf. Bieling 2014): the first point is given by the implicit functionalism and stability orientation of much regulationist work which shows a receptiveness to adopting a socio-technological and regulatory problem-solving perspective instead of critically analyzing the generation of conflict, (dis)consent and hegemony; and the second point refers to the problem that, by and large, the regulationist views, in similar fashion to institutionalist CPE, remain trapped within a dichotomous view of the nation state, on the one hand, and the world market, on the other.

We assume that both of these problems might be overcome by extending the regulationist perspective by a neo-Gramscian IPE, as this kind of theoretical current is congenial to regulation theory. The elective affinity comes to the fore if one looks closely at the work of Robert Cox, one of the most prominent neo-Gramscian IPE scholars. Cox (1989, p. 39) has a very broad perception of production which:

> [I]s not confined to the production of physical goods used or consumed. It covers also the production and reproduction of knowledge and of the social relations, morals, and institutions that are prerequisites to the production of physical goods.

In addition, Cox also emphasizes the social configuration of diverse forms of power which are inscribed into the different modes of production and repro- duction. At the same time, this implies that hegemony and hegemonic strug- gles within society have a certain "material core." Hegemony needs to offer a more or less attractive form of living in order to generate active consensus or, at least, to make alternatives – for instance, via the techniques of dis- cursive disarticulation – less viable (Gramsci 1991ff., pp. 499, 1567; Laclau 1977, p. 161).

Next to the emphasis on social power relations and societal conflicts, neo- Gramscian IPE can contribute to correcting the dichotomy of the nation-state and the world market. Particularly in the context of globalization, neo- Gramscian IPE advances an understanding of hegemony as a consensually supported mode of transnational development that transcends inter-state relations (cf. Cox 1983, p. 171). Transnational hegemonic relations are fun- damentally shaped by the "uneven and combined" patterns of economic penetration and interdependence. Like in the domestic realm, they also include manifold social relations and corresponding forms of the discursive, cultural, and politico-institutional organization of domination and consensus.

Neo-Gramscian IPE illuminates another aspect of austerity by highlighting the extension of the domestic "integral state," i.e. state–civil society relations, thus identifying an emerging transnational civil society. This transnational civil society is dominated but not completely controlled by transnational corporations and their respective business associations (cf. Sklair 2001) which – in close collaboration with academics, think tanks, and most influ- ential governments – push for international arrangements such as treaties, institutions, or regimes in order to strengthen capital freedoms and investor rights. For Stephen Gill (2003, p. 132) such processes are the expression of a "new constitutionalism," which:

> [...] imply or mandate the insulation of key aspects of the economy from the influence of politicians or the mass of citizens by imposing, internally and externally, "binding constraints" on the conduct of fiscal, monetary and trade and investment policies. [...] Central, therefore, to new con- stitutionalism is the imposition of discipline on public institutions, partly to prevent national interference with the property rights and entry and exit options of holders of mobile capital with regard to particular political jurisdictions.

As the "new constitutionalism" facilitates the establishment of nodes of statehood beyond the nation-state, it also promotes the emergence of transnational state–civil society complexes. Such new, more complex and transnational, state-backed regulatory dynamics are, however, not fully grasped by most neo-Gramscian IPE scholars since they tend to shy away from more systematic state theoretical considerations.

New forms of regulation due to multi-scalar statehood

In contrast to the dominant understanding of the state as a rule-setter and regulator within institutionalist Political Economy, from a historical materialist perspective, the state should be regarded as an unstable institutional, discursive, and subjectivizing structure and practice (Jessop 2007; Gallas *et al.* 2012). It plays an important role in regulating the manifold societal tensions and conflicts and gives certain durability to dominant or even hegemonic societal orientations and relationships of forces. As Poulantzas (2002, p. 159) put it, the state can be understood as "a relationship of forces, or more precisely the material condensation of such a relationship among classes and class factions, such as this is expressed in the state in a necessarily specific form."

A general will – the general interest in and of a society to maintain and enhance economic competitiveness in the world market – somehow appears to exist autonomously from society. In fact, the state consists mainly of the generalized interests of ruling forces. This important, historically created, and contested dimension of the state is fetishizised by institutionalist perspectives which are not interested in a class (or gender or race) perspective and instead primarily focus on institutional complementarities. For current reflections on the crisis and austerity politics it is important to note that the state is the strategic terrain which is by and large, albeit not completely, controlled by dominant forces, i.e., those who dispose of the means of production. In this sense, it represents a terrain of struggle, but also a social and institutional arrangement that can fail.

In contrast to most state theory and analysis, from the historical materialist perspective developed here, the state should be seen as a multiscalar social relation. It should not be equated with national or subnational levels but its modes of existence and functions can also be performed at the international level and especially via international state apparatuses (Brand 2009). In view of the increasing amount of international legal standards and norms, and sometimes considerable resources and instruments of political steering and intervention, this internationalization can be interpreted, enhancing Poulantzas, as a "second-order condensation of societal power relations" (Brand *et al.* 2011). This "second-order condensation" can be specified in two regards (cf. Bieling 2007): first, it differs from the domestic arena, however, to the extent that the structures of transnational civil society and public spheres remain nationally fragmented. Next to increasing transnational activities of business associations, political parties, social movements, NGOs or academic and

journalist practices, national state apparatuses such as governments, minis-
tries, or administrations represent therefore a constitutive dimension of the
condensation process. The second specification refers to the kind of statehood
which tends to emerge in the international realm. Here, we have seen that the
"new constitutionalism" generates a type of a market-liberal oriented state in
line with inter- or supranational rule of law which primarily focuses on
property rights, investor freedoms, and predictable trade relations, and perhaps takes into consideration some aspects of *checks and balances*. Prominent
examples such as the European Union show that quite a few competencies
moved up to the inter- or supranational level, while most administrative
tasks remain settled within the domestic arenas. However, as we will show
below, the internationalized state is key in imposing austerity politics and to
legitimize it.

Capitalist hegemony and regulation in times of austerity

In a way, the EU represents a prototypical emerging supranational state. As
an increasingly institutionalized political arena, the EU can be interpreted as
a form of "second-order condensation of societal power relations" strongly
based on "new constitutionalist" arrangements. Most of these arrangements
are closely related to projects of economic integration such as the Single
Market, the Economic and Monetary Union (EMU) or financial market
integration and, more generally, to the emergence of the transnational formation of "European financial capitalism" (Bieling 2013). The development
of this formation was economically facilitated by a structural over-accumulation
of capital and an increasing amount of financial assets. Politically, it implied
increasing power of transnational financial market players such as (investment)
banks, institutional investors, rating agencies, consultants and managers of
different types which all cultivated close ties with political decision makers in
order to generalize a market-liberal reform agenda. As a consequence of the
implementation of this reform agenda – for instance, the privatization of
pensions, public services, and transport, or the deregulation of labor markets
and the spread of precarious employment – concrete forms of production,
living, and communication changed remarkably. Overall, people from different
social classes have become more dependent on financial market developments.
At the same time, and in comparison to former periods, the new capitalist
formation is even more crisis-prone due to the inherent tendency of highly
integrated but de-regulated financial markets to generate financial bubbles.
Recent developments within the EU, as a result of an institutionally ill-
designed EMU (cf. Aglietta 2012), reflect the difficulties of politically moder-
ating financial instability. On the contrary, the mode of operation of EMU
facilitated the spatially and temporarily uneven development within the
European political economy and has brought about the emergence of a
"European crisis constitutionalism" (Bieling 2013) which modifies the previous
new constitutionalist arrangement only to uphold inherited transnational

inter-dependencies, power relations, and forms of finance-led capitalist reproduction.

At the same time and due to the resource and climate dimension of the multiple crisis, political strategies in the EU remain focused on competitiveness which seems to have intensified in recent years. Given the uncertain availability of natural resources, strategies tend to prevail that promote efficient use of them (especially recycling) as well as strategies that prioritize a mid- and long-term secure access to those resources. Not by chance, in the last years, the EU Commission formulated for the first time several strategies concerning access to and availability of resources (e.g. European Commission 2011). Behind this stands a consensus not to question the predominant mode of production and living.

European crisis management

All measures and initiatives which have been taken to politically mediate and balance the financial crisis have to be placed in the broader context of European financial capitalism. By and large, they can be grouped into two periods. The first period began with the outbreak of the financial crisis in 2007–08 and was characterized by the bursting of the financial bubble and its broader economic consequences, that is, collapsing housing prices, stock market crashes and manifold ways of contagion, insolvent banks, and a deep economic recession. Most European governments and other political authorities tried to soften the impact of these crises phenomena by mobilizing a set of specific instruments. For instance, they became very active in rescuing illiquid – presumably systemic – banks by ad hoc measures and the establishment of specific rescue funds. In addition, they launched fairly comprehensive economic stimulus packages whose content was, however, structurally conservative as they mainly aimed to defensively stabilize production and employment of the established economic sectors. And finally, both kinds of activities (bank rescues and economic stimulus programs) have been flanked by an accommodating monetary central bank policy lowering key interest rates and injecting additional money in the economy in cases of emergency (cf. Lapavitsas *et al.* 2012).

With the benefit of hindsight, it can be said that the transnational alliances of social forces – composed of governments, (central) bankers and financial players, transnational corporations and their respective business associations as well as intellectuals, journalists, and parts of trade unions – have been quite successful in inventing instruments and measures characteristic of an emergency-driven Keynesian state interventionism to ward off a fundamental collapse of the global economy. At the same time, however, the mobilized instruments and resources were far from sufficient to overcome the economic, let alone the ecological, crisis. Due to the high public costs of bank rescues and economic stimulus packages, the crisis was only mitigated and shifted to the public sector. In view of continued economic stagnation and skyrocketing public debt, market-liberal observers and politicians started to talk about a so-called "sovereign debt crisis" and "euro crisis." This change in public discourse happened in early 2010. It signaled the transition towards the second period of crisis management, in which supranational reform measures became increasingly important. The frequency of EU summits and initiatives taken since then are quite impressive. They paved the way to a typical but highly complex European compromise.

This compromise is mainly composed of three major components. One component, the governments of highly indebted countries were primarily concerned about, was alleviating the their burden of indebtedness by mobilizing more common resources. More concretely, they pushed for establishing new interventionist instruments such as the European Financial Stability Facility (EFSF) and the European Stability Mechanism (ESM), whose operation was further flanked by ECB measures such as the Outright Monetary Transaction Programme (OMTP), aiming to bring down add-on interest for highly indebted governments. All these instruments which point to the direction of a union of shared liability were, however, balanced by a second component, namely, a whole bunch of European reform measures that aim to establish a common agenda of a permanent austerity detrimental to public employees, recipients of social benefits, and users of public services. The austerity agenda was mainly promoted by current account surplus countries, the international creditor community, and supranational actors such as the European Commission (cf. Konecny 2012). They not only made the credits provided by the EFSF and ESM conditional on structural adjustment programs supervised and controlled by the so-called Troika of European Commission, ECB, and IMF. They also administratively strengthened the control of insufficiently austerity-minded governments: by the institutionalizing a so-called "European semester," a mechanism of ex-ante coordination of national budgetary plans; by adopting a so-called "Sixpack" of legislative reforms, all aiming to further strengthen and rigidify the Stability and Growth Pact (SGP); by the agreement on a – however, not binding – "Euro plus Pact" which extends market-liberal reform dynamics to labor markets, collective bargaining, and social security systems; and by the "Fiscal compact" treaty which binds signatory countries to introduce mechanisms like the German "debt brake" and to constitutionalize such rules in national legal arrangements. The third component flanked the other ones, as it mainly aims to strengthen the European system of financial market control through more comprehensive but not too strict financial market regulations and some new bodies and competencies of financial supervision and control (cf. Bieling 2013).

The intricate processes of deliberation and negotiation which brought forth these results reflect both the capitalist dynamics of "uneven and combined development" and the corresponding socio-economic interests of influential national as well as trans- and supranational political actors. Both aspects indicate that European crisis constitutionalism, i.e., the generation of additional elements of European statehood, represents a contested "second-order condensation of societal power relations" which is generally in line with the "new constitutionalist" arrangements of the pre-crisis period. Its policy content is, however, more ambiguous which differentiates the European crisis constitutionalism from new constitutionalism: one difference is that the crisis constitutionalist reforms do not simply accompany capitalist globalization but represent a much more politicized and contested reaction to it. Besides, they generate not only new forms of supranational rule of law, but also some elements of active economic intervention and control, including additional resources which have far-reaching transnational redistributive effects. And finally, European crisis constitutionalism is much more – domestically as well as internationally – contested. Quite a few developments such as more intense intergovernmental conflicts, the ongoing redistribution from labor to capital, and rise of right-wing populist movements underscore the eroding hegemonic social basis of transnational financial capitalism. One reason for this erosion is that there are more and more difficulties in externalizing the huge economic, democratic, and ecological costs of system stabilizing crisis management measures; a process which still partially works in the European core, i.e., the current account surplus countries, but less so in the countries of the European periphery (cf. Busch *et al.* 2013).

Imperial mode of living in times of austerity

Crisis and the dominant ways of dealing with it through austerity politics needs to be put into a wider context. Although in some respects the externalization of crisis costs becomes more difficult, it still takes place in space and time. Therefore, we would like to stress some aspects of the crisis and crisis politics which are usually overseen in institutionalist and even in historical materialist Political Economy: the bio-physical basis of social-economic life and its relatedness to capitalist dynamics and capitalist crises (Altvater 1993; Foster 2000; Brand and Wissen 2013). Our point here is not to complain about the ecological crisis and weak environmental politics. We are asking in what sense industrial and fossilist capitalism and their crisis tendencies are combined with the economic and financial crisis and austerity politics. This leads to some important paradoxes when we consider the outlined theoretical perspective of the unifying and fragmenting dynamics of capitalist development.

Gramsci argued that hegemony requires a "material core," i.e. needs to offer a more or less attractive form of living in order to get active consensus or, at least, to make alternatives less viable. This leads to our first remark: even under conditions of the outlined crisis management there is still a strong implicit assumption of an ongoing growth-oriented, industrialist, extractivist, and fossilist mode of production. This is complemented by an "imperial mode of living," that is, economic, political, and cultural practices in the capitalist centers which, in principle, are based upon the availability of cheap resources and labor (Brand and Wissen 2013). The imperial mode of living is an integral part of capitalist globalization in the sense that it not only profoundly restructured the international division of labor in the last three decades but also that the middle classes of the emerging and developing countries strive for such a mode of living. Therefore, it is a good example for the unifying tendencies which, at the same time, articulate themselves temporarily and spatially in uneven ways. The unifying tendency is that the imperial mode of living is enhanced within the countries with so-called emerging economies. But it also creates an enormous fragmentation within particular societies and globally.

This is an important continuity of the capitalist mode of production which partly stabilizes current social relations and developments. This mode of production, living, and related orientations towards growth and competitiveness – in order to secure this mode of living – gives current crisis management a certain legitimacy: the global resource and environmental order is not questioned and it is largely secured by international political institutions which we understand as a "second-order condensation of social power relations."

Second, right after the beginning of the financial and economic crisis and due to a high level of uncertainty as well as the strong politicization of the ecological crisis, for some time there seemed to be political space for more ambitious environmental politics. Governments in the US and China spent billions of dollars in the construction of public transport and renewable energies. In Europe, optimistic signs quickly gave way to pessimism. In Germany and Austria the automobile industry was stabilized through car scrappage schemes (partly justified by environmental concerns, yet car scrappage schemes were absurd because of the ecological cost of constructing cars). The chance in 2009 and 2010 to transform the economy in a more serious way towards an ecologically sustainable path was lost. The major means to deal with the crisis remains in the corridor of growth, competitiveness, and, in Europe, austerity and, at the same time, they are capitalist, i.e., they imply a further valorization of nature. We can see this quite explicitly in climate change politics with the mechanisms of emission trading and REED+. Different ways by which the ecological crisis is dealt with become *a moment* of the socio-economic crisis and strategies to overcome it. One prominent political strategy, for instance, was the proposal of a Green Economy or a Green New Deal in order to overcome the financial crisis (overview in Brand 2012). With respect to the appropriation of nature and the forms to deal with the unintended effects it becomes clear that, as an overarching tendency, the state secures the dominant forms of the appropriation of nature for the expansive capitalist mode of production. Hence, even if environmental politics became an important, highly politicized, and contested issue, dealing with environmental problems largely takes place in the corridor of ecological modernization (Brand and Wissen 2014).

However, and third, even the very modest approaches to an ecological modernization of capitalism are under pressure. Austerity politics leads to a shrinking of the state's capacity to promote the politics of sustainable development in the sense of an ecological modernization of capitalism, i.e. even inner-capitalist progressive alternatives are blocked. We can see this in Spain where the strong support for renewable energy was suspended. In Greece, one widely discussed way out of the crisis is the search for mineral resources like gold or fossil fuels or to industrialize agriculture further. The imperial mode of production and living is still predominant. On the one hand, austerity policies and politics are based in a way on the imperial mode of living. Especially for those whose standard of living is lower, access to products based on cheap labor and resources remain important. Their interest groups like trade unions tend to defend such a way of living and its material basis. In the future, on the other hand, orientations to growth, competitiveness, and cut backs tend to strengthen the brown economy with its negative implications for the use of resources and sinks. We could name this constellation a "fragmented hegemony" to indicate that austerity politics is more or less hegemonic in those countries with a stronger economic performance and able to externalize the costs of the existing mode of production and living to the European and global (semi-)periphery.

In sum, what we currently experience in Europe is not an effective dealing with the root causes of the crisis but the predominance of political actions which stabilize existing power relations, orientations, and practices. The pressure of multiple crisis remains.

Outlook: contradictions, conflicts, and emancipatory alternatives

Institutionalist approaches attempt to analyze current capitalist development from a micro-perspective of firms and the institutional settings which embed them in order to secure or enhance competitiveness. Economic restructuring is and should occur mainly under conditions of supply-side economics and is considered as path-dependent. Political consequences of capitalist restructuring of the last decades are seen in an accommodation of labor relations to changing conditions. As we argued, institutionalist Political Economy has an insufficient social theoretical foundation, reduces social complexity via a flat ontology, and has proved incapable of formulating clear hypotheses and identifying causalities. The term capitalism is applied in a fairly narrow manner, as it is equated with market relations almost exclusively shaped by the profit orientation of (private) firms which represents the major orientation for relevant actors, especially management. Moreover, it tends to favor with its normative assumptions the existing constellation of austerity and the imperial mode of living: the explicit orientation at competitiveness, the implicit acceptance of the dominant capitalist mode of production with its imperative of capital accumulation, related social and nature relations as well as power relations, inclusion, and exclusion. Contradictions and the manifold forms of domination are mainly overlooked. What seems to be a differentia specifica of historical materialist approaches in contrast to institutionalist ones is the theoretical advertence of contradictions, social forces and, hence, for opposition and counter-hegemonic actors, especially actors with emancipatory goals and strategies.

Some arguments developed in this article can help us understand why, despite the crisis, alternatives, especially emancipatory ones, are difficult to pursue. One answer is that the existing "imperial mode of living" is deeply inscribed into manifold societal relations like production, distribution, and consumption, class relations, and more or less viable forms of compromising, gender relations, and respective forms of hegemonic identities, social status, and again the division of labor. There is still a strong "Fordist" experience and dispositive of well-being which makes the overcoming of material conformism, inert consciousness, and practices difficult. The latter remain intrinsically tied to existing production and power structures.

At the political level, politics of scale at the EU level are mainly pursued by dominant forces. Potentially counter-hegemonic actors develop their political concepts and strategies largely at the national or local scale. However, important contradictions and forms of contestation exist and prepare the terrain for alternatives. We can observe intense resistances against austerity politics in those countries and among those social strata which are mostly affected. It becomes more and more clear that competitiveness policies do not work any longer. While in economically stronger countries "competitive corporatism" converted into a new mode of "crisis corporatism" (Urban 2012), i.e., a constellation in which the representatives of the subaltern act to soften the most severe negative consequences of austerity politics, in the hard-hit crisis countries of the European periphery corporatist arrangements almost completely dissolved due to a structural inability to forge viable compromises (Bieling and Lux 2014).

Conceptually, there are quite a few ideas and practices which point towards a solidarity or sufficiency economy composed of cooperatives, open source production, urban gardening, and localized production and consumption. Concrete initiatives are launched to reduce work time and establish a basic income or a minimum wage. Particular concepts intend to condense practices of resistance and formulate alternative horizons: food sovereignty, energy democracy, commons, climate justice, and many others. Identities are shaped via queering or daily practices against the affluent society. Currently, the debate about degrowth is an important focus for strategies and experiences of alternatives (Muraca 2013). All this shows that many of these and other alternative ideas are abundant in today's capitalism. Moreover, due to capitalism's inherent contradictions these alternatives are systematically generated and nourished. However, whereas struggles against a further commodification of social relations and societal nature relations are intense, those within the already commodified spheres seem to remain weak. We still need to strengthen the political articulation of different struggles and spread emancipatory projects throughout more segments of capitalist societies and inform or even transform the political agenda. It is a possibility that such processes will take place as the conditions of permanent austerity and market-liberal reforms accelerate the ongoing self-de-legitimation of European financial capitalism.

Notes

1 We would like to thank Tobias Haas, Julia Lux, Markus Wissen, and Richard Westra for their useful comments, and Etienne Schneider for his assistance with research.
2 In terms of the institutional settings, the VoC approach focuses on the following five spheres: industrial relations, vocational training and education, financial markets and corporate governance, inter-firm relationships, and the involvement of employees.

References

Aglietta, M. (2001 [1979]) *A Theory of Capitalist Regulation: The US Experience* (London: Verso).
——(2012) "The European Vortex," *New Left Review* (75): 15–36.
Albert, M. (1993) *Capitalism Against Capitalism* (London: Whurr).
Albritton, R., M. Itoh, R. Westra and A. Zuege (eds) (2001) *Phases of Capitalist Development: Booms, Crisis and Globalizations* (Basingstoke: Palgrave Macmillan).
Altvater, E. (1993) *The Future of the Market* (London: Verso).
Amable, B. (2003) *The Diversity of Modern Capitalism* (Oxford: Oxford University Press).
Atzmüller, R., J. Becker, U. Brand, L. Oberndorfer, V. Redak and T. Sablowski (eds) (2013) *Fit für die Krise? Perspektiven der Regulationstheorie* (Münster: Westfälisches Dampfboot).
Aulenbacher, B. and B. Riegraf (2013) "Kapitalismus und Krise – eine Frage von Ökonomie und Klasse?" in R. Atzmüller, *et al.* (eds) *Fit für die Krise?* (Münster: Westfälisches Dampfboot, pp. 90–110).
Beck, S. and C. Scherrer (2013) "Varieties of Capitalism." Konzeptionelle Schwächen angesichts der Finanzkrise, in J. Wullweber, A. Graf and M. Behrens (eds) *Theorien der Internationalen Politischen Ökonomie* (Wiesbaden: Verlag für Sozialwissenschaften, pp. 151–66).
Becker, J. (2002) *Akkumulation, Regulation, Territorium* (Marburg: Metropolis).
Becker, J. and J. Jäger (2012): "Integration in Crisis: A Regulationist Perspective on the Interaction of European Varieties of Capitalism," *Competition & Change*, 16(3): 169–87.
Bieling, H. J. (2007) "Die Konstitutionalisierung der Weltwirtschaft als Prozess hegemonialer Verstaatlichung," in S. Buckel and A. Fischer-Lescano (eds) *Die Organisation der Hegemonie. Zum Staatsverständnis Antonio Gramscis* (Baden-Baden: Nomos, pp. 143–60).
——(2011) "Varieties of Capitalism, Regulationstheorie und neogramscianische IPÖ – komplementäre oder gegensätzliche Perspektiven des globalisierten Kapitalismus?" *Zentrum für Ökonomische und Soziologische Studien der Universität Hamburg*, Discussion Paper 23 (Hamburg: ZÖSS).
——(2013) "European Financial Capitalism and the Politics of (De-) financialization," *Competition & Change*, 17(3): 283–98.
——(2014) "Comparative analysis of capitalism from a regulationist perspective extended by neo-Gramscian IPE," *Capital & Class*, 38(1): 31–43.

Bieling, H. J. and J. Lux (2014) "Crisis-induced social conflicts in the European Union – trade union perspectives: the emergence of 'crisis corporatism' or the failure of corporatist arrangements?" *Global Labour Journal*, 5(2): 153–75.

Bohle, D. and B. Greskowits (2012) *Capitalist Diversity on Europe's Periphery* (New York: Cornell University Press).

Brand, U. (2009) "The Internationalised State and its Functions and Modes in the Global Governance of Biodiversity," in G. Kütting and R. Lipschutz (eds) *Power, knowledge and governance in international environmental policy* (London: Routledge, pp. 100–123).

——(2012) "After Sustainable Development: Green Economy as the Next Oxymoron?" *GAIA*, 21(1): 28–32.

Brand, U., C. Görg and M. Wissen (2011) "Second-Order Condensations of Societal Power Relations. Environmental Politics and the Internationalization of the State from a Neo-Poulantzian Perspective," *Antipode*, 43(1): 149–75.

Brand, U. and W. Raza (eds) (2003) *Fit für den Postfordismus? Theoretisch-politische Perspektiven des Regulationsansatzes* (Münster: Westfälisches Dampfboot).

Brand, U. and M. Wissen (2013) "Crisis and continuity of capitalist society-nature relationships. The imperial mode of living and the limits to environmental governance," *Review of International Political Economy*, 20(4): 687–711.

Brand, U. and M. Wissen (2014) "Strategies of a Green Economy, Contours of a Green Capitalism," in K. van der Pijl (ed.) *The International Political Economy of Production* (Cheltenham: Edward Elgar), forthcoming.

Brie, M. (2013) "Vorwärts in die Vergangenheit? Wolfgang Streecks verfehlte Wiederentdeckung der marxistischen Kapitalismuskritik," *Blätter für deutsche und internationale Politik*, 7/2013: 59–70.

Bruff, I. (2011) "What About the Elephant in the Room? Varieties of Capitalism. Varieties in Capitalism," *New Political Economy*, 16(4): 481–500.

Busch, K., C. Hermann, K. Hinrichs and T. Schulten (2013) "Euro Crisis, Austerity Policy and the European Social Model. How Crisis Policies in Southern Europe Threaten the EU's Social Dimension," *International Policy Analysis*, February 2013 (Berlin: Friedrich-Ebert-Stiftung).

Coates, D. (2014) "Studying comparative capitalisms by going left and by going deeper," *Capital & Class*, 38(1): 18–30.

Cox, R. W. (1983) "Gramsci, Hegemony and International Relations: An Essay in Method," *Millennium*, 12(2): 162–75.

——(1989) "Production, the State, and Change in World Order," in E.-O. Czempiel, and J. N. Rosenau (eds) *Global Changes and Theoretical Challenges. Approaches to World Politics for the 1990s* (Toronto: Lexington Books, pp. 37–50).

Demirovic, A. (2013) "Keine Zeit mehr. Das Ende des sozialdemokratischen Projekts," *Prokla*, 171: 305–16.

European Commission (2011) *Roadmap to a Resource Efficient Europe*. Communication from the Commission. Com (2011) 571 final, available at: http://ec.europa.eu/environ ment/resource_efficiency/pdf/com2011_571.pdf [accessed March 29, 2014].

Foster, J. B. (2000) *Marx's Ecology: Materialism and Nature* (New York: Monthly Review Press).

Gallas, A., L. Bretthauer, J. Kannankulam and I. Stützle (eds) (2012) *Reading Poulantzas.* (London: Merlin Press).

Gill, S. (2003) *Power and Resistance in the New World Order* (New York: Palgrave).

Gramsci, A. (1991ff): *Prison Notebooks, German Edition* (Hamburg and Berlin: Argument).

Hall, P. A. (2012) "The Economics and Politics of the Euro Crisis" *German Politics*, 21 (4): 355–71.

Hall, P. A. and D. Soskice (2001) "An Introduction to Varieties of Capitalism," in P. Hall and D. Soskice (eds) *Varieties of Capitalism* (Oxford: Oxford University Press, pp. 1–68).

Hall, P. A. and K. Thelen (2009) "Institutional change in varieties of capitalism," *Socio-Economic Review*, 7(1): 7–34.

Hancké, B., M. Rhodes and M. Thatcher (eds) (2007) *Beyond Varieties of Capitalism. Conflict, Contradictions, and Complementarities in the European Economy* (Oxford: Oxford University Press).

Hirsch, J. (1997) "Globalization of capital, nation-states and democracy," *Studies in Political Economy*, 54: 39–58.

Höpner, M. (2009) "'Spielarten des Kapitalismus' als Schule der vergleichenden Kapitalismusforschung," *Zeitschrift für vergleichende Politikwissenschaft*, 3(2): 303–27.

Jackson, G. and R. Deeg (2012) "The Long-Term Trajectories of Institutional Change in European Capitalism," *Journal of European Public Policy*, 19(8): 1109–25.

Jessop, B. (1996) "Veränderte Staatlichkeit. Veränderungen von Staatlichkeit und Staatsprojekten," in D. Grimm (ed.) *Staatsaufgaben* (Frankfurt a.M.: Suhrkamp, pp. 43–73).

——(2007) *State Power* (Cambridge: Polity Press).

Kalinowski, T. (2013) "Regulating international finance and the diversity of capitalism," *Socioeconomic Review*, 11(3): 471–96.

Kang, N. (2006): "A Critique of the 'Varieties of Capitalism' Approach," ICCSR Research Paper No. 45 (Nottingham: University of Nottingham).

Konecny, M. (2012) "Die Herausbildung einer neuen Economic Governance als Strategie zur autoritären Krisenbearbeitung in Europa – gesellschaftliche Akteure und ihre Strategien," *Prokla*, 168: 377–94.

Laclau, E. (1977) *Politics and Ideology in Marxist Theory: Capitalism, Fascism, Populism*, (London: Verso).

Lapavitsas, C., *et al.* (2012) *Crisis in the Eurozone* (London: Verso).

Lipietz, A. (1988) "Accumulation, Crises, and Ways Out. Some Methodological Reflections on the Concept of 'Regulation'," *International Journal of Political Economy*, 18(2): 10–43.

——(1994) "Post-Fordism and Democracy," in A. Amin, (ed.) *Post-Fordism: A Reader* (Oxford: Blackwell, pp. 338–57).

Marx, K. (1968 [1875]) "Critique of the Gotha Program," in: *Marx and Engels Selected Works* (New York: International Publishers, pp. 315–35).

——(1973 [1857–61]) *Grundrisse, Foundations of the Critique of Political Economy* (London: Penguin Books).

——(1976 [1867]) Capital. *A Critique of Political Economy, Volume One* (London: Penguin Books).

——(1996 [1894]) *Capital. A Critique of Political Economy. Volume III* (New York: International Publishers),

Marx, K. and F. Engels, (1998 [1848]) "The Communist Manifesto," in L. Panitch and C. Leys (eds) *The Communist Manifesto now*, Socialist Register 1998 (New York: Merlin Press, pp. 240–68).

Muraca, B. (2013) "Décroissance: A Project for a Radical Transformation of Society," *Environmental Values*, 22(2): 147–69.

Nölke, A., C. May and S. Claar (eds) (2013) *Die großen Schwellenländer* (Wiesbaden: Springer VS).

Porter, M. (1990) *The Competitive Advantage of Nations* (New York: Free Press).

Poulantzas, N. (2002 [1978]) *State, Power, Socialism* (quoted from German edition "Staatstheorie") (Hamburg: VSA).

Röttger, B. (2008) Entry "Kapitalismen", in *HKWM – Historical-Critical Dictionary of Marxism*, 7/I (Hamburg: Argument, pp. 227–38).

Sauer, B. (2013) "Putting patriarchy in its place," in R. Atzmüller, *et al.* (eds) *Fit für die Krise?* (Münster: Westfälisches Dampfboot, pp. 111–31).

Shonfield, A. (1965) *Modern Capitalism* (London: Oxford University Press).

Sklair, L. (2001) *The Transnational Capitalist Class* (Oxford: Blackwell Publishers).

Smith, N. (1984) *Uneven Development* (Oxford: Basil Blackwell).

Streeck, W. (2010) *E Pluribus Unum? Varieties and Commonalities of Capitalism*, MPIfG Discussion Paper 1012 (Köln: MPIfG).

——(2011a) "Taking capitalism seriously: Towards an institutionalist approach to contemporary political economy," *Socioeconomic Review*, 9(1): 137–67.

——(2011b) "The Crisis of Democratic Capitalism," *New Left Review*, Second Series No. 71, 5–29.

——(2013) *Gekaufte Zeit. Die vertagte Krise des demokratischen Kapitalismus* (Frankfurt a.M.: Suhrkamp).

Trotsky, L (1977 [1932]) *The History of the Russian Revolution* (London: Pluto Press).

Urban, H. J. (2012) "Crisis corporatism and trade union revitalisation in Europe," in S. Lehndorff (ed.) "A triumph of failed ideas," *European models of capitalism in crisis* (Brussels: ETUI, pp. 219–41).

12 Profitability and modern capitalism

Guglielmo Carchedi

The last couple of decennia have seen dramatic changes in capitalism: The brutal reaffirmation by capital of its power over labor, the enhanced importance of finance capital as a consequence of the increasingly deeper difficulties of productive capital, and the reassertion of capital's rule over the whole world, also called globalization, after the fall of the Soviet Union. This has led some authors to believe that these changes have ushered in a new phase of capitalist development in which the law of the tendential fall of the profit rate (from now on, the Law) has ceased operating. Other authors have submitted that "monopoly capitalism" has marked the demise of the Law. Yet other authors believe that a fusion of Marx and Keynes is not only possible but also desirable as an alternative to the Law. This chapter argues for the persistent theoretical and empirical validity of the Law as the unsurpassed theory of crises in modern capitalism.

The focus is on the most important economy worldwide, the US.[1] The US economy has been subdivided into productive and unproductive sectors and the sectors producing material goods have been chosen as a proxy for the former.[2] As for the unproductive sectors, the focus is only on finance and speculation. Commerce has been disregarded because it is not central to contemporary debates.

Special attention has been given to the average rate of profit (from now on, ARP) realized in the productive sectors because they produce the vital lymph of capital, value, and surplus value. In what follows, ARP refers to the ARP in these sectors, unless otherwise indicated.[3] But as other studies have emphasized, the ARP for the whole economy – or *general* ARP – is also an important indicator. Another important distinction is between nominal and deflated values. Here the data refer to deflated values.[4] Finally, the focus is on the two fundamental classes, capital and labor. This is not to say that there are no other classes in capitalism. Rather, for the present purposes it is sufficient to focus on the producers of value and surplus value (labor) and on the appropriator of surplus value (capital).[5] The latter shares the booty, directly or indirectly and in a variety of ways, with other classes and social groups.

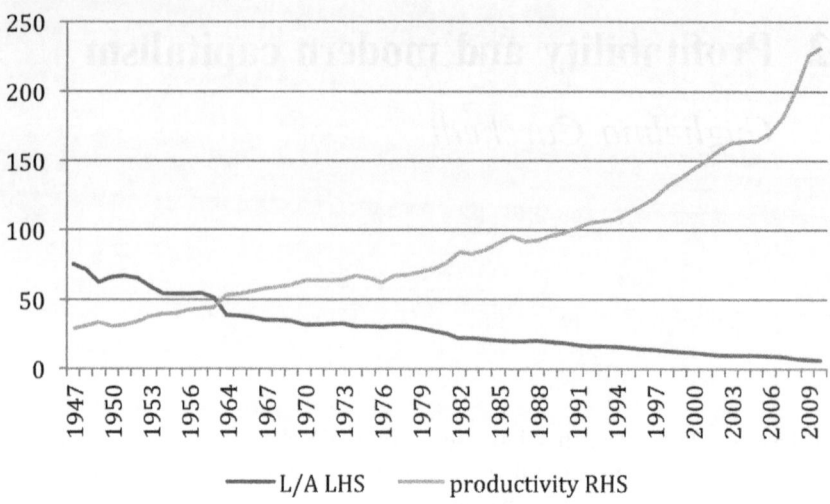

Figure 12.1 Capital efficiency (L/A) and actual productivity

A sketch of the Law

Technological innovations increase *efficiency*, i.e. the effect of science and technology incorporated in the means of production (or assets) on employment.[6] More efficient means of production reduce the number of laborers per unit of capital invested. So efficiency is measured as the number of laborers working with a certain quantity of assets. In Figure 12.1 increased efficiency is indicated by falling Labor/Assets ratio. The laborers working with assets worth 1 million dollars (deflated figures) drop from 75 in 1947 to 6 in 2010.

Through the use of more efficient assets, the laborers increase their *productivity*, the output per unit of capital and thus per laborer, given that the number of laborers per unit of capital has decreased. But the output per laborer can increase also because of higher exploitation. To calculate the increase in output per laborer due only to higher efficiency, productivity has been computed by holding the rate of exploitation constant. This is called constant exploitation productivity.[7] This is shown in Figure 12.1. The output per laborer climbs from deflated $28.9 million in 1947 to $231.5 million in 2010. Thus, more efficient assets cause on the one hand the shedding of labor and on the other greater output.

The replacement of labor by means of production, or greater efficiency, causes average profitability (ARP) to fall.[8] In fact, if only labor produces value (a fundamental assumption to be empirically substantiated below), the more efficient capitalists, by replacing labor with more efficient means of production, generate *less* (surplus) value per unit of capital invested. The non-financial ARP falls on this account. At the same time, the more efficient capitals' rate of profit rises. In fact, due to the assets' higher efficiency, the laborers' productivity rises. They produce a greater output (use values) per unit of capital invested than the laggards. Since unit prices tend to equalize within sectors, the innovators, by selling to other sectors a higher output at the same price as that of the lower output of the low-productivity capitalists, realize a share of the latter's surplus value.[9] Their rate of profit rises while the laggards' rate of profit and the ARP fall. Thus, a falling ARP indicates that, given a lower mass of surplus value produced, the profitability of the inno-vators rises while that of the technological laggards and the ARP fall. As more and more capitalists introduce the new technologies, increasingly less labor is employed and less surplus value is generated. As expanded repro-duction comes to an end, many capitals go bankrupt while a few prosper. Generalized *bankruptcies* and *unemployment*, i.e. *the destruction of capital* and thus the crisis, follow.[10] After the crisis, labor power increases relative to the means of production, capital starts generating more value and surplus value, and the rate of profit rises. Downward cycles alternate with upward cycles. This is the kernel of Marx's theory of crises.[11]

The reverse of L/A is the A/L ratio. If L is expressed in wages rather than in labor units, we obtain Marx's organic capital composition (from now on OCC), the ratio of constant capital (capital invested in assets) to variable capital (capital invested in labor power). In Figure 12.2, C and V are constant capital and variable capital respectively, and C/V is the OCC.[12] This is how Marx relates rising efficiency (the substitution of labor power by means of production) to profitability. Tendentially, as shown by the trend, if the OCC rises, the ARP falls.

Even though the secular trend is downward, the ARP starts rising from the mid-1980s. This does not contradict the Law, provided it is understood (as in

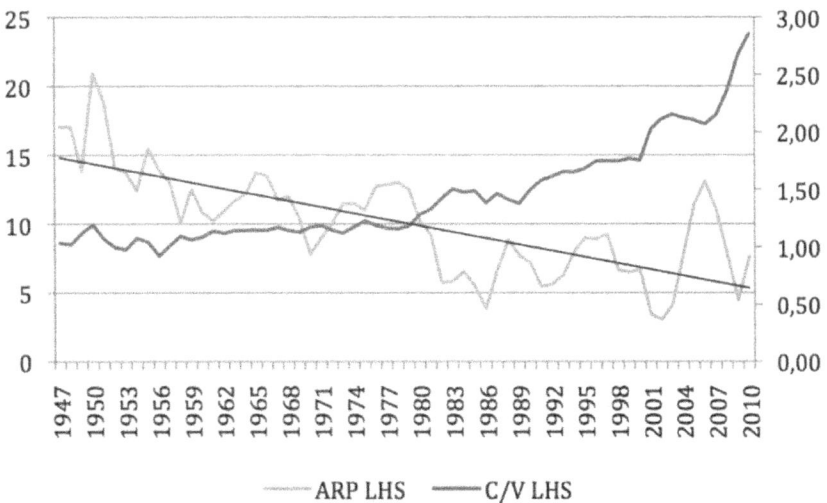

Figure 12.2 ARP and OCC (i.e. C/V)

Marx) as a tendential movement. The whole secular trend is downwards, and that includes the period of rising profitability starting around the mid-1980s. It follows that this period is a counter-tendency. This point will become clearer below when the effects of the tendency will be separated from those of the countertendencies.

Average profitability and capital mobility

Many objections have been raised against the Law.[13] One in particular should be mentioned. Supposedly, the equalization of the rates of profits into an average requires capital mobility across sectors and (price) competition within sectors. But in a monopolized economy these conditions are lacking so there is no (movement towards an) ARP. The Law cannot apply to monopolies and thus to modern economies.

However, modern economies are oligopolistic rather than monopolistic. And oligopolies do penetrate each other's sphere of production. But assume for the sake of argument that each sector of production is a monopoly. Each monopoly must sell its output to other monopolies (sectors). If a monopoly innovates, it produces a greater output at lower unit costs while reducing labor power. It produces less value and surplus value but more use values. Each use value incorporates less value and surplus value. If the innovator can sell its greater output to the other monopolies at the same price as before the innovation, it appropriates a part of the surplus value contained in the other monopolies' output. The former increases its profits at the cost of the latter. The latter's profitability falls and they are forced to innovate. The different profit rates tend towards an average. This average tends to fall because the innovators, by replacing labor force with assets, generate less surplus value. The crisis is in the making. The Law operates.[14]

Money and value average rates of profit

The validity of the Law has been shown on the basis of the official US data, which are deflated money prices of *use* values. But the Law should hold also in terms of values (i.e. abstract labor quantities). Figure 12.3 shows the ARP in money and in value terms.[15]

Since money quantities can be converted into value magnitudes, the results of the analysis in money terms apply also to the value dimension. The Law holds both in money and in value terms. This is why the two ARPs not only move in the same direction (tendentially downward) but also track each other very closely.[16]

The constant exploitation average rate of profit

Figures 12.2 and 12.3 show a rise in the ARP since the mid-1980s. For some authors this is a sign of economic recovery. However, the recovery requires not only a rising ARP but also a mounting *generation* of new value. There is no recovery if the ARP increases because of *redistribution* of value, because a greater

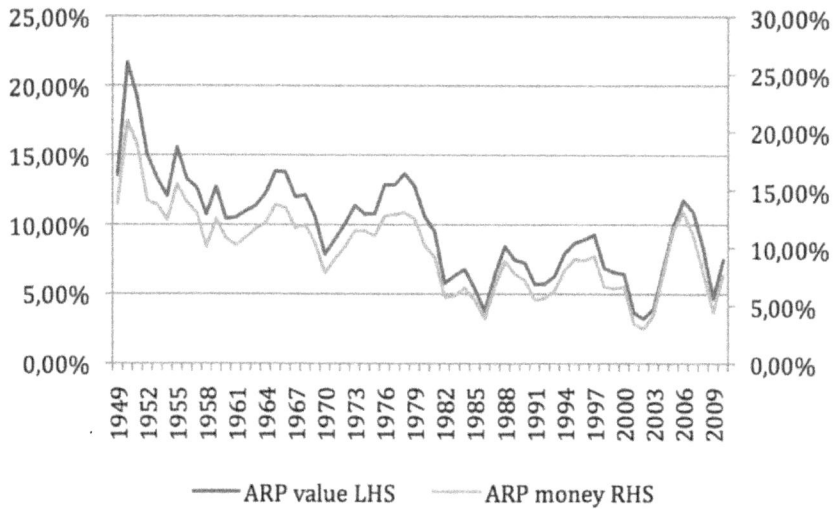

Figure 12.3 Money ARP and value ARP

share of that smaller quantity goes to capital due to a greater rate of exploitation. And this is what happened in the period of the so-called neo-liberalism.

Figure 12.4 shows that while tendentially the ARP rises, the new value generated falls. Then, what is the ARP if the effects of an increased rate of exploitation are removed? The official data do not tell us whether profits are due to changes in the rate of exploitation or not. The ARP is unsuitable to deal with this issue. We need a measure of profitability whose numerator is independent of the fluctuations in the rate of exploitation. This is the *constant exploitation ARP (CE-ARP)*, the ARP whose numerator has been computed by holding the rate of exploitation constant throughout the secular period.[17] See Figure 12.5.

Even though the ARP increased between 1986 and 2010, the CE-ARP decreased, so, as mentioned above, the former does not indicate economic recovery.[18] Simply, a greater share of the shrinking new value has been redistributed from labor to capital. And this is why the ARP has risen.

The Law has a tendential nature. The tendency is an inverse relation between the OCC and profitability. One of the countertendencies is the increase in the rate of exploitation. Then, it is the CE-ARP rather than the ARP that is better suited to test the validity of the Law. Figure 12.6 shows the secular inverse relation between the CE-ARP and the OCC.

An all-important point emerges from this figure. If the OCC and thus the assets relative to labor rise persistently while the ARP falls persistently, assets cannot produce surplus value. So they do not produce value either. Given that there are only two factors of production, means of production and labor, it is labor and only labor that produces value and surplus value.[19] *The law of value is empirically substantiated.*

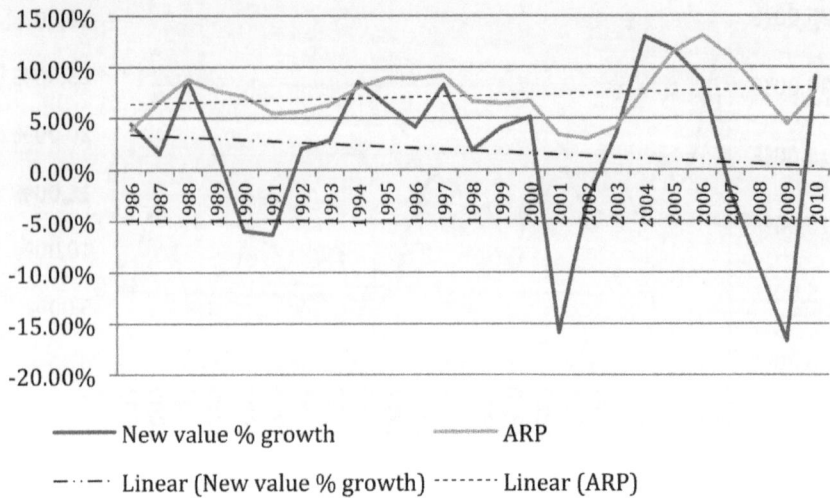

Figure 12.4 New value percentage growth and ARP

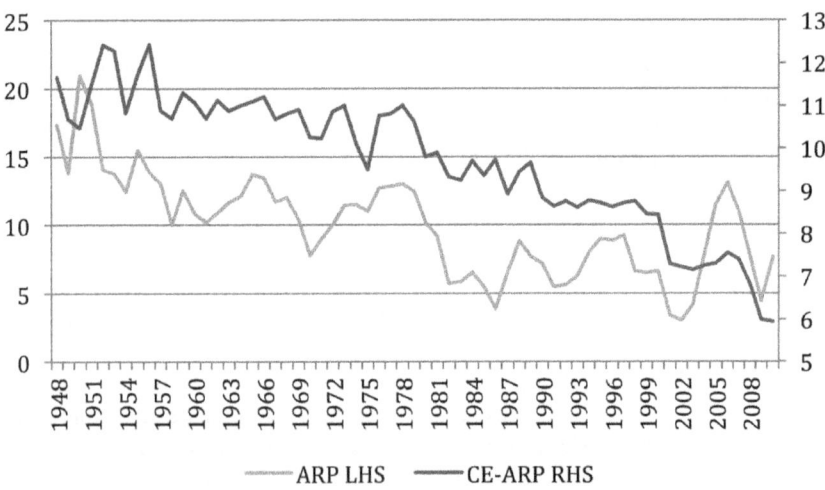

Figure 12.5 ARP and CE-ARP

Keynesian and neo-liberalist vulgates

Let us now consider the two major alternatives to the Law. First, the Keynesian vulgate. It ascribes crises to persistently falling wages, i.e. to the losses deriving from unsold commodities. However, crises are persistently preceded by *rising* wages. See Table 12.1.

This table shows that all crises are preceded by at least two years of rising wages and in all cases wages fall from the last pre-crisis year to the first crisis year, except for 2007.[20]

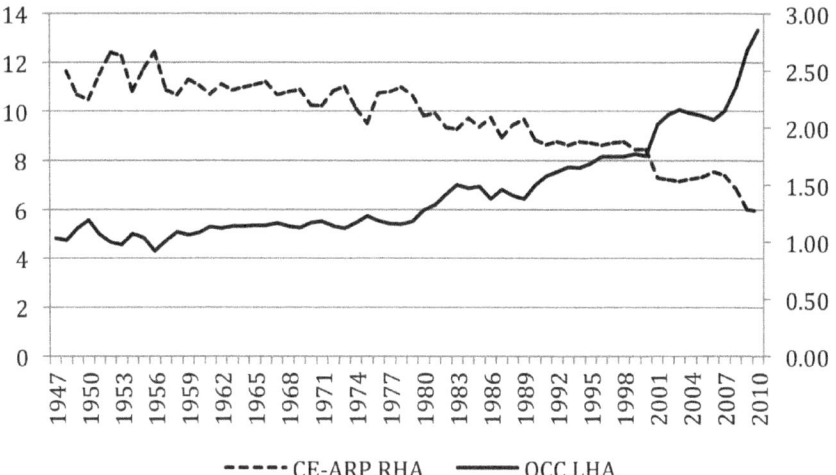

Figure 12.6 CE-ARP and OCC

Table 12.1 Wages in pre-crisis years and in first crisis year

Wages in pre-crisis years		Wages in first crisis year	
1950–53	231.4–331.1	1954	317.5
1955–56	347.3–395.4	1957–58	370.6
1962–69	415.0–591.0	1970	578.6
1971–73	576.7–649.4	1974–75	623.8
1976–79	622.1–724.6	1980–82	695.4
1983–89	690.8–885.2	1990–91	834.6
1992–2000	819.8–1186.8	2001–02	1069.8
2003–06	1047.8–1159.2	2007–09	1180.7

Empirically, Table 12.1 refutes the Keynesian vulgate. Theoretically, lower wages cannot cause or worsen the crisis because lower wages imply not only higher profits but also a higher ARP. This is conceded, but it is argued that lower wages on the one hand increase profitability but on the other depress it due to unsold wage goods. Failed realization, then, is the cause of crises. But it can be shown that on balance the positive effect prevails. Suppose that wages are cut and that all the goods whose prices correspond to that cut remain unsold (the most favorable case for the Keynesian thesis). Sector II (the producer of the means of consumption) suffers a double loss. First, the loss due to unsold commodities to its own laborers. But this loss is cancelled by an equal gain because of lower wages. Second, the loss due to the unsold commodities to sector I's laborers (the producer of the means of production). But this is sector I's gain due to lower wages in that sector. The combined numerators in both sectors do not change but the combined denominators fall because of lower investments in labor power. The ARP rises as a result of falling wages, *in spite of completely failed realization.* Lower wages cannot cause or worsen the crisis. The Keynesian cannot understand why governments and international institutions keep holding onto austerity policies instead of the pro-labor redistributions they demand. They miss the point that lower wages increase, rather than decrease, profits and that this is what interests capital.[21]

Lower wages increase average profitability but have an opposite effect on the two sectors. Profitability mounts in sector I but falls in sector II. The greater the wage cut, the greater the gain for sector I, the higher the ARP, but the heavier are sector II's losses. Then could the crisis not originate in sector II and spread to sector I? It cannot because profitability rises in sector I. However, the two rates of profit cannot continue to diverge if wages keep falling. Growth in sector I causes higher demand for means of consumption. Prices of means of consumption rise and profitability rises in sector II. The balance can be restored. But what is gained by sector II is lost by sector I. The movement is thus towards an equalization of the two rates of profit. But the higher average profitability is not lessened.

The Keynesian thesis also submits that higher wages can lessen the depression and end the slump. But this too is wrong. Let us assume unsold consumption goods. Suppose wages are raised and wholly spent by labor in both sectors on those goods (the most favorable hypothesis for the Keynesian thesis). Sector II suffers a loss due to higher wages but it can sell an equivalent quantity of means of consumption to its own laborers. It can also sell more commodities to the workers of sector I. This is a net gain. But sector I suffers an equal loss due to higher wages. This loss compensates sector II's gain. There is no change in the two numerators conjointly. But both denominators rise due to higher investment in variable capital. Rising wages decrease average profitability *in spite of the sale of all the previously unsold commodities.* Sector-wide, the greater the advantage for sector II, the greater profitability deteriorates in sector I. The rise in profitability due to greater realization in sector II cannot spread to sector I. Here too the movement has its own correcting mechanism. Higher profitability in sector II increases the demand for sector I's output. If sector II offers higher prices for the means of production, profitability grows in sector I but falls in sector II. The average is not changed while the two rates of profit tend to converge. Higher wages cannot end the slump. Keynesian redistribution policies are doomed to failure.

Three considerations follow. First, given that Marx and the Keynesians reach diametrically opposite conclusions, any attempt to combine the former with the latter is theoretically inconsistent. Second, the foundation of conventional economics, that increasing demand spurs greater supply and so the economy tends toward the equilibrium between demand and supply, does not hold if labor's demand increases due to a pro-labor redistribution of value. Within the context of a two-sector model, a higher wages to profits ratio decreases profitability. Eventually, closures follow and supply falls.

Third, in the Keynesian view recovery can be achieved not only through pro-labor redistribution but also through capital-financed, state-induced investment policies, i.e. through the Keynesian multiplier. This thesis is invalidated by the Marxist multiplier (Carchedi 2011b). But this aside, state-induced production is capitalist production, even if it focuses on "creative" or "useful" industries. It does not eliminate the deleterious features of capitalist production, including the destruction of nature. The aim should not be to help this system to stand on its feet again, but to change it. Pro-labor polices are useful only if framed within this perspective, as elements of a strategy aimed at weakening, rather than strengthening, capital.

Consider now the neo-liberal vulgate. It holds that crises are due to rising wages. However, to explain how crises are endogenous to the system, one has to start from economic growth, when both the rate of profit and the new value rise and see how economic growth turns into its opposite. But the inverse relation between wages and profits holds if the mass of new value is unchanged or falling. It does not necessarily hold if the new value rises, i.e. when the economy is recovering. If the new value produced rises, *both* wages and the profit rate can rise. There is no inherent necessity for the rate of profit (ROP) to fall, only a possibility. Then, there must be a factor that *necessarily* undermines the increase in the rate of growth of the new value created. This is the increase in the OCC due to labor shedding and productivity increasing techniques. Rising wages can only detonate the crisis and worsen it. But the ground has to be prepared by the rising OCC.

Neo-liberal economics is also mistaken in holding that lower wages can spur the economy. As seen above, profits and the ARP rise as a result of pro-capital redistribution. However, the rise in the ARP is only one of the two conditions for economic recovery. The other condition is that the new value grows. In an economic crisis, lower wages increase not the new value produced but capital's share of a decreasing quantity of new value. They increase the ARP but not the CE-ARP. This is why crises emerge while wages are constantly reduced, a puzzle for the champions of austerity measures which can be solved by focusing of the CE-ARP. In the US, the wage share has persistently fallen from 44.7 percent in 1973 to 24.09 percent in 2010. Yet, the secular fall in the CE-ARP is still to be reversed.

If profitability is falling in the productive sectors and if wages are reduced as a counter-tendency, the higher profits are increasingly invested in finance and speculation where higher rates of profits can be reaped, as Figure 12.7 shows.

What is taken from labor goes to unproductive investments. The lesson for labor is clear. Neither Keynesian nor neo-liberal policies can end the slump. The former because they decrease profitability. The latter because they increase profitability but not the new value created (i.e. they increase the ARP but not the CE-ARP), thus contributing to the formation of financial and speculative bubbles. Contrary to the apostles of neo-liberalism, labor's sacrifices are useless. If redistribution policies cannot end the slump, what should be labor's strategy? Labor should fight for pro-labor redistribution and other reforms because these policies improve labor's conditions. But it should

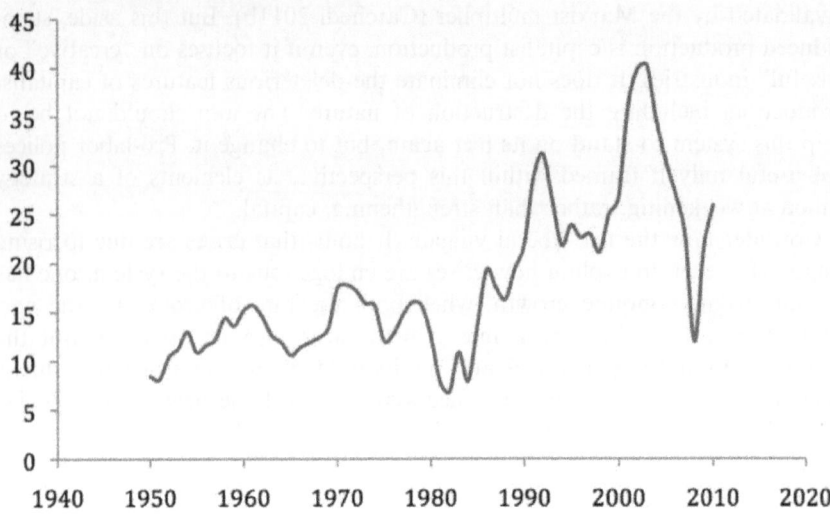

Figure 12.7 Financial profits as a percentage of the economy-wide profits, US 13 corporations

conceive them as weapons to weaken capital rather then as ways to help it end the slump.[22]

The short cycles

It has been shown that the Law is valid for the long, secular period. But the CE-ARP does not fall in a straight line. It falls through a succession of upward and downward cycles. To understand this movement we must consider the interplay of technological competition, capital composition, the ARP, and employment.

A review of the thirty-four short cycles from 1948 to 2010 shows that in twenty-eight out of the thirty-three cases, as the CE-ARP climbs to a peak, the OCC falls, and vice versa.[23] This is a replica on a micro-scale of the long-term, secular movement. The following example – the 1954–56 upward cycle and the following 1956–58 downward cycle – illustrates the recurrent pattern

Table 12.2 depicts the 1954–56 upward cycle. Its starting point is the 1954 trough in profitability (10.8 percent). Some capitals have closed down. Wages have fallen by 3.92 percent and total value has also fallen by 0.3 percent. Other capitalists can now fill the economic space left vacant. In 1955 production, as measured by total value, increases. Initially, net fixed investments do not rise. Rather, capitalists increase their assets' capacity utilization. More laborers are now employed by the same (previously under-utilized) means of production. Increased production with unchanged efficiency implies greater employment (from 18.5 to 19.9 million). Wages rise by +9.11 percent. The

Table 12.2 The 1954–56 upward cycle

Upward cycle	CE-ARP %	OCC	E	TV %	Wages %
1954	10.8	1.08	18.5	−0.3	−3.92
1955	11.7	1.04	19.6	+10.4	9.11
1956	12.4	0.92	19.9	+5.6	13.83

denominator of the OCC rises. As for the numerator, due to higher capacity utilization, assets are subject to increasing wear and tear, which reduces their value. Also, the capitalists buy the means of production, raw materials, semi-finished products, etc. of the bankrupt capitalists at reduced prices. These means of production do not incorporate new technologies and thus do not shed any extra labor. Constant fixed capital falls. The numerator of the OCC falls. The OCC falls on both accounts (from 1.08 to 1.04 to 0.92). The CE-ARP rises from 10.8 percent to 11.7 percent to 12.4 percent. Rising employment increases labor's purchasing power and rising profitability increases that of capital. Both factors facilitate the realization of the greater output. This process describes economic recovery.

At this point, the movement changes direction illustrated by the start of the 1957–58 downward cycle. Spurred by higher profit rates and hindered by high capacity utilization, capitals start investing in higher OCC assets. Constant capital rises and employment falls and with it wages. The OCC rises from 0.92 to 1.09 and the CE-ARP falls from 12.4 percent in 1956 to 10.6 percent in 1958 (while the profitability of the innovators rises). The percentage growth of total value falls from +5.6 to-2.3. Some capitals cease operating, i.e. some capital is destroyed. Due to falling employment and to falling profitability, both labor's and capital's purchasing power falls. Difficulties of realization follow. This process describes the slump.

The example above highlights three fundamental points. First, the upward profitability cycle generates *from within itself* the downward cycle. This latter, in its turn, generates *from within itself* the next upward profitability cycle. Second, there is an inverse relation between the OCC, and thus technological innovations on the one hand, and profitability and employment, on the other. Third, these fluctuations do not move around an equilibrium average, as it would seem if we focus on short-term cycles (in this example, the ARP starts at 10.8 percent in 1954 and ends at 10.6 percent in 1958). Rather, *each cycle is a further station on the path of the long-term secular fall in profitability,* as Figure 12.6 shows.

Crises and recoveries

We can now deal with crises and recoveries in more detail. Crises are manifestations of falling average profitability. However, falling profitability does not necessarily unfold into a crisis. Crises are a *negative percentage growth of new value created.*[24] They emerge within downward cycles of the CE-ARP *but only when this downward movement culminates in a negative growth of new value*. It is commonly accepted that a crisis must necessarily be preceded by a period of falling profitability. Not so. A crisis can emerge after the ARP has been falling because the OCC has been rising for some time. But since a downward cycle is always preceded by an upward cycle, the OCC can start increasing right after the last year of an upward cycle, i.e. right after the last year of rising profitability. Conversely, recoveries imply not only growing profit rates but also rising percentage growth of new value. As Figure 12.8 shows, both the short-term crises and the short-term booms are embedded within a long-term, secular fall in the CE-ARP, i.e. short-terms recoveries cannot counter the secular fall in the CE-ARP. Figure 12.8 lists all the crises since the end of WWII.

The depth of a crisis is indicated not so much by the fall in the general rate of profit or in the CE-ARP but by the negative percentage growth of new value.

Let us now consider the 2007–09 Great Recession. Let us first look at the 2003–06 recovery preceding it.

In those four years, the CE-ARP grows by a very modest 0.4 percentage points, but the ARP grows much more, by 9 percentage points, due to the jump in the rate of exploitation by 27.1 percentage points. The new value percentage growth is robust but in 2006 it slows down (from 11.68 percent to 8.67 percent), in anticipation of the coming crisis.

Some critics argue that the 2007 financial crisis emerged after a four-year rise in the general ARP such that, presumably, the fall in the ARP cannot be the (ultimate) cause of (all) crises.[25] But there is nothing special about this crisis. As Table 12.3 shows, in seven out of ten cases, the first crisis year is also the first year of falling profitability, i.e. the first crisis year is preceded by a

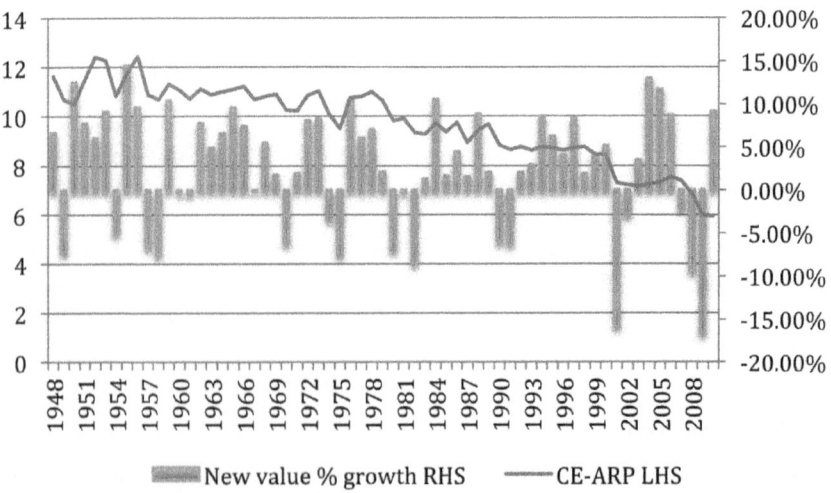

Figure 12.8 CE-ARP, growth of new value (%), and crises (negative % growth 15 of new value, RHS)

Table 12.3 Crises

Downwards CE-ARP cycle	Crisis years	Negative growth of new value %[1]
1949–50	1949	–7.2
1953–54	1954	–5.1
1957–58	1957–58	–13.9
1960–61	1960–61	–0.6
1970–71	1970	–6.1
1974–75	1974–75	–8.0
1979–83	1980–82	–15.7
1990–91	1990–91	–12.3
1999–2003	2001–02	–18.8
2007–10	2007–09	–28.4

Note [1] From the first year before the crisis to the last crisis year. In 1981, the CE-ARP rises minimally. This is only an insignificant interruption of the downward cycle.

Table 12.4 Recoveries (%)

Recoveries	CE–ARP	New value growth
1961–62	10.7 –> 11.1	–0.4 –> 7.7
1963–66	10.8 –> 11.2	4.9 –> 7.4
1971–73	10.2 –> 11.0	1.9 –> 8.2
1975–78	9.0 –> 11.0	–7.6 –> 7.0
1987–89	8.9 –> 9.6	1.5 –> 2.0
1991–92	8.6 –> 8.7	–6.3 –> 2.0
1993–94	8.6 –> 8.7	2.8 –> 8.5
2002–06	7.2 –> 7.5	–2.9 –> 8.6
2009–10	5.9 –> 5.9	–16.7 –> 9.1

Note: Negative growth rates of the new vale indicate crises years. They are also the start of the recovery.

Table 12.5 The 2003–06 recovery

Upward cycle	Exploitation rate	ARP	CE-ARP	OCC	New value % growth
2003	13.1%	4.1%	7.1%	2.15	3.48
2004	24.4%	7.8%	7.2%	2.12	12.97
2005	35.5%	11.4%	7.3%	2.10	11.68
2006	40.2%	13.1%	7.5%	2.07	8.67
Ppt difference	27.1	9	0.4		

year of rising profitability. This falls perfectly in line with the Law. The Law does not hold that a period of a falling ARP must *necessarily* precede crises. It may or it may not. The Law establishes a necessarily causal relation and not a necessary temporal relation between falling profitability and crises. The *necessary* conditions for the crisis are *rising OCC, falling profitability, and negative percentage growth of new value,* whether the rising OCC and falling ARP precede temporally the negative growth in new value or not. As Table 12.6 shows, starting from 2007, the OCC rises, the ARP falls, the new value grows negatively, and thus the crisis emerges.

The fall in the ARP and in employment is very serious; however, in terms of new value production and mass of profits, the crisis is unparalleled.

There is one further element: while falling profitability is the cause of crises, their detonation is caused by the conscious attempts to hold them back. This is the topic of the next section.

Figure 12.9 shows the relation between profitability (ARP) and capital accumulation (CA). The focus is on the ARP and not the CE-ARP, because the decision to re-invest a part of profits (accumulate) is determined by empirically observable profitability (which includes the effects of higher exploitation) and this is what the capitalists see. Figure 12.9 shows that both the ARP and CA trend downwards and move in a roughly similar pattern, especially after 1974–75.

Profitability leads capital accumulation, not vice versa. The ARP peaks in 1948 and CA in 1949; the ARP troughs in 1949 and CA in 1950; the ARP

Table 12.6 The 2007–09 Great Depression

Crisis years	New value % growth	ARP	OCC	mass of profits % growth	Employment % growth
2006	8.6	13.10	2.07	18.7	0.13
2007	−2.2	11.01	2.15	−12.2	−1.93
2008	−9.5	7.80	2.36	−27.0	−7.53
2009	−16.7	4.45	2.67	−43.8	−12.54

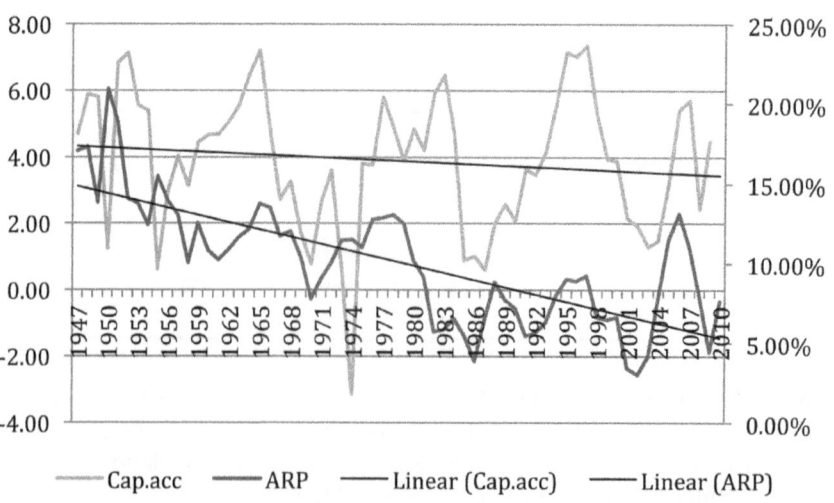

Figure 12.9 ARP and capital accumulation (CA)

peaks in 1950 and CA in 1952; the ARP troughs in 1954 and CA in 1955; the ARP peaks in 1955 and CA in 1957; the ARP and CA trough in 1958; the ARP and CA peak in 1965; the ARP and CA trough in 1970; the ARP peaks in 1978 and CA peaks in 1977;[26] the ARP peaks in 1978 and CA in 1983; the ARP troughs in 1986 and CA in 1987; the ARP and CA peak in 1997; the ARP troughs in 2002 and CA in 2003; the ARP peaks in 2006 and CA in 2007. Of the fourteen observations, the turning points in the ARP led those in CA in nine cases. In four cases, the turning points are contemporaneous. And only in one case the ARP peak (in 1978) follows that in capital accumulation (in 1977). So there is reasonably strong evidence that profitability determines capital accumulation.

Capitalists see increasing profits and accumulate. And yet they generate a decreasing share of surplus value relative to assets. The ARP (computed on profits either before or after taxes) explains the capitalists' behavior while the CE-ARP explains the way capitalism works.

Money, profitability, and inflation

The factors determining the timing of the crisis are many. Here only monetary policies will be considered. Figure 12.10 shows that they are ineffective anti-crises policies.

While the quantity of money (M1+M2) grows persistently, the ARP falls up to the mid-1980s and rises afterwards while the CE-ARP falls continuously. The quantity of money has no influence on long-term average profitability no matter how it is measured.[27]

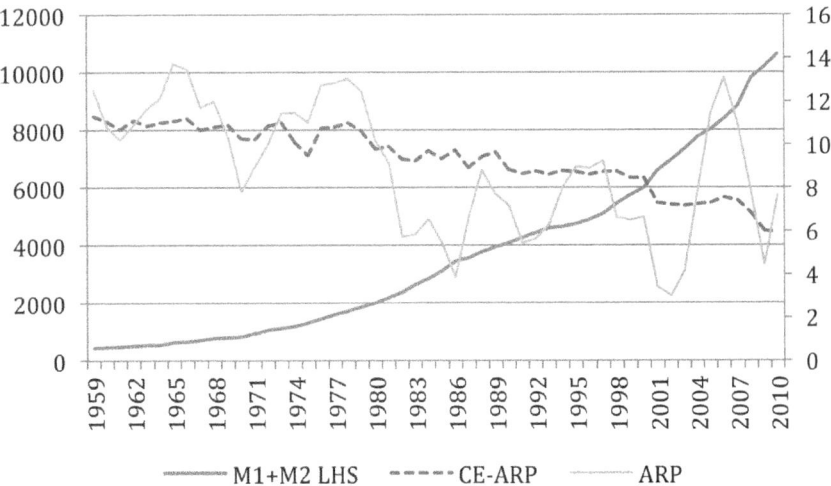

Figure 12.10 ARP, CE-ARP, and money quantity

When output, i.e. total value, grows as a result of growing productivity, the monetary authorities increase the money quantity to make possible the realization of the larger output without monetary prices having to fall. But the money quantity increases by 2329.7 percent while the total value grows by 376.4 percent from 1959 to 2010. This upsurge is due to the exponential increase in M2 due to the incorrect belief that increasing credit (and thus debt) can stimulate the economy. Since debt must be repaid, this is only a postponement of the inevitable.

If the increase in the quantity of money cannot hold back the fall in profitability, does a shrinking quantity of money cause the crisis? It would seem so. Tables 12.7 and 12.8 show that contractions of money supply or credit crunches preceded the crises in the productive sectors since 1970.

This would seem to indicate a causal relation. However, there is one element missing – the fall in new value. As Table 12.9 shows, this fall either precedes or is contemporaneous with restrictive monetary and credit policies. It also precedes and determines the crises in the productive sectors.

The question then is the following: Given that the monetary authorities are ignorant of value in the Marxist sense, how does their action reflect the fall in new value and catalyze crises? The monetary authorities react to inflation and inflation is the empirically observable index of the worsening of the economy. We have seen that the technological leaders appropriate value from the backward capitalists. The latter, inasmuch as they cannot innovate, react by raising their prices. This is why, in times of vigorous growth, the need to resort to price increases is smaller than in times of economic distress. This is very clear if we consider the history of post-WWII US capitalism. This secular period can be subdivided in a first phase of strong growth of new and total value, the so-called Golden Age of capitalism lasting up to the 1970s, and a second phase in which new and total value slow down considerably. From 1947 to 1965, the average annual inflation rate is 1.96 percent while from 1966 to 2010 it is 4.28 percent.[28]

In all six cases in Table 12.9, restrictive monetary policies are contemporaneous with a rise in inflation and, in five out of six cases, inflation rises while the new value produced falls percentage-wise. Moreover, in two of out of these five cases, new value starts falling before inflation starts rising.

Table 12.7 Money supply

Crisis year in productive sectors	% change in money supply in the pre–crisis peak year	% change in money supply in the year prior to the crisis	Contraction in money supply
1970	1965 (13.61%)	1969 (3.31%)	1965–69 (10.00%)
1974–75	1972 (12.03%)	1973 (6.36%)	1972–73 (5.67%)
1980–82	1967 (11.89%)	1979 (7.67%)	1976–79 (4.22%)
1990–91	1986 (10.97%)	1989 (4.50%)	1986–89 (6.47%)
2001–02	1998 (7.13%)	2000 (4.27%)	1998–2000 (2.86%)
2007–09	2004 (5.73%)	2006 (4.78%)	2004–06 (0.95%)

Table 12.8 Federal fund rate

Crisis year (ARP) in the productive sectors	Federal fund rate in the pre-crisis peak year	Federal fund rate in the year before the crisis	Credit crunch
1970	1968 (5.64%)	1969 (8.18%)	2.54%
1974–75	1973 (8.69%)	1973 (8.69%)	+
1980–82	1978 (7.90%)	1979 (11.16%)	3.26%
1990–91	1988 (7.56%)	1989 (9.23%)	1.67%
2001–02	200 (6.23%)	2000 (6.23%)	=
2007–09	2004 (1.35%)	2006 (4.96%)	3.61%

Table 12.9 Restrictive monetary policies and new value

Contraction in M1+M2	Credit Crunch	inflation rate[1]	New value % growth[2]	Crisis	Downward CE-ARP cycles
1965–69	1968–69	Upward 1965–69	Downward 1965–68	1970	1969–71
1972–73		Upward 1972–73	(a)	1974–75	1973–75
1976–79	1978–79	Upward 1976–79	Downward 1976–79	1980–81	1978–83[1]
1986–89	1988–89	Upward 1986–89	Downward 1984–89	1990–91	1989–91
1998–2000		Upward 1988–200	Downward 1994–2000	2001–02	1998–2003
2004–06	2004–06	Upward 2004–06	Downward 2004–06	2007–09	2006–10

Notes: [1] Rise from previous low. [2] Fall from previous peak. (a)The 1974–75 crisis is an exception. The collapse in new value (-3.43% in 1974) is preceded by a three-year rise.

Then, *the line of causation goes from technologically determined falling new value, to its manifestation as the technological laggards' profitability difficulties, to their resorting to price rises as a means to increase faltering profitability, to monetary policies meant to slow down the inflationary movement, to further difficulties for the laggards, to crises.* For example, consider the 1970 crisis. The new value starts falling in 1965. The laggards start experiencing economic difficulties. In the same year, inflation starts rising and the quantity of money is contracted.[29] Two years later credit is contracted. As a result, in 1970 the crisis emerges. Its cause is the previous fall in new value, its manifestation is inflation, and its catalyst is monetary policies. These latter are meant to subdue inflation but by aggravating the already wavering finances of the less competitive capitalists, cause their bankruptcies, unemployment, and thus the crisis.

Table 12.10 Financial crises[1]

Downward CE–ARP cycle	Crises in the productive sectors	Financial crises
1969–71	1970	1970
1973–75	1974–75	1974–75
1978–80	1980	1979
1981–83	1981–82	1982
1974–75		1984–85
1986–87		1987
989–91	1990–91	1989–91
1998–2003	2001–02	1998
1998–2003		2000
2006–10	2007–09	2007–09

Note [1] For the downward CE–ARP cycles, see table 12.3. The financial crises are: the 1970 Pennsylvania Central Railroad failure, the 1974 Franklin National Bank failure, the 1979 silver crisis, the 1982 failure of Drysdale Government Securities, inc., the 1982 failure of Penn Square Bank, the 1982 Mexican bailout, the 1984 bailout of Continental Illinois Bank, the 1984–85 savings and loans crisis, the 1987 stock market crash, the 1989–91 thrift bailout and commercial bank lending excesses, the 1998 malfunctioning of Long-term Capital Management and Russian debt moratorium, the 2000 high-tech bubble, and the 2007–09 junk bonds crisis. The dates of financial crises are taken from Kaufman, 2009, p.134. For a detailed analysis, see Reinhard and Roghoss, 2009.

Consider finally the relation between financial crises and profitability crises. Table 12.10 shows that the downward movement in the CE-ARP causes both types of crises because they emerge within this movement.[30]

There does not seem to be a clear-cut pattern of determination of financial crises by crises in the value producing sectors or vice versa. The reason is that the crises in the productive sectors can precede the financial crises because the flow of new value to the financial sectors dries up. But the financial crises can precede the non-financial crises because the financial sector's reduced lending capacity catalyzes closures and unemployment. The point is that, no matter which one precedes the other, *financial crises* too emerge within and thus *are determined by the falling movement of CE-ARP.*

Some concluding questions

If this is the case, then what can we infer from the tendential but persistent fall in profitability since the end of WWII, not only in the US but also in all advanced capitalist countries? More specifically, does this secular replacement of living labor by dead labor imply a coming breakdown of capitalism? This is a possibility, which however throws up the question as to what will come afterwards. Yet capitalism overcame the 1929 crisis through a massive destruction of capital. It might be able to achieve the same feat and not necessarily through a war. One thing seems certain – that capitalism is increasingly exhausting its capacity to create surplus value and that only a massive destruction of capital and its consequent reorganization on the basis of new technologies, perhaps in a new center of capital accumulation, might give this system a new lease of life. In this case, new and more horrible forms of exploitation will be ushered in. Or will labor take over and direct a new course in human history?

Appendix

Profits are from NIPA tables 6.17A, 6.17B, 6.17C, 6.17D: Corporate Profits before tax by Industry

[Billions of dollars]. In the first three tables utilities are listed apart but in table 6.17D they are listed together with, and cannot be separated from, transportation. I have decided to disregard utilities in all four tables. See note 4.

Constant capital is here the same as fixed capital (see note 12). The BEA defines *fixed assets* as "equipment, software, and structures, including owner-occupied housing" (www.bea.gov/national/pdf/Fixed_Assets_1925_97.pdf). The data considered in this paper comprises agriculture, mining, construction, and manufacturing (but not utilities, see above). Fixed assets are obtained from BEA, Table 3.3ES: Historical-Cost Net Stock of Private Fixed Assets by Industry [Billions of dollars; yearend estimates].

Wages for goods producing industries are obtained from NIPA Tables 2.2A and 2.2B: wages and salaries disbursements by industry [billions of dollars].

Employment in goods producing industries is obtained from: US Department of Labor, Bureau of Labor Statistics, series ID CES0600000001.

Money ARP is computed by dividing profits of a certain year by fixed and variable capital of the preceding year conforming to the temporal approach. It is computed for the productive sectors. The best approximations are the goods producing industries. These are defined as agriculture, mining, utilities, construction and manufacturing. However, in this paper utilities are disregarded (see above). See note 15.

Money and value ARP. Suppose we want to compute the ARP in value (i.e. labor) terms as the end point of period t2-t3. We must start our data collection one period earlier, t1-t2. At t2, the price of the means of production as outputs of t1-t2, the units of labor employed during that period, the money wages paid, and the profits realized are known. Then, first we divide the total of money wages and profits by the labor units (or hours) of new labor and obtain the units of new labor corresponding to one unit of money wages plus profits. Given the inherent homogeneity of value (as abstract labor) and of money, we apply this ratio to the price of the means of production at t2. This is the value of those means of production as outputs of t1-t2. They enter t2-t3 as inputs and thus with the same value. So we have the labor content of the means of production at t2 as the beginning of t2-t3. Next, we compute at t3 wages as a percentage of total wages plus profits. We do the same with profits. If we multiply these percentages by the units of labor expended, we obtain the value of labor power and of profits in terms of labor. We now have assets in terms of labor at t2 as the initial point of t2-t3 plus wages and profits also in terms of labor at t3. The *temporal* ARP in terms of labor (value) follows.

Notes

1 But the features highlighted in this work, beyond their specificity, characterize also other countries and even the world economy. See Roberts (2012).
2 The generation of knowledge too can be productive of surplus value (Carchedi 2011a, Chapter 4). However, no estimates can be made due to the lack of suitable statistics.
3 Some authors believe that it is impossible to separate the profits in the productive from those in the unproductive sectors because corporations in the former sectors operate also in the latter sectors. But fictitious capital does not produce profits. Then again, the profits realized by productive capitals through their operations in finance and speculation have been previously generated in the productive sectors and should be added to the rate of profit for these sectors.
4 Carchedi (2011b) uses nominal values. The conclusions are similar.
5 For a theory of old and new middle classes, see Carchedi (1971).
6 "The accumulation of knowledge and skill, of the general productive forces of the social brain ... [are] absorbed into capital" (Marx 1973, p. 694).
7 It is $(c+v+s)/E$, where c = constant capital, v = variable capital, s = v times average rate of exploitation, and E = employment. It could be objected that this is not the real productivity. But it is a more accurate estimate than a measure of productivity that mixes up efficiency and exploitation. It is in the interest of capital to overlook this distinction.
8 Okishio (1961) is the main critic of this thesis. Okishio's flaw is that he substitutes Marx's labor as a cost for labor as value creating activity (see Carchedi 2011a, Chapter 2). Thus he does not deliver an internal critique of the Law. Many authors follow in the footsteps of Okishio. For example, for David Harvey the innovators produce more use values, realize higher rates of profit, reduce the *cost* of the wage goods, and raise the material level of living of the laborers even if (monetary) wages can fall (2010, pp. 88–89). Shaikh (1999, pp. 121–22) holds that the innovative capitals reduce their *costs* and thus their prices. A generalized fall in prices follows. Average profitability falls too. Since the innovators' costs are lower than the competitors', the former's rate of profit is higher than the reduced general profit rate. The objection is that if the costs of some capitalists' output fall, so do the costs of other capitalists' inputs. The ARP is unaffected.
9 The assumption is that the distribution of purchasing power among sectors is unchanged. But this assumption can be dropped without altering the outcome of the analysis.
10 For Grossman the falling rate of profit is a threat to capitalism because at the limit "The capitalist class has nothing left for its own personal consumption because all existing means of subsistence have to be devoted to accumulation" (1992, Chapter 2). But capital accumulation falls during crises and rises during recoveries.
11 See the section "The Short Cycles". Each crisis has its own distinctiveness. The specificity of the present crisis is that it has developed from a crisis of profitability to a financial crisis and then to a sovereign state and to the euro crisis. See Carchedi 2013. For the long roots of the present crisis, see Carchedi and Roberts 2013.
12 There are many ways to measure constant capital. See Deepankar Basu and Ramaa Vasudevan 2011. Constant capital is both fixed and circulating. Here, only fixed capital is considered. Thus in what follows constant and fixed capital are synonymous. Carchedi and Roberts (unpublished), deals with circulating capital.

13 See note 8 concerning Okishio. Heinrich 2013 is a recent example of a rehearsal of old critiques. See Carchedi and Roberts 2013.

14 For the Monopoly Capital School the *surplus* generated by monopolies rises because of realization difficulties. See Foster 2012.

15 See the Appendix for the methodology.

16 The correlation coefficient is 0.8935.

17 It has been argued that the CE-ARP is not a "real," but a hypothetical measure of profitability because it measures what profitability would have been under the assumption of a constant rate of exploitation, rather than what it has actually been. If correct, this objection would invalidate, say, the computation of the ARP with deflated prices. The point is whether the CE-ARP, just as deflated prices, helps us understand features of reality that the ARP with variable rates of exploitation cannot disclose.

18 Paitaradis and Tsoulfidis find that their net profit rate starts increasing around the early 1980s but conclude that there is no recovery because the 1997 peak is far below that of the 1960s (2012, p. 224). Nevertheless, the trend *is* rising. The reason why there has not been a recovery is the fall in the CE-ARP.

19 The point is not to show that labor produces value. Marx had already given an answer: "Every child knows that any nation that stopped working, not for a year, but let us say, just for a few weeks, would perish" (Marx 1969, p. 416). The point is to show that *only* human labor, and not the means of production, produces value. Like man-made means of production, animals, the forces of nature, etc. affect efficiency and productivity and thus quantity of use values produced, but do not affect value.

20 The 1949 and 1960–61 crises are disregarded because preceded by only one pre-crisis year.

21 Husson (2013, p. 7) mentions some possible "explanations": the policy makers' lack of information, "analphabetism," holding onto obsolete paradigms, vested interests.

22 In stating, "the oddity of this position is that it implies that the defence of wages and of social expenditures would be anti-Marxist or at least non-Marxist" Housson (2013, p. 4) shows that he profoundly misunderstands this position.

23 The five exceptions are: 1980–81 and 1990–92 when both the CE-ARP and the OCC rise; and 1960–63, 1993–94, and 1996–98 when the CE-ARP rises but the OCC remains constant.

24 The crisis years so defined coincide with the NBER (define) data. The chronology does not change if crises are defined as negative growth of total value. Tapia Granados (2013) identifies five world recessions starting from the mis-1970s, which coincide with the crisis years in this paper.

25 See for example Duménil and Levy 2011; Husson 2010.

26 CA rises from the 1970 trough to a peak in 1972, then to a trough in 1974 before it reaches its 1977 peak.

27 I use the conventional definition of money, as M1+M2, to show that not only money proper (bills and coins) but also credit (which is not money) are impotent against the tendency towards the fall in profitability and thus crises.

28 There are, of course, other causes of inflation such as a rise in the price of raw materials (oil). Also, the above does not exclude occasional price reductions by the technological leaders in order to get a larger share of the market at the expense of the laggards. But while other causes and occurrences are occasional, the need to prop up profits by the technological laggards by raising their output's prices is a constant.

29 Actually, inflation was at its lowest in 1961. However, from 1961 to 1965 it increased minimally (by 0.6 percentage points). But in 1965 it started accelerating and in 1969 it had risen by 3.9 percentage points.

30 For the downward CE-ARP cycles, see Table 12.3. The financial crises are: the 1970 Pennsylvania Central Railroad failure, the 1974 Franklin National Bank

failure, the 1979 silver crisis, the 1982 failure of Drysdale Government Securities, inc., the 1982 failure of Penn Square Bank, the 1982 Mexican bailout, the 1984 bailout of Continental Illinois Bank, the 1984–85 savings and loans crisis, the 1987 stock market crash, the 1989–91 thrift bailout and commercial bank lending excesses, the 1998 malfunctioning of Long-term Capital Management and Russian debt moratorium, the 2000 high-tech bubble, and the 2007–09 junk bonds crisis. The dates of financial crises are taken from Kaufman 2009, p. 134. For a detailed analysis, see Reinhart and Roghoff 2009.

References

Albo, G., S. Gindin and L. Panitch (2010) *In and out of crisis* (Oakland, CA: PM Press).

Basu, D. and R. Vasudevan (2011) *Technology, Distribution and the rate of profit in the US economy: Understanding the current crisis*, available at: http://gesd.free.fr/basuvasu.pdf.

Bellamy Foster, J. and R.W. McChesney (2012) *The Endless Crisis* (New York: Monthly Review).

Bernstein, J., L. Mishel and H. Shierholz (2006–07) *The State of Working America* (Washington, DC: Economic Policy Review).

Carchedi, G. (1971) *On the Economic Identification of Social Classes* (London: Routledge and Kegan Paul).

——(2011a) *Behind the Crisis* (Leiden: Brill).

——(2011b) "Behind and beyond the crisis," *International Socialism*, 32.

——(2012a) "Could Keynes end the slump. Introducing the Marxist multiplier," *International Socialism*, 136 (October 8).

——(2012b) "From the crisis of surplus value to the crisis of the euro," *World Review of Political Economy*, 3: 288–312.

——(2014) "Krise und Fall der Profitrate – empirische Belege", *Das Argument* (forthcoming).

——(unpublished) *Value and Class Knowledge in the Age of the Internet*, available at: www.Marx2010.weebly.com.

Carchedi, G. and M. Roberts (2013) "The Long Roots Of The Present Crisis: Keynesians, Austerians, And Marx's Law," *World Review Of Political Economy*, forthcoming.

——(unpublished) *The rate of profit and circulating capital*, available at: www.Marx2010.weebly.com.

——(forthcoming) "Marx's law of profitability: answering old and new misconceptions," *Critique*.

Duménil, G. and D. Lévy (2004) *Capital Resurgent* (Cambridge, MA: Harvard University Press).

——(2011) *The Crisis of neoliberalism* (Cambridge, MA: Harvard University Press).

Foster, J. B. and R. W. McChesney (2012) *The endless Crisis* (New York: Monthly Review Press).

Freeman, A. (2009) *What makes the US profit rate fall?* Available at: http://mpra.ub.uni-muenchen.de/14147/1/MPRA_paper_14147.pdf.

Harvey, D. (2010) *The Enigma of Capital and Crisis of Capitalism* (Oxford: Oxford University Press).

Heinrich, M. (2013) "Crisis theory, the law of the tendency of the rate of profit to fall, and Marx's studies in the 1870s", *Monthly Review*, 64(11). Available at: http://monthlyreview.org/2013/04/01/crisis-theory-the-law-of-the-tendency-of-the-profit-rate-to-fall-and-marxs-studies-in-the-1870s.

Husson, M. (2010) "The Debate on the Rate of Profit," *International Viewpoint*, 426. Available at: www.internationalviewpoint.org/spip.php?article1894.

——(2013) *A gauche de la crise: les discours heterodoxies*, available at: http://hussonet. free.fr.

Grossman, H. (1992) *The law of accumulation and the breakdown of the capitalist system* (London: Pluto Press).

Kaufman, H. (2009) *The Road to Financial Reformation* (Hoboken, NJ: John Wiley and Sons).

Kliman, A. (2007) *Reclaiming Marx's capital* (Lanham, MD: Lexington Books).

Marx, K. (1967) *Capital, Vol. III* (New York: International Publishers).

——(1973) *Grundrisse* (London: Penguin Books).

Moseley, F. (2009) "The US economic crisis: causes and solutions," *International Socialist Review*. Available at: www.isreview.org/issues/64/feat-moseley.shtml.

Okishio, N. (1961) "Technical Changes and the rate of profit," *Kobe University Economic Review*, 7: 85–99.

Paitaridis, D. and L. Tsoulfidis (2012) "The Growth of Unproductive Activities, the Rate of Profit, and the Phase-Change of the U.S. Economy," *Review of Radical Political Economics*, 44(2): 213–33).

Reinhart, C. M. and K. S. Rogoff (2009) *This time is different* (Princeton, NJ: Princeton University Press).

Roberts, M. (2012) *A world rate of profit* (paper to the WAPE/AHE/IIPPE conference).

Shaikh, A. (1999) "Explaining the global economic crisis," *Historical Materialism*, 103–44, available at: http://excellentfuture.ca/sites/default/files/Explaining%20the%20Global%20 Economic%20Crisis.pdf.

Shaikh, A. (2011) "The first great depression of the 21st century," *Socialist Register*, 47.

Smith, E. G. and J. Butovsky (2012) "Profitability and the Roots of global crisis," *Historical Materialism*, 20(4): 4–39.

Tabuki, H. (2013) "Back in Power, Abe Aims to Spend Japan Back to Economic Vitality," *New York Times*, January 22, available at: http://dealbook.nytimes.com/2013/01/22/back-in-power-abe-aims-to-spend-japan-back-to-economic-vitality.

Tapia Granados, J. A. (2013) "From the Oil Crisis to the Great Recession: Five crises of the world economy," available at: http://sitemaker.umich.edu/tapia_granados/files/from_the_oil_ crisis_to_the_great_recession_h1.pdf.

Index